A Common Spring
Crime Novel and Classic

A Common Spring
Crime Novel and Classic

NADYA AISENBERG

Bowling Green University Popular Press
Bowling Green, Ohio 43403
1979

ACKNOWLEDGEMENTS

Grateful acknowledgment is made to the following for permission to reprint previously published material:

Atheneum Press: Excerpt from Stanley Hyman, *The Tangled Bank,* 1962.

Doubleday and Co.: Excerpt from Edmund Bergler, M.D., "Reader Participation in the Whodunit," *The Writer and Psychoanalysis,* 1950.

Faber and Faber, Ltd.: Excerpt from Robert Graves and Alan Hodge, *The Long Weekend,* 1940.

Grove Press, Inc.: Excerpt from Eugene Ionesco, "Victims of Duty," from *Three Plays,* 1958.

Indiana University Press, *Indiana University Studies:* Excerpt from Stitch Thompson, "Motif - Index," Vol. XIX studies no. 96, 97, 1932.

Alfred A. Knopf, Inc.: Excerpt from Albert Camus, *The Rebel,* 1956.

Oxford University Press: Excerpt from Raymond Williams, *The Country and the City,* 1973.

The Psychoanalytic Quarterly, Inc., *Psychoanalytic Quarterly:* Excerpt from Charles Rycroft, "A Detective Story: Psychoanalytic Observations," Vol. 26, 1957.

Purdue University, *Modern Fiction Studies:* Excerpt from Ursula Spier, "Melodrama in Graham Greene's *The End of the Affair,* "Vol. III (Autumn 1957).

and to the following museums for permission to reprint material from their collections:

The Metropolitan Museum of Art, N.Y.C., N.Y.: Gustave Moreau, *Oedipus and the Sphinx.*

The Museum of Modern Art, N.Y.C., N.Y.: Odilon Redon, *The Eye like a Strange Balloon Moves Towards Infinity,* Plate I of *To Edgar Poe;* Henri Rousseau, *La Reve.*

Private Collector: Giorgio de Chirico, *The Mystery and Melancholy of the Street.*

Thanks are due to the late Professor Paul Wiley, Department of English, University of Wisconsin, Madison, Wisconsin, for his encouragement and patient guidance through the initial stage of this manuscript and to Ms. Megan Marshall for her scrupulous and skillful editorial assistance and indexing.

To Alan
sine quem non

CONTENTS

LIST OF TABLES

LIST OF NOTES

LIST OF ILLUSTRATIONS

CHAPTER I
INTRODUCTION

Detective novels differ from some other kinds of novel, in having to have a rather hard structure built in logical coherence. But the structure will fail to satisfy the mind, writer's or reader's, unless the logic of imagination, tempered by feelings and rooted in the unconscious, is tied to it, often subverting it.

Ross Macdonald, *On Crime Writing*

*   *   *

Our fears are infinitely more precise than our hopes.

Paul Valéry

Human fears are covertly expressed in the detective story. Detective fiction is inseparable from certain myth-making faculties, particularly the imposition of order, through narrative formulae, upon collective fears and uncertainties, and the provision of rational explanation for inexplicable phenomena. Scholes and Kellogg have claimed in *The Nature of Narrative,* ". . . myths are not solely projections of human aspirations. They are projections of human fear as well."[1]

1

This same attribute which links the detective story to collective imaginative constructions of the past such as myth, fairy tale, and fable, makes it a natural vehicle for expressing and coping with the moral ambiguities of our continuing present, "The Age of Anxiety," as Auden designated it. In the twentieth century we have seen detective fiction rise to one-fourth of the total publishing output in the English language, not a surprising statistic when public opinion polls report that 53 percent of all college graduates are mystery buffs.[2] Although generally categorized as entertainment, the crime novel actually describes the landscape of our deepest fears.

Despite its formulae and archetypes, crime fiction discloses larger truths about the society for which it is written. It can even, upon analysis, be seen to work out the human conflicts and fears which provide its daily nourishment. Thus, while "the reading of an individual romance, say a detective story . . . may be in itself a trivial imaginative experience . . . a study of the whole convention of . . . detective stories would tell us a good deal about the shape of stories as a whole, and that, in its turn, would begin to give us some glimpse of still larger verbal structures, eventually of the mythological universe itself."[3] The crime novel is intimately related to such mythologies because any formulaic novel sticks closer to established narrative conventions; a story "that proceed[s] very simply to its obviously predestined end [is] nearer myth than novel or drama."[4] By understanding the crime novel's own mythologies, we come closer to understanding the society itself. Myths relate individual lives to grander beginnings and ends.

I will begin with only a brief look at the evolution of the form (including a compressed chronological table—Table I, Chapter I), since this is an aspect which has been considered by others.[5] I will also separate the catch-all phrase "crime novel" into its two more exact designations, "detective story" and "thriller," an important distinction which parallels cultural changes—for example, linguistic changes. A discussion of the potentialities of the crime novel, its implications, principles, and scope, and its analogy to myth and fairy tale (Chapter II) will alert the reader to the ways in which three major writers, Dickens, Conrad, and Greene, borrowed many important ingredients from the formulaic novel.

2

Introduction

A thorough comparison of motifs will substantiate my contention that the detective story reassembles components of myth and fairy tale in a manner hitherto undocumented.

With supporting illustrations drawn from Rex Warner, T.S. Eliot, Jorge Luis Borges and other twentieth-century authors, I propose that the detective story and the thriller have made an unacknowledged contribution to "serious" modern literature. These contributions will be found to consist importantly, but not completely, in its systems of imagery—i.e., the visualization of the motifs of Chapter II. The formulae of the crime novel will be summarized in order to trace their origins in past traditions and to stress universal emotions they still express. In my attempt to arrive at an understanding of crime fiction, I will define its relation to other allegorical forms, the participatory role which the reader plays, and the resonance of the crime novel we hear in the literature to which we attend more closely.

The present practice which consigns detective novels to a special shelf in the library and to a separate page in newspaper and magazine book reviews, is deplored by many who point out that it has no more justification now than it had when Dickens, Collins, and Poe published. Although Edmund Wilson, a powerful prosecutor, charges that the detective novel has dropped the social burden of Dickens or even the social analysis of Collins, such reading seems to me extraordinarily narrow. Ellery Queen's attack on the artificial distinction between "entertainment" and "literature" in his discussion of Faulkner's *Knight's Gambit* sets the tone for our chronological survey:

> The publication, advertising and critical review of Faulkner's *Knight's Gambit* have emphasized once more the shameful literary snobbishness that has always existed, and still exists, in America. . . . The pure and simple truth is, *Knight's Gambit* is a book of detective stories, and far from being scorned as such, should be judged on its larger merits. . . . The criminological cornerstones of 110 years were laid not only by detective story writers . . . but also by such world-famous literary figures as Stevenson, G.K. Chesterton, O. Henry, and W. Somerset Maugham, to say nothing of important contributions made by Thomas Hardy, Oscar Wilde, Rudyard Kipling,

3

H.G. Wells, John Galsworthy, Anton Chekhov, Sinclair Lewis, Pearl Buck, Edna St. Vincent Millay, John Steinbeck, Ernest Hemingway—and William Faulkner.[6]

Chronological Survey

The flood of detective fiction unleashed yearly in America and Great Britain makes it hard to realize that this form did not even exist until the nineteenth century. The very word "detective" did not gain common currency until the middle of the nineteenth century, in spite of literary forerunners in the works of Tom Taylor and William Goodwin.

The nineteenth century crime novel was the offspring of two older literary types or attitudes. The first is the picaresque or rogue tale, typified by *Lazarillo de Tormes,* and told by Cervantes, Smollett, Fielding, and Le Sage. (In England an additional source was *The Newgate Calendar.*) The sympathetic outlaw, who may be traced to Robin Hood as well, is taken up at the end of the eighteenth century in the pre-Romantic period. Assuming the character of a "fallen angel" and secret benefactor, he employs bandits as instruments of justice for the benefit of mankind, though he may possess a "dark secret" himself. This hero was adopted by Eugène Sue (Sue's *The Mysteries of Paris* may just be the most commercially successful novel of all time), Paul Frence, Byron, and countless others, and underlies the conception of Dostoevsky's Raskolnikov. The second legacy inherited by the nineteenth century was a new attitude toward Nature, exemplified in the poetry of William Collins and the novels of Ann Radcliffe—an attraction toward a wild, remote landscape with pseudo-medieval architectural features. This new view provided a most suitable setting for melodrama,[7] and remains the background for the Gothic novel which has had a renaissance in our day. This landscape induced a feeling of terror exploited in the Tale of Terror (which we still encounter in the nineteenth century—e.g., Bulwer-Lytton's *The Haunted and the Hunters,* 1859), and developed slowly into the *roman-feuilleton* or serial-romance, influencing so many of the greatest nineteenth-century novels—for instance, those of Dickens.

Introduction

Of course the crime novel's emergence in the nineteenth century was in large part due to a new consciousness of what might be called the social contract. Most of the English-speaking world, and indeed much of Western Europe, had come to expect law and order in daily life. A body of laws and regulations were understood and accepted by most of this society which could now afford to organize special institutions for keeping the peace. In 1829, the town of London established its first Metropolitan Police Force, initially known as the Bow Street Runners and later the "Bobbies," after their eponymous founder, Sir Robert Peel. Detective fiction, and indeed fiction in general in the nineteenth century, was able to draw upon a new source, the workings of a police force. Dickens has clearly demonstrated his fascination for this new material not only in such well-known novels as *Bleak House,* but also in three essays about the methodology of police work, "The Detective Police," "On Duty with Inspector Field" (a personal friend), and "Three Detective Anecdotes" printed in *Household Words* (1850).

The infusion of the spirit of modern science into police procedure increased the crime novel's scope: e.g., the development of fingerprint techniques, poison detection tests, ballistics information—in short, the use of the scientific method by the official bureaus of investigation such as the Sûreté and Scotland Yard. The publication of the romantic memoirs of Vidocq, head of the Sûreté (1829), and some sensational memoirs of erstwhile Bow Street Runners whetted the public's appetite for stories of crime.[8] In addition, innovative theories about the workings of the unconscious mind provided a new source of motivation in the novels of Wilkie Collins and Sheridan Le Fanu.

A new genre, the *roman policier,* grew out of this material. These novels focused on detection rather than on the commission of the crime itself. Paul Féval (1818-1887) pioneered with his accounts of the Paris police force; the *roman policier* has become the police procedural fictionalized by such writers as Georges Simenon, J.J. Marric, Nicholas Freeling, and others.

The modern detective story is generally conceded to have been fathered by Edgar Allan Poe with his influential "The Murders in the Rue Morgue" (1841), "The Mystery of Marie Rogêt" (1842), "The Gold-Bug" (1843), and "The Purloined Letter" (1845). On July 16, 1856, the Goncourts entered in their *Journal*, ". . . he [Poe] ushers in the scientific and analytic literature . . . in which things play a more important part than people; love gives way to deduction; and the basis of the novel is transferred from the heart to the head."[9]

Poe not only concerned himself with the creation of detective stories, establishing criteria that were to obtain thenceforward for a hundred years, but also helped shape the genre with his criticism of the attempts of other authors, rejecting variously Stevenson, Balzac, Bourget, and Dickens. (In his essay "Dickens and Mystery in the Novel, Apropos of *Barnaby Rudge*," Poe charges Dickens with many of the deficiencies I will discuss in Chapter III.) Poe required the detective tale to contain a single detective hero (in his case the renowned Auguste Dupin), analytical deduction, and the combination of suspense with an unemotional tone. Poe's Dupin also set the precedent for a clever amateur who, using his intuitive powers, proves himself shrewder and more effective than the police force with all its methodology. From this we infer the detective hero is "above and outside the law as the crooks are outside and beneath it."[10]

Bypassing minor figures whom I have included in the chronological table (Table I), we come to Wilkie Collins, whose book *The Moonstone* (1868) has been hailed by T.S. Eliot as "the greatest English detective story." Collins' *The Woman in White* (1860) was the first of his series of experiments with the detective genre, all of which featured meticulous plotting, solid characterization, and narrative skill. Most important, Collins helped to establish the "fair play" rules of the detective writing game: no false clues; no amnesia; no esoteric knowledge required; no vital clue withheld; all characters act; no supernatural solution. There did not exist at that time the rigid system of classifying fiction which is accepted now, and the work of Sheridan Le Fanu, Wilkie Collins, and Edgar Allan Poe was not considered inferior in their day. Rather the reverse—Dickens emulated Collins, and in *Barnaby Rudge* used a detective who, like that of Collins in

The Woman in White, was an amateur and did not appear until the last third of the book. "When Dickens sat down to write *Bleak House* ('the golden age of melodramatic literature,' says Eliot) we must not suppose that he was greatly troubled by the exact definition of the book he was writing. . . . Romance, satire, pure fantasy, the detailed transcription of life; there they all are, improvidently flung together upon the bones of a detective story. It is the underlying detective story which keeps the tale moving. . . ." [11]

The nineteenth century's most famous detective-hero was Sherlock Holmes, who mirrors the Romantic cult of the individual. Ross Macdonald writes:

> Holmes had other ancestors [e.g., Gaboriau and Scott] and collateral relations which reinforce the idea that he was a portrait of the artist as a great detective. His drugs, his secrecy and solitude, his moods of depression (which he shared with Dupin), are earmarks of the Romantic rebel then and now. Behind Holmes lurk the figures of nineteenth century poets, Byron certainly, probably Baudelaire, who translated Poe and pressed Poe's guilty knowledge to new limits. [12]

Conan Doyle, Holmes' creator, retained Poe's innovation of the single detective hero, and retained also many trappings of the Gothic novel, including the revenge motive. Gothic trappings notwithstanding, Doyle's work is read now with a feeling of coziness and nostalgia, not only as a period piece but because of its implicit assumption that the status quo is correct and unchanging. The success of Holmes inevitably made him the model for the spate of eccentric, rich, cultivated amateur detectives so enjoyed in the Golden Age of detective fiction, 1920-1940: e.g., Lord Peter Wimsey (Dorothy L. Sayers); Sir Roderick Alleyn (Ngaio Marsh); Albert Campion (Margery Allingham); Nigel Strangeways (Nicholas Blake). His immense popularity assured the perpetuation of the genre, and implanted a new figure securely in the collective Western imagination.

In the twentieth century the most striking single addition to detective fiction has been psychology. The reader has learned to credit the evil potentialities of his fellow man—the criminal may be the rector, the doctor, or the gardener. Detective fiction can rely on a truth that is stranger than fiction. Such novels or stories often depend upon psychological horror or inner mystery (e.g., Margaret Millar and Anthony Berkeley), and might even pivot around a murderer-narrator, (e.g., in the work of Francis Iles, Nicholas Blake, Richard Hull, and F.W. Crofts); Patrick Hamilton's *Hangover Square,* dealing with a schizophrenic criminal, has become a classic of this type. In a way that is reminiscent of *The Mysteries of Udolpho* and the Gothic tale, such works reveal their plots from the outset, and substitute an atmosphere of horror for mystery of plot. Thus what inaugurated a more realistic trend (i.e., the psychological motivation of crime) came full circle, with the ''unnatural'' in man replacing the ''supernatural'' of the earlier Gothic. The new blend was indubitably tied also to the collapse of the Dream of Reason, the pure puzzle form of detection which was its expression, and the detective hero who was its Apostle.

The donnish entertainment which was constructed around the pure puzzle and held the field in the early part of this century persists more as an anachronism than a vital force. The novel of manners which Agatha Christie, Dorothy L. Sayers, S.S. Van Dine, *et al.,* attempted to integrate with the puzzle, thereby hearkening back to Le Fanu and Collins, has been replaced by an interest in the criminal act itself. An unfortunate side effect of the movement away from the detective novel as a novel of manners has been the loss of important women characters, since traditionally the female role in the epic or adventure is a marginal one. More significant is the shift from the eccentric leisured detective, who belonged to the novel of manners, to the plodder, from whimsey to realistic procedure, culminating in the figure of police-detective hero—a holdover from the old strain of the *roman policier.* This switch brings to the foreground qualities to which we may all aspire: patience, thoroughness, competence on the job. Although as late as 1944 Raymond Chandler could complain that two-thirds of detective fiction still obeyed the Golden Age rules, the sweeping away of pseudo-gentility began as early as the end of World War I, as Robert Graves and Alan Hodge cogently describe in *The Long Week-end* (see Note 1, Chapter I).

Introduction

The "tough guy" novel made its official appearance in the 1930s. This type was rooted in the economic strivings of the Twenties, and did not create a new hero in any case. As Ross Macdonald, whose own Lew Archer is of this strain, points out, "[The] hardboiled heroes were deeply rooted in the popular and literary tradition of the American frontier, going back as far as Washington Irving and James Fenimore Cooper, and have been considered inimical to the American way of life. . . ."[13] But actually many of these characteristics are recognizable in the distant rogue figure of Robin Hood: the conviviality of outlawry in the forest masks his misanthropic leavetaking of society; the swashbuckling action of his band is initiated because society cannot be entrusted with redressing injustice; his unquestionable personal integrity contrasts with the venality of the victims; and his imperviousness to danger is the result not just of wit but also of frontier hardihood.

The twentieth century has also seen a proliferation of other formulaic fictions. An outgrowth of two World Wars, the spy story, developed by John Buchan and W. Somerset Maugham and carried on succcessfully by Eric Ambler, John le Carré, and Len Deighton, stars a maverick hero at odds with authority and the Establishment which employs him—a return to the picaresque. Science fiction, the offspring of Mary Shelley's *Frankenstein* (1818), gained popularity with the advance of modern technology, uniting the older elements of horror and the supernatural with urgent and immediate fears for the future of man; the science fiction of H.G. Wells, George Orwell, C.S. Lewis, and Aldous Huxley inspired Isaac Asimov, Ray Bradbury, and H.P. Lovecraft in the next generation. A number of authors have practiced the allegorical adventure, whether political or religious: Friedrich Dürrenmatt, Max Frisch, Charles Williams, Graham Greene, and Rex Warner, among others. And Daphne du Maurier, Phyllis Whitney, Dorothy Eden, and their sisters have brought about the rivival of the Gothic itself.

We may add that the deliberate manipulation of excitement, which existed in nineteenth century fiction, has become cruder and even sadistic, while the novel of manners or character-dominated novel has become so subtle that it frequently bears little trace of plot at all (Virginia Woolf) or has turned its back on both plot and character (Alain Robbe-Grillet). The *nouveau roman* has to be phenomenological. This perhaps accounts for the present highly successful re-publication of French nineteenth century thrillers, and the popularity of the journalistic novel (Norman Mailer).

Of the myriad varieties and combinations of varieties extant, only two major forms lie within the scope of this study: the pure puzzle, or classic tale of detection derived from Poe, and the thriller, a latter-day picaresque grafted onto the modern scene, but ultimately a reincarnation of the Robin Hood theme. These are the bifurcations of the *crime novel.*

TABLE I - CHAPTER I
Chronology

gar Allan Poe — "The Murders in the Rue Morgue" (1841)

arles Dickens — *Barnaby Rudge* (1841)

gar Allan Poe — "The Mystery of Marie Rogêt" (1842) · "The Gold-Bug" (1843) · "The Purloined Letter" (1845)

> Auguste Dupin, detective and his chronicler

exandre Dumas — *Le Vicomte de Bragelonne* (1848)

Sherlock Holmes: Watson

arles Dickens — *Bleak House* (1853)

Martin Hewitt: Brett

lkie Collins — *The Woman in White* (1860)

Raffles: Bunny

eridan Le Fanu — *Uncle Silas* (1864)

Poirot: Capt. Hastings

ile Gaboriau — *L'Affaire Lerouge* (1866) · *Le Dossier No. 113* (1867) · *Monsieur Lecoq* (1869) | *roman policier*

Hanaud: Mr. Ricardo

arles Dickens — *The Mystery of Edwin Drood* (1870)

rtuné du Boisgobey — *roman policier* (1872-9)

nan Doyle — "A Study in Scarlet" (1887)

bert Louis Stevenson — *The Wrong Box* (1889)

nan Doyle — "The Sign of the Four" (1890), etc.

na K. Green — *The Circular Study* (etc.) (1900-15)

W. Hornung — *Raffles* (1901) (criminal-detective)

urice LeBlanc — (rogue literature - Arsène Lupin, criminal-detective)

J. Crofts — (*roman policier* - Inspector French)

Austin Freeman — (scientific method - Dr. Thorndyke, detective) (1913-40)

0s-1940 — Classic Tale:

Tough Guy thriller - 1930s ff.

A.C. Bentley	Dashiell Hammett
Dorothy L. Sayers	Raymond Chandler
Margery Allingham	Ross Macdonald
Nicholas Blake	Ian Fleming
S.S. Van Dine	
Ngaio Marsh	Spy
G.K. Chesterton	Adam Hall
Richard Hull	Len Deighton
Agatha Christie	John le Carré
Michael Innes	Eric Ambler

chological

ia Fremlin

roman policier

argaret Millar — Georges Simenon

ancis Iles — Nicholas Freeling

len Eustis — Maurice Proctor

orges Simenon — J.J. Marric

edrich Dürenmatt

ax Frisch

Note 1

CHAPTER I

Robert Graves and Alan Hodge, *The Long Week-end* (Faber and Faber, London, 1940), p.p. 300-303.

Low-brow reading was now dominated by the detective novel. A large number of writers made comfortable incomes from this fashion, and a curious situation arose. In Great Britain, though a few score murders and acts of grand larceny took place every year, not more than two or three of these had features in the least interesting to the criminologist as regards either motive or method; nor in any of these, did private detectives play a decisive part in bringing the culprits to justice—this was done by the competent routine procedure of the C.I.D. Yet from the middle Twenties onwards some 1000's of detective novels were annually published, all of them concerned with extraordinary and baffling crimes, and only a very small number gave the police the least credit for the solution. These books were designed not as realistic accounts of crime, but as puzzles to test the reader's acuteness in following up disguised clues. It is safe to say that not one in 100 showed any first-hand knowledge of the elements that comprised them—police organization, the coroner's court, fingerprints, firearms, poison, the laws of evidence—and not one in 1000 had any verisimilitude. The most fanciful and unprofessional stories (criminologically speaking) were the most popular. Detective novels, however, were no more intended to be judged by realistic standards than one would judge Watteau's shepherds and shepherdesses in terms of contemporary sheep-farming. Of all the detective novelists of the period only one, the American Dashiell Hammett, happened to be both a first-rate writer and to have had a long experience of crime, in his capacity as a Pinkerton Agency Manager. . . .

Agatha Christie remained true in her detective novels to the romantic cumbersome English style of the early Twenties. There were numberless other styles, including even the coldly scientific, in which microscopic examinations of fluff in people's pockets yielded beautiful results. But the norm was the breathless, familiar, undistinguished, emotional style of the Sunday newspaper special reporting. A detective story was considered well-written if the denouement was a legitimate deduction from a small piece of evidence unobtrusively introduced in an early chapter, and if the suspicion successively cast on a number of persons in the story were plausible enough to divert attention from the criminal till the last moment. . . . The chain of reasoning was all that mattered. For the cultured public, Dorothy Sayers topped the bill with her case stories of 'Lord Peter Wimsey'; he derived from the Baroness Orczy's lackadaisacal 'Sir Peter Blakeney' and outclassed all other detective heroes, at least in the fantastic complication of his cases. Dorothy Sayers gave her lordling a love of rare books as an endearing foible . . . and made him the hook on which to hang incidental dissertations on art, music, the poets, and good food and drink. She was also an earnest publicist of the Anglican faith.[a]

Introduction

a. There has been a gradual introduction of ethnic variety—e.g., Harry Kemelman's rabbi-detective; Lesley Egan's Mexican policeman-detective; Arthur Upfield's Australian half-aborigine detective.

CHAPTER I

[1]Robert Scholes and Robert Kellogg, *The Nature of Narrative*, (New York: Oxford University Press, 1966), pp. 218-219.

[2]Margo Miller, "White Collar Life and a Bit of Murder," *Boston Globe*, Sunday August 20, 1978, p. B-1.

[3]Northrop Frye, *The Secular Scripture*, (Cambridge, Mass.: Harvard University Press, 1976), p. 60.

[4]Frank Kermode, *The Sense of an Ending* (New York: Oxford University Press, 1968), p. 18.

[5]A.E. Murch's *The Development of the Detective Novel* and Fritz Wölchen's *Der Literarische Mord* both give competent chronological surveys of the genre. There have, of course, been many partial approaches to explicating the literature itself: biographies and explications of individual writers—e.g., Agatha Christie, James Bond, Rex Stout—and naturally the more important Conan Doyle and Edgar Allan Poe; anthologies with varying organizing principles—e.g., *My Best Mystery Story;* manuals such as Carolyn Wells's *The Technique of the Mystery Story;* consideration of specialized aspects—e.g., Roger Callois's *Le Roman Policier;* and personal apologias and defenses—e.g., G.K. Chesterton's *The Defendant.* 1971 saw the publication of the first catalogue *raisonné, A Catalogue of Crime,* edited by Jacques Barzun and Wendell Hertig Taylor, followed by Julian Symons' *Mortal Consequences: A History from the Detective Story to the Crime Novel,* in 1972. Until the publication of this book no comprehensive catalogue of the field existed, and even those of narrower scope—e.g., the Greene-Osborne catalogue, *Victorian Detective Fiction,* were few. The preceding year, 1970, *The Mystery Writer's Art,* edited by Francis M. Nevins, Jr., appeared, the first collection of essays on this subject since Howard Haycraft's classic *The Art of the Mystery Story* in 1945. The Nevins book is an anthology of uneven quality but interesting diversity; moreover, it contains some of the only original and provocative speculation about the detective novel that I have encountered outside of W.H. Auden's cogent essay, "The Guilty Vicarage." Publication data for these works appear in the bibliography.

Since undertaking this study, four books have appeared which more or less direct themselves to the subject. I will be referring occasionally to these books: Northrop Frye's *The Secular Scripture;* Gavin Lambert's *The Dangerous Edge* (New York: Viking Press, 1976); Ian Ousby's *The Bloodhounds of Heaven* (Cambridge, Mass.: Harvard University Press, 1976); John G. Cawelti's *Adventure, Mystery, and Romance* (Chicago: University of Chicago Press, 1976).

[6]"The Renaissance," *Queen's Quorum* (Boston: Little, Brown & Co., 1951), p. 109.

[7]Melodrama and the criminal fused in the Victorian plays about the "ticket-of-leave man," or parolee.

[8]For the first full-length biography of Vidocq, see *Vidocq Dossier: The Story of The World's First Detective,* Samuel Edwards, (Boston: Houghton Mifflin, 1977).

[9]*Goncourt Journal,* ed. and trans. Robert Baldick (London: Oxford University Press, 1962), p. 20.

[10]Daniel Hoffman, *Poe Poe Poe Poe Poe Poe Poe,* (Garden City, New York: Doubleday and Co., 1972), p. 121. Edgar Allan Poe took Dickens to task for the lapses in *Barnaby Rudge qua* mystery novel: the characters undergo changes which are unaccountable (e.g., Mrs. Varden changes from shrew to patient wife; Chester from gentleman to brute; Rudge's sting of conscience is not consistent with his crime); the mystery and horror of the private or domestic murder are eclipsed by the mystery and horror of the public Gordon Riots; a five-year lapse between two appearances of Rudge is too long for interest in him to be sustained; the raven, although adding atmospheric interest, should have been awarded a more prophetic role; the stain upon Barnaby's hand is at variance with medical knowledge. These and other structural misdemeanors led Poe to conclude that the detective story was not Dickens' metier after all, despite his considerable talents. More astonishing is that if we recall the extreme diffuseness of *Our Mutual Friend,* the novel which immediately preceded *The Mystery of Edwin Drood,* the latter seems a model of connection and necessity, with irrelevancy and inconsistency stripped away.

[11]*London Times Literary Supplement,* Feb. 25, 1955, "The Secret Attraction," p. i.

[12]Ross Macdonald, "The Writer as Detective Hero," *The Mystery Writer's Art,* ed. Francis M. Nevins, Jr. (Bowling Green, Ohio: Bowling Green University Press, 1970), p. 298.

While Sherlock Holmes's characterization endows him with a personality we may loosely term, "romantic," Ian Ousby points out that "Holmes's approach to detection participates intimately in that spirit of scientific rationalism which had come to dominate the intellectual climate of the late Victorian Period." *The Bloodhounds of Heaven,* p. 153. But in a most interesting essay which attempts to interpret the detective as a metaphor for society, Elliott Gilbert seizes upon this very belief in ratiocination as the weathervane pointing to change: "Can it be that in the end even Sherlock Holmes, whose creator—Conan Doyle—was himself to move from the realm of reason to the world of the occult, had come to doubt the efficacy of the intellect, had come to see that if the detective was a metaphor for the nineteenth century's faith in ratiocination he was also symbolic of the age's profound disillusionment with human reason?" Elliott Gilbert, "The Detective as Metaphor," *The Mystery Writer's Art,* p. 292.

[13]Ross Macdonald, *N.Y. Times Book Review,* May 16, 1971.

CHAPTER II
Myth, Fairy Tale, and the Crime Novel

In folk tales plots, themes, and motifs are predictable enough to be counted and indexed. . . . These reveries, daydreams, conscious sexual fantasies are formulaic and the formulaic unit of phrase or story is the cornerstone of the creative imagination. . . .

John G. Cawelti, *Adventure, Mystery, and Romance*

We can now proceed to the more engaging problem: not what in the past fostered the crime novel, but what in the present sustains it? Or, more exactly, what unchanging, non-temporal properties does it possess which continue to attract us?

It is my object here to show that there exist basic but unsuspected connections between myth, fairy tale, and the crime novel. Although they remain largely unexplored, these connections hover in the background as felt resemblances and echoes. I will be drawing on the works of psychoanalyst C.G. Jung, anthropologist Claude Lévi-Strauss, formalist critic Vladimir Propp, historiographer Angus Fletcher, hermeneutist Northrop Frye, and others who are the early pioneers of such investigation.

In his comprehensive and searching study *Allegory,* Angus Fletcher rightly makes the point that allegory is a continuing stream in

16

literature, with unrecognized modern expressions. Twice he singles out the detective story as such a modern allegory:

> While allegory in the middle ages came to the people from the pulpit it comes to the modern reader in secular, but no less popular, form. The modern romance and the detective story with its solution, also carry double meanings that are no less important to the completion of their plots than is the *moralitas* of the preacher's parable.[1]

And again:

> The older iconographic languages of the religious parable now need a good deal of interpretation, because their worlds are remote from our world. . . . Even though the twentieth-century reader has no experience with detectives and murderers, he understands the world of the private eye. . . .[2]

The third time Fletcher mentions the detective story, it is as part of a list of allegorical variants—westerns, romances, utopias, fairy tales. Many other writers have noted a glancing likeness between the detective story and the fairy tale;[3] it may well be that our sense of precognition as readers of the crime novel derives from the fact that the fairy tale is a prior version of the allegorical mode. For these correspondences among different narrative modes will be found to rest, ultimately, on an identical function that is allegorical.

The fiction I am considering is closely allied to myth, which in turn is sustained by the performance of ritual magic, and is ultimately religious in derivation. In one of the first penetrating analyses ever devoted to detective fiction *per se,* W.H. Auden speaks of its "magical function."[4] It is primarily on the grounds of this "magical function" (though on other grounds also) that the detective story can be read as a twentieth century fairy or folk tale, or fable as Fletcher calls it, (bearing in mind the etymological link between "fable" and "fabulous"). Jorge Luis Borges also denominates this magical function as he distinguishes between two forms of contemporary novels:

A Common Spring

> One kind of novel, the slow-moving psychological variety, attempts
> to frame an intricate chain of motives akin to those of real life. This,
> however, is not generally the case. In the adventure novel, cumber-
> some motivation of this kind is inappropriate. . . . A quite different
> sort of order rules them, one based not on reason but on association
> and suggestion—the ancient light of magic.
>
> Magic . . . has been reduced by Frazer to a convenient general law,
> the Law of Sympathy, which assumes that "things act on each other
> at a distance through a secret sympathy," either because their form is
> similar (imitative, or homeopathic magic) or because of previous
> physical contact (contagious, or contact, magic).[5]

Fiction is a method of denying determinism by substituting a different alternative, similar in method to the child's make-believe,
what Frank Kermode calls "the establishment of an accepted
freedom by magic."[6]

The detective story is linked with myth and other allegories
structurally. Both are concerned with enigma, myth obliquely and
the detective story directly; the detective novel (and the fairy tale)
share with myth the use of archetypal figures. Indeed, Northrop
Frye uses the ability to reduce fictional characters to archetypal
figures as a criterion for distinguishing between novel and romance
(the category in which he would include the detective novel):

> The essential difference between the novel and romance lies in the
> conception of characterization, the romancer does not attempt to
> create 'real people' so much as stylized figures which expand into
> psychological archetypes. It is in the romance that we find Jung's
> libido, anima, and shadow reflected in the hero, heroine, and villain
> respectively.[7]

Archetypal characterization is one of the charges argued
repeatedly against the detective story, but it is no more valid in this
context than it would be if levied against Cinderella, Prince Char-
ming, or the characters of any more accepted allegorical form. In
The Morphology of the Folktale the structuralist critic Vladimir
Propp arrives at the same conclusion about fairy tales, namely that
two of its characteristics are uniformity and recurrence. While the
dramatis personae of the fairy tale or myth vary, their function
does not. Lévi-Strauss, in fact, interprets all of Greek mythology

as being co-substantial; the various stories are all summarized by him: "King, Queen, Mother, Father, Brother, Sister, Daughter, Son, Son-in-law, Paramour, etc., are all seen to exhibit permutations of a single plot."[8]

The hero is one of the oldest and most universal archetypes. Jung views the hero myth in its ongoing tradition as exemplum. Lord Raglan believes that to the hero accrue those themes which encapsulate the universal rites of passage—birth, initiation, and death. Jung concurs, "the archetypal pattern of initiation in the religious sense—known since ancient times as 'the mysteries'—[is] woven into the texture of all ecclesiastical rituals. . . ."[9]

The search for common literary denominators leads not only to the consideration of archetypal characters, but also suggests a literary interpretation centered about themes and motifs. In modern times, new anthropological material substantiating comparative mythology has made this approach possible. Claude Lévi-Strauss has said, "if we consider any corpus of mythological tales at their face value, we get the impression of an enormous variety of trivial incident, associated with a great deal of repetition and a recurrent harping on very elementary themes."[10]

Propp elaborates:

> The steed, the eagle, the ship, are forms of bearers of dead souls, and one may suppose that one of the first bases of folktale composition, travelling in particular, reflects notions about the travelling of souls to the other world.[11]

William Aydelotte senses the sempiternal:

> The fantasies of the detective story appear in recognizable form in the popular literature of other ages, in folklore for example, and the drives they reveal are therefore by no means recent in origin but might rather be regarded as traditional elements of the human character as it has developed in our civilization.[12]

If these themes *are* based on ritual, then they are ultimately religious, sacred, and have in common the "magical function" to which we alluded earlier.

The structuralist approach of looking for "deeper structures" within literary works (a method resembling that of the semiologists and anthropologist Lévi-Strauss) is immediately useful in this context. We can search out analogies among genres, comparing written or oral myth, fairy and folk tale with the later allegory, the crime novel. We have a method that discloses their formulaic connection. Whereas mimetic literature attempts to make us "see" ourselves and our world, the formulaic novel substitutes a different vision: an ideal world. It does this by severe moral simplification—disorder, ambiguity, lack of resolution are extirpated. We are transported into a world secure in its certainties. Formulaic literature, for example, is one of the last refuges of the idealized hero. The reader does not have to confront himself, but an idealized version of himself, more fortunate or more powerful. Thus the reader is enabled to transcend his own limitations, and escape from himself. The imagination creates in surprisingly conventional modes.

What are these motifs and these eidetic images? Who are these heroes? What is this "magical function"? What is this landscape against which these figures move and these themes are played out? And, finally, if they are all subsumed under allegory, what is their allegorical intention?

I have drawn the list which follows (Table I, Chapter II) from Stith Thompson's longer compilation of motifs from folk tale, myth, ballad, fable, medieval romance, and exemplum. These motifs seem to be amazingly applicable to the detective story, requiring the minimum adaptation of detail to fit a modern context. Furthermore, the extraordinary quantity of such motifs establishes an immediate sense of relationship between the earlier and anonymous folk material and the detective story.

Stith Thompson's list could well be summarized by de Vries' statement, made in his book *Poe and After*, ". . . the fairy story, lyric in origin, bristles with crime."[13] There are so many motifs from our folk inheritance which apply to the crime novel that it is impossible to enumerate them all: H1210 Quest assigned/police investigation; H1220 Quest voluntarily undertaken/amateur detective; J50-1180 Wisdom and cleverness/handbook for the successful detective; KO-K1999 Deception/handbook for successful criminal; and N 270-800 could well be a list of plot hints for the aspiring crime novelist.

Perhaps a more fruitful way to assess the significance these motifs have for our inquiry is to re-group them under larger thematic headings which indicate their relevance to the detective story and provide a basis for discussion: Pursuit, The Quest, Identity and Recognition, The Scapegoat, Poetic Justice (Order). Tautology is difficult to avoid, these motifs are so intertwined.

I. The Pursuit Theme

One of the most common allegorical themes is Pursuit, and we have only to think of the range from Francis Thompson's religious allegory *The Hound of Heaven* to Rex Warner's political allegory *The Aerodrome* to remind ourselves how variously it has been employed. Pursuit stories are found all over Europe as well as in *The Arabian Nights,* and are allied to the stories of disenchantment by disguise or shape-shifting, a motif which Lord Raglan attributes to superstition. In its simplest terms, pursuit suggests movement; the hero is pursued and subsequently rescued from pursuit. This, of course, is a basic constituent of the fairy tale. Both the detective story and the fairy tale are set in motion by an act of villainy; their subsequent movement differs, however. In the fairy tale (and the myth for that matter) the movement is mainly physical, and thus more naturally lends itself to the theme of pursuit. For this reason it is more closely allied to the thriller, which as we have shown is, *sui generis,* wide-ranging and episodic, even comedic, retaining vestiges of its picaresque inheritance (Defoe, Smollett, and Fielding). The thriller can become more interested in, and sympathetic to, the id; it has an interior landscape, and can contain developed characterization. The detective story, on the other hand, glorifies the superego. It does not rely on action, but rather on the intellectual activity of deduction

> . . . wherein a fictional character solves a fictional mystery through
> the use of inductive and deductive reasoning—ratiocination, as this

operation was called in the early nineteenth century. Such a story
might indeed include thrilling events and action, but in no way does
the solution of the mystery depend on action.[14]

The "whodunit," no matter how long, is one episode, a single
working out of a problem.

Because the thriller, but not the detective story, has incorporated elements of the Gothic novel, in which melodramatic effects are permitted for their own sake, the thriller allows fortuitous
personal peril whereas the detective novel does not. Though the
detective story and the thriller share a movement through danger
to security, the detective story emphasizes the security and the
thriller, the danger. In the thriller the hero is often *obliged* to move
on because of his illicit activities (e.g., Robin Hood, Don Juan);
thus the mechanics of the structure insure its physical mobility.

Another difference between the fairy tale or thriller and the
detective tale is that the detective story's form of pursuit may be
the intellectual explanation of a riddle. Though the fairy tale may
contain a riddle, to solve it by analytic observation runs counter to
its propensity for magical solutions. For the writer of the classic
detective novel, however, magic and the supernatural are outlawed; they violate the canons of fair play between writer and reader
whereby the reader is given all the information necessary for a rational solution of the mystery.

The detective novel does permit one magical device: the
(magically) infallible detective. Angus Fletcher views him as a
watered-down medicine man, a magus who restores the health of
the community:

> Although the principle of magical contagion, by which characters in
> allegories interact, infecting each other with various vices and virtues
> . . . need not involve direct reference to magical practices or to magi-
> cians . . . the author does present . . . a mad scientist in science fic-
> tions, a Hercule Poirot in detective fiction, a wise country doctor in
> romantic westerns, a sage in all cases.[15]

Auden agrees that the appeal of the detective story lies in its
cathartic effect, implemented by such a figure: "The reader of the

22

thriller may exorcise his fantasies of violence, but the reader of the detective story is exorcising his sense of sin . . . by the miraculous intervention of a genius from outside who removes guilt by giving knowledge of guilt."[16] This genius from outside tallies exactly with Fletcher's allegorical magus; both critics discern a magical agent. Both use the metaphor of disease, Fletcher with the terms "contagion" and "infecting," and Auden with the term "cure." In the same vein, Gavin Lambert speaks of the ultimate identification of the murderer in the Sherlock Holmes stories as, "a practical and symbolic act . . . preclud[ing] the removal of an infection of the system."[17]

Largely through the offices of such an agent implementing such an act, the detective story *does* share with the fairy tale a movement through danger to ultimate security, despite its different form of pursuit.

II. The Quest Theme

"The allegorical journey may first of all be understood in the narrow sense of a questing journey," writes Fletcher.[18] A progress, then, need not be an actual journey, but may be a ranging of the mind, the creating of a new cosmography, a movement towards the ideal. It is to this last type of "progress" that the detective story truly belongs. If the allegorical quest, in general terms, is undertaken by a protagonist seeking something which he lacks, then in the specific instance of the detective story what is sought is the restoration of innocence. This innocence, achieved by exonerating the many through identifying the guilty one, establishes the security which was temporarily displaced. Restoration of innocence is the avowed goal of detection narrative, which therefore can be classified as a movement towards the ideal.

C. Day-Lewis, who under the pseudonym Nicholas Blake wrote scores of "whodunits," leans to the same anagogical view, investing the detective story with sin, a high priest, and a judgment. He claims that the detective story provides a needed locus of guilt which the offices of religious belief no longer commonly provide. The sense of sin which seems to lie at the base of the detective story is a sin against God, since murder is unique—the one irremediable crime and the one crime for which the victim can extend no pardon. (The thriller, on the other hand, presents sins of man against man, and does not *have* to cope with the central fact of murder.) Thus the quest for a return to innocence which is enacted in the detective story duplicates, in a contemporary form, a moral progress such as that inaugurating *The Pilgrim's Progress*. "Whenever there prevails a mood of intense piety, and wherever life beyond is regarded as the true one, and life here as merely transitory, this life is experienced and shaped as a migration."[19]

III. The Identity and Recognition Theme

It is hardly necessary to point out that identity is the central theme of the detective novel, since the mystery of the criminal's identity is its *raison d'être;* furthermore, the identities of the innocent bystanders are deliberately obfuscated to postpone the resolution; and even the identity of the detective is sometimes withheld, if not from the reader, then from the other characters. This deliberate retardation is one of the characteristic features of the detective novel and is structurally antithetical to traditions of Restoration comedy and French farce, in which the audience is privy from the outset to the mistaken identity which precipitates the action of the novel or play. In his article "Who Cares Who Killed Roger Ackroyd?" Edmund Wilson complains that the "device of retardation" stalls the movement of the detective novel and makes it less compelling reading than the thriller.[20] But deliberate retardation makes possible multiple interpretations during the process of reading; the narrative must remain open on many levels, corresponding to layers of meaning in allegory.

Kafka has tellingly demonstrated how the identity theme can be presented allegorically. In *The Trial* he has written about a man, K, certain of his guilt but not of the *identity* of his crime; in "The Metamorphosis" Gregor Samsa's change of physical *identity,* a good illustration of the shape-shifting motif, is made the allegorical referent of moral ambivalence and guilt. Both of these works trace quests for identity.

As we noted earlier in this chapter, stories of pursuit frequently employ enchantment or disenchantment, disguise or shape-shifting. The identity theme in the crime novel leans on the device of disguise. Thus Conan Doyle, in "Scandal in Bohemia," shows us the leading characters, Holmes and Irene Adler, in garments of disguise; in *"A Study in Scarlet"* he disguises identity behind a false name, a common offshoot of intrigue, but, in Doyle, the means to escape a criminal past. The crime novel involves both literal and metaphysical cover-ups (i.e., the mask and the persona), often indications of the author's own psychological defenses. Thus Gavin Lambert sees Wilkie Collins as exorcising his own "buried lives and secrets" in "the masked child, the imprisoned daughter, the false beggar . . . the wigs and cosmetics" of his fiction.[21] But in the twentieth century, disguise spreads among whole groups as individual identity becomes increasingly difficult to establish.

The identity theme has, of course, been a mainstay of literature of all types in all ages.

> From the Bible and Greek dramatists to Dickens and Henry James, the discovery of who is who and what his actions mean has been a mainstay of great narratives. The stories of Joseph and Oedipus, the plots of *Bleak House* and *In the Cage,* pose questions of identification and work out puzzles in the most exact sense of these terms. . . .[22]

Attempting a definition, Northrop Frye writes:

> [Identity] is existence before 'once upon a time,' and subsequent to the 'and they lived happily ever after.' What happens in between are adventures, or collisions with external circumstances [once upon a crime] and the return to identity is a release from the tyranny of these circumstances. . . . Most romances end happily with the return to the state of identity, and begin with the departure from it.[23]

Still, two different "questions of identity" are coupled in the modern crime novel: the older, more literal question, often mirrored in an exterior journey (e.g., Samuel Johnson's *Rasselas*) and the newer, interior and psychological question derived from the Romantic legacy of the nineteenth century and the psychoanalytic and philosophical concepts of the twentieth, most particularly existentialism and phenomenology. Scholes and Kellogg write:

> The discovery of the self, the recovery from the trauma or wound in the psyche, offered narrative artists a new kind of comic formulation referable to psychology rather than to myth. Destruction of the

individual due to trauma rather than *hamartia* offered a new scheme for tragedy. The ritualistic-romantic quest for the Grail is metamorphosed in modern fiction into the search for identity . . . But its general effect has been to drive the old romantic formulations out of serious fiction and into the realm Graham Greene called 'entertainment.'[24]

Thus Sophocles' *Oedipus,* for example, has been reinterpreted by the modern sensibility as a tragedy of character (or internal tragedy), rather than a tragedy of fate (or external tragedy).

Clearly the detective novel and the tragedy must face common questions. Whether the theme of identity is approached internally or externally, there are certain structural conditions which both forms fulfill as the search for identity is enacted. The element of surprise is integral to both tragedy and detective fiction, for example. Aristotle's dictum about tragic drama, namely that it must create expectations it can reasonably fulfill, contingencies which may introduce surprise, but nothing, finally, incongruous or extravagant to confuse the process of discovery—this could be applied verbatim to the detective novel.

As some critics have remarked, insofar as the detective novel contains fewer narrative byways, a static environment, less firmly delineated character, and a *deus ex machina* in the shape of the detective, it is closer to drama than to the regular novel. The detective story, like classical drama, has a beginning, middle and end, and adheres to the principle of poetic justice. W.H. Auden, in the essay to which we have already drawn attention, "The Guilty Vicarage," notes specific structural parallels with Greek tragedy: first, concealment; secondly, manifestation *(hamartia);* thirdly, reversal *(peripeteia).* Auden goes on to say that in both Greek tragedy and the detective story the characters are not changed by their actions; in Greek tragedy their actions are fixed; in the detective story the decisive event has already taken place (this is sometimes also true of Greek tragedy). He also distinguishes between the detective story which obeys the classical unities closely, and the thriller which demands constant changes of time and place.

26

Although in these ways the crime novel does resemble tragedy structurally, there are basic conditions of tragedy it cannot fulfill. Neither its hero nor its outcome partakes of these structural resemblances. While it is true that, unlike the picaresque hero, who submits to blind chance, neither choosing nor deliberating but acting under compulsion (e.g., Don Juan), the murderer presumably does choose and deliberate, does precipitate the action, nevertheless we cannot say of the criminal that his deeds, like those of a tragic hero, are the work of a noble character. Thus, even if we hold to the conception of tragedy as a tragedy of fate, the detective novel is not a tragedy, because it recounts the fall of the least good man, not the best man. The author cannot enlist our identification with the murderer to a degree which would make us reject his punishment. If, contrariwise, we believe that the detective is the protagonist (this is the premise of Raymond Chandler, Dashiell Hammett, and other writers of the "realistic" thriller, who have cast their detective-protagonists as "the great good man") then he in turn cannot be said either to precipitate the action or to embody a "fatal flaw." There remains the important problem of the final outcome and its consequences for the other actors. If the downfall of the murderer is an outcome unequivocally to be desired (as it is in the detective novel but not in *Lear, Hamlet,* or *Oedipus* for whose heroes we mourn the lost potential for greatness), then this accomplishment makes the detective novel "a tragedy with a happy ending," as Raymond Chandler phrased it.[25] The comedic atmosphere results from arresting an advance towards death or impotence via the explanation of a riddle.

But a more complex work which deals with murder—e.g., *Crime and Punishment*—compels the reader into an identification with the murderer. In fantasy one avoids one's suffering; in works like *Crime and Punishment* one can not. As we have previously established, part of the magic of the detective novel lies in effecting our *disassociation* from the murderer. The detective story therefore cannot produce the catharsis of tragedy. The detective novel's central focus is on a riddle or mystery—inevitably an intellectual problem, which Marjorie Nicholson, among others, likens to a game of chess. Clearly, passions are not its proper

27

province.[26] In classical drama, Fletcher writes, we learn of "discoveries and reversals [that] are not mere intellectual changes from 'ignorance to knowledge' but more important from 'love to hate,' or 'hate to love.' "[27] Such emotional changes are undergone neither by the detective, who remains professionally dispassionate, nor by the murderer, whose state of mind is fixed. This may be attributable, in part, to the fact that the detective story is never concerned with a whole life, but rather, as already noted, with an episode. The enjoyment of reading a detective novel may, in lieu of any identification with a character, lie in the sagacity that the reader, like the detective, is called upon to bring to the problem.

Another important aspect of the identity theme is a special sort of recognition: that attraction between hunter and hunted for which the crime novel provides a most sympathetic, though not exclusive, milieu. This bond between pursuer and pursued may, for example, be channelled either into psychological insight or social criticism, or may reach the province of tragedy. The relationship may be extended so far as to result in a confusion of identities between the two, or in the "doubling" or "doppelganger," motif. The ironic extreme is a character such as Oedipus, who functions simultaneously as criminal and detective, hunter and hunted. (See Notes 1 and 2, Chapter II.) As Eric Ambler writes, "There is a criminal and a policeman inside every human being."[28]

Jung traces the roots of the doppelgänger theme to the magic of ancient hunting cultures. Analyzing their cave paintings he observes:

> These pictures suggest a hunting-magic like that still practiced by hunting tribes in Africa. The painted animal has the function of a 'double'; by its symbolic slaughter, the hunters attempt to anticipate and ensure the death of the real animal. This is a form of sympathetic magic, which is based on the 'reality' of a double represented in a picture: what happens to the picture will happen to the original.[29]

Fletcher identifies later literary versions of the archetype:

> Symmetrical plot structure abounds through literature wherever struggles of a radical kind occur . . . When the author divides his

28

major character into two antithetical aspects, he is bound to create double stories, one for each half. This is what happens in the Jekyll and Hyde stories, which abound in German prose literature . . . Hoffman [E.T.A. Hoffmann] and others developed the idea of the doppelgänger with such psychological precision that the allegorical character of this writing is not apparent. The fact is, however, that these antitheses which the German Romantic double depend upon are always antitheses of good and evil.[30]

Thus doubling may work as a device for dramatizing a moral struggle which takes place in the course of an identity search. In the rigid morality of the detective novel the two halves remain disparate; there is no rapprochement essayed or desired. The only trace of moral ambivalence may lie in the artistic sublimation of evil, when, as Schiller says, "the base element disappears in the terrible," so that the murderer is often not punished literally, but left to commit suicide or be handed over to authorities outside the scope of the book; in this way neither the reader nor the detective is forced to witness the punishment of the opponent, our "double."

Dostoevsky's *Crime and Punishment* introduces a further permutation of the once rigid concept of the doppelgänger as divisible into good and evil personalities. Raskolnikov's diminished sense of identity necessitates an act of assertion, but he commits a crime which is unworthy of him. Therefore his proof waits upon a worthy opponent: the investigator, Porfiry.

The extent to which the doppelgänger can reveal an attraction between the hunted and the hunter is shown in a central scene of the Japanese movie "High and Low," (the title itself suggests doubling), made from an American thriller. The injured party, Mifune, goes to see the criminal and, faced with the kidnapper of his son, asks him, "Why are you so convinced that it is right that we hate each other?"[31]

This special attraction between the hunter and the hunted is also a by-product of the chase as "game," sportsmanship between oponents, codifying of rules, indeed sport becomes ritual. Roles are carefully defined, and each side plays by the rules; the professionalism constitutes a bond in itself.

29

Within the looser framework of the thriller, with its margin for digression and exploration, the "doubling" may be more subtle or ambiguous. The thriller enables us to close the gap between the two halves, to experience vicariously the guilt of 'the other.' In the crime story both our anti-social impulses and our consciences find satisfaction. We can hunt with the hounds and flee with the hare.

From the problem of blurring of identities presented through the doppelgänger, it is an easy step to consideration of communal identity and guilt. George Orwell, whose own books were vehicles for social criticism, looks at the rather brutal *No Orchids for Miss Blandish* from a social vantage point:

> *Miss Blandish* takes for granted sexual sophistication in its readers, as well as corruption and self-seeking norms of behavior. The detectives are almost as great rogues as the criminals, and motivated only by payment. If ultimately one sides with the police against the gangsters, it is mainly because they are better organized and more powerful, because, in fact, the law is a bigger racket than crime.[32]

Orwell uses Chase's book to make the generalization that the problem is no longer to affix the deed to the doer but the blame to society. Though drawing their conclusions from diverse sources, many commentators have drawn our attention to this phenomenon. In contemporary literature, and life as well, Frederick Hoffman writes,

> The basic problem is to distinguish between assailant and victim, accurately to locate each, and to distribute the onus of guilt between them. These problems are often not solved; they are referred to [an] essential absurdity. . . .

Absurdity is antithetical to the assumptions of the strictly formulaic detective novel, in which morality is never questioned, but is always enforced. Furthermore, the importance attached to plot in detective fiction assures that a logical explanation of events will be forthcoming. But in the work of Eugene Ionesco, for instance, the ubiquitous problem of absurdity becomes more pronounced as it is placed ironically within the confines of the detective formula. Thus in the play *Victims of Duty* the policeman as well as the man

30

he has come to arrest are shown as victims referred to in the title (see Note 3, Chapter II). In his play *The Lesson* a school teacher murders forty pupils a day; melodrama, made even more hyperbolic, depicts absurdity.

The failure to ascribe guilt, to solve the problem of identity as the detective novel prescribes, is seen by some observers to be a relatively modern condition. Eric Hobsbawm, in a special issue of the *Times Literary Supplement* devoted to detective fiction asserts, "Modern private enterprise and modern civilization leave blurred what is criminal, and hence our own picture is complicated by the relation between crime and social revolt."[34] An extreme case is depicted in Daniel Berrigan's *The Trial of the Catonsville Nine* in which social conscience initiates the criminal act.

Though we may perceive an exacerbation of the problem in contemporary values, we cannot see it as a uniquely modern problem. Elliot L. Gilbert perceives this same moral confusion in Dickens' *Bleak House:*

> For it is clear from *Bleak House* just as a jailer becomes a prisoner of the man he guards, so Inspector Bucket is as much the creature of crime as he is its nemesis . . . Bucket . . . succeeds in avenging the inhumanity of murder only by coldly perverting the human obligations of friendship and sympathy.[35]

And Hannah Arendt, in *The Origins of Totalitarianism,* draws the same conclusion from different materials:

> They (the type of white observer in South Africa) were irresistibly attracted by a world where everything was a joke, which could teach them 'The Great Joke,' that is, the mastery of despair.[36] The perfect gentleman and the perfect scoundrel came to know each other well, in the 'great wild jungle without law,' and they found themselves well-matched in their enormous dissimilarity, *identical souls in different disguises.* We have seen the behavior of high society during the Dreyfus affair and watched Disraeli discover the social relationship between vice and crime; here, too, we have essentially the same story of high society falling in love with its own underworld. . . . The play, *Dreigroschenoper* [1928, based on Gay's *The Beggar's Opera,* 1728], presented gangsters as respectable businessmen and respectable

31

businessmen as gangsters. This was accepted as true wisdom, masks discarded, and the standards of the work openly accepted.[37]

This non-fictive inversion is the unstated premise of the fiction of such writers as Hammett and Chandler, as well as Graham Greene, who incorporated society's linkage of criminal and respectable. *"L'enfer, c'est nous-mêmes."*

We have arrived at the opposite pole from whence we started; the detective story requires a closed and innocent milieu, so that the murder precipitates a crisis and a temporary fall from grace for the whole community. Hence in a police state, or an anarchic state, murder could have no real significance; where murder is expected there can be no judgment of individual instances of life and death.

The preoccupation of major nineteenth and twentieth century writers (e.g., Faulkner, Greene, Conrad, Dickens, Dostoevsky, James) with detectives as thinking beings whose intellects cannot cope with the communal guilt and disorder of the world may in part explain the period's great interest in two literary figures—Hamlet and Oedipus. Both of these characters are, as has frequently been remarked, detectives of a sort; that is, they are both obliged to solve murder mysteries, and their roles, which make them ideally suited to the job, eventuate ironically in their doom.

IV. The Scapegoat Theme

The idea of a scapegoat, old enough to have probably originated with human sacrifice, is prescribed in Leviticus:

> And Aaron shall lay both his hands upon the head of the live goat, and confess over him all the inequities of the children of Israel, and all their transgressions in all their sins, putting them upon the head of the goat, and shall send *him* away by the hand of a fit man into the wilderness.

Acknowledgment of communal guilt produces a functional scapegoat. For a multiplicity of reasons, the figure of Oedipus is extraordinarily suitable for elaborating on the Scapegoat theme. In the mythical story of Oedipus, we find many of the motifs of allegory commingled: the Oedipus plot is a quest; it is obviously related to the enigma; and, as we have already remarked, the strange role assigned to Oedipus, who paradoxically functions as both criminal and detective, unites the two halves of the doppelgänger (these two roles, of course, tie him more intimately to the detective novel than would the mere overlapping of allegorical conventions). The allegorical implications of the Oedipus story were captured by the painter Gustave Moreau, whose *Oedipus and the Sphinx* (Illustration I, Chapter II) shows the Sphinx (itself an allegorical figure with its bestial lower and human upper half) growing out of the body of Oedipus.

The story of Oedipus is so well-known that we may just outline the events of his drama. His sin, though unwitting, brings misfortune upon Thebes, and it is not until Oedipus himself garners evidence in his role as king and guardian of the city that he realizes he is the scapegoat who must atone. He is exiled from the city and also blinded.

This theme of the scapegoat, derived from mythology, is without doubt one of the archetypal themes of literature. The insurance of fertility by the ritual slaughter of the king-priest has been documented by anthropologists, among them Sir James Frazer, author of *The Golden Bough,* one of the most powerful shapers of the twentieth-century imagination. This mythological material has been utilized by critics (e.g., Jessie Weston's *From Ritual to Romance*) in the explication of texts, as well as incorporated into primary material (e.g., T.S. Eliot's *The Waste Land,* in which the scapegoat is personified as a Fisher King,[38] implicitly placing the sacrifice of Christ within a larger tradition.)

The centrality of the Oedipus legend to western folklore has been established ingeniously by Lord Raglan in a survey designed to illustrate the dependence of myth upon ritual. In this survey, *The Hero,* Lord Raglan puts together a kind of conglomerate model for a heroic career, consisting of twenty-two crises, turning points, or motifs (e.g., exile and return).[39] He applied this pattern to various heroes starting with Oedipus, and proceeding to Theseus, Romulus, Hercules, Perseus, Jason, Asclepius, Dionysios, Apollo, Zeus, Joseph, Moses, Sigurd, Arthur, and many more, ranking them by the degree to which they fulfilled his enumerated conditions. Oedipus ranked highest with twenty-one, which may lend statistical corroboration to the primacy he was accorded by Freud.[40]

Curiously enough, in a book which aimed to prove that the legendary Oedipus was really the historical king Akhnaton, Immanuel Velikovsky, independently of Lord Raglan, devised a similar approach whereby the Oedipus legend is viewed as a composition of certain motifs garnered from the vast storehouse of Indo-European mythology. This approach provides a way of placing the specific hero-myth within a tradition, thus detaching it from a too-literal or singular interpretation.[41]

From the scapegoat of myth and fairy tale to that of detective fiction is a plausible modulation. In fact, the scapegoat, whose expulsion and expiation is necessary for the continued well-being of the society, is indispensable to the detective novel. Those critics, particularly William Aydelotte, interested in probing the psychological or sociological foundations of the detective novel have had no trouble in identifying him:

> The criminal is a *scapegoat*. He is the cause of and can justly be blamed for all the troubles of the detective story world, the murder and everything that follows from it. . . . He shares something of the ambiguous character of the scapegoat of mythology who is both a friend and enemy to society, who commits the act of sin or disobedience that helps us all and then removes the taint or penalty attached thereto by himself undergoing punishment [as did Oedipus], a punishment that is occasionally inflicted by the beneficiaries.[42]

Twice more Aydelotte couples the two, criminal and scapegoat:

> The criminal is a fantasy developing out of a competitive, uncohesive society. He is a personalization of our grievances, as we like to personalize them in the atmosphere of political or social crises in real

34

life. We have toward the criminal the same or comparable feelings
that we have toward any one of the commonly accepted scapegoats
of our day, the Jew, the Labor agitator, 'Wall Street,' etc. . . .[43]

and finally,

By unearthing the criminal [the detective] sets in motion the
scapegoat mechanism which shifts the burden of guilt from our
shoulders. He can do all these things because he has control over the
world we know and the destinies of men in it.[44]

Because of the ethical bias of the detective story, the figure of
the scapegoat and the concept of taboo, both of which emerge
from ideas about good and evil, are predictably present. The motif
of the plague such as we find in *Oedipus,* symbolizing the dominant Greek idea that "murder pollutes the land,"[45] is the concomitant of the theme of the scapegoat. We have already encountered
this image of the plague, engendering fear of contagion and conse-
quent isolation, in both Auden and Fletcher's vocabulary of illness
and infection. Lévi-Strauss sees the system of limitation by taboos
(imposed on human behavior by moral codes, by law, by fear
itself) on the one hand, and man's will to overcome inhibition on
the other, as a basic opposition of any society. This polarization is
indigenous to allegory, and thus natural for the detective story.
The scapegoat functions in the allegory of crime as the outcast
whose banishment and subsequent isolation will enable the rest of
the community to cohere.

Whether we construe isolation physically, as exile, or symbolically, as taboo, the ordering or disunifying of images, agents,
assumptions, and even linguistic systems within the novel is
shaped by it. Isolation is manifest not only in the figure of the
scapegoat, but in the ordering of the artist's materials. Fletcher
claims that "Surrealist art is surreal precisely because its images
are all isolated. . . ." In the detective story, the images (or 'clues'),
though presented in isolation, must "add up"; the detective story
is teleological, surrealism dysteleological. Fletcher elaborates, "A
riddle, after all, is a verbalized surrealist collage, with a hidden
meaning that draws the parts together 'under the surface'. . . ."[46]

(See Illustration 2, Chapter II.) The detective story is, in a sense, a latterday version of the enigma. In the detective story, details are purposely isolated: the landscape is dotted with unconnected people and objects in order to contribute to mystification and suspense. As in melodrama, or the sensationalism of mannerist imagery in poetry and painting, there is a "dialectic of violent contrast."[47] This isolation of images is an intrinsic part of the detective story; it is an intrinsic part of the allegorical process, as Fletcher would assure us. And it calls into question the whole issue of place and order which we will discuss under our final thematic heading, *Poetic Justice (Order)*.

V. Poetic Justice (Order)

A dominant sense of moral order, strong enough to impose itself upon the landscape and even to be responsible for patterns of language, pervades all forms of allegory. We must not be led astray by the act of violence which is the crime novel's initial impulse; we still inhabit a world where "God's in His Heaven,/All's right with the world."

The moral order in detective fiction acts as a kind of Prime Mover: "Behind the crime artist's obsession with melodrama lies another obsession, which is to imagine punishment as well as crime."[48] The discussion will begin with a definition and explanation of how Poetic Justice operates in the context of the detective novel proper. Having recently resorted to the phrase "crime novel," the differences between the detective novel proper and the thriller must be re-emphasized, for the latter does not share this passion for formal disposition. As system in art counteracts the extravagance of modern fantastic art, so in the detective novel system counteracts any inclination toward the supernatural, the Gothic, the extravagant—the province of the thriller or romance. Fletcher extends the analogy between the effects of system in literature and in the visual arts, "A visualizing, isolating, tendency is bound to appear wherever system is desired, since the perfect form of imagery for such purposes will be something like a geometric shape."[49] This geometrizing may be equated with the paraphernalia of the detective novel, maps and timetables and diagrams, which Auden interprets as rituals of space and time. However, its "isolating, visualizing tendency" is antithetical to surrealism. The crucial difference is between the permanent dislocation of surrealism (whether in art or literature) and the shifting dislocations of crime narrative. The former defies rational solution; its static composition or movement cannot be termed a "progress toward the ideal" as can that of the detective novel. Though they display superficial similarities and both can be interpreted allegorically, they are dissimilar in their conclusion, and in the conclusions we draw from them. The order of surrealism is both private (vs. societal or public for the detective novel) and intuitive (vs. rational or logical for the detective novel).

Many writers have attested to the implacable sense of order in detective fiction: Julian Symons, "The detective story reduces the unruly shape of life to an ideal order"; Margery Nicholson, "The detective story is a revolt . . . from a smart and easy pessimism, which interprets men and the universe in terms of unmoral purposelessness, to a re-belief in a universe governed by cause and effect"; Nicholas Blake, "The detective story's clientele are relatively prosperous persons, who have a stake in the social system."[50]

Whether we believe that this order compensates for Western democratic *angst* produced by the disorder, even incipient failure of Western society, or on the contrary, that this order is the fruit of a belief in the functioning of the democratic process itself, there is no gainsaying the tightness of the form which has developed. There are no loose ends; all is explained; the murderer is always caught. We are dealing not with justice, but with poetic justice. In this sense, of course, the detective novel is as much an escape form as the more adventurous thriller—that is, it is neater than life.

The simplest of all allegorical combats takes place in the detective novel. As we noted in our discussion of the doppelgänger, the moral dichotomy posed in the detective novel is never bridged. This is at once its simplicity and its security, for there can be no impediment to the administration of justice when guilt is so clearly assigned, good is so clearly superior, and all is predictable. Since we are only out to track down the murderer, it makes little

37

difference what the rest of the characters are like. Everything is black or white because it can only be considered in relation to the one specific question: "Who did it?"

This order eventuates in certain rules. For example, since the detective novel is not to be a novel of ideas (i.e., there is no exploration), the murder should not be committed by a gang, because murder will not be presented as a social problem—e.g., the "criminal classes." Similarly, the victim cannot be someone to whom the reader has become attached, nor can he be a gangster himself (in which case the game would be reduced to an internecine warfare, excluding the reader). The detective novel's impulse is the wish to see justice done, and the murder, as we have said, is simply the point of departure. Therefore the concern of the detective novel ends with the dispensation of poetic justice; it never looks ahead to the consequences of its judgments in the world outside the novel.

The detective novel is a ritualistic game, and the rules must be observed unwaveringly, as in the execution of any ritual. (This aspect of its "gamesmanship" is attributed, by George Orwell, to its Englishness. In his essay on the *Raffles* stories he stresses their sociological implications: "The *Raffles* stories, written from the angle of the criminal, are much less antisocial than many modern stories written from the angle of the detective. Their key phrase is 'not done' [i.e., in society]. The line they draw between good and evil is as senseless as a Polynesian taboo, but, at least, like the taboo, it has the advantage that everyone accepts it.")[51] This ritual gamesmanship excludes not only ambiguity, but humor as well; certainly it cannot admit mercy or error into its charmed circle. In short, the detective novel can never say, *"Tout comprendre, tout à pardonner."*

In many of these features of order the detective story is manifesting its allegorical nature. Fletcher writes:

> Allegory seems often to be more orderly than any other mode of literature. The 'reason' behind the allegorist's destruction of evil, which he accomplished by sending a daemonically-powered agent of death against the camp of the evildoers, is an overpowered reason, no way balancing the claims of abstraction of experience. The expression of utopian good and utopian evil (Sir Thomas More vs. George Orwell) provides no solid grounding in experience.[52]

In this quotation about the nature of allegory, we observe the same rigid dichotomy of moral forces, the same insistence upon rationality, the same sense that whatever the scene we are shown a specially constructed reality, which we have attributed to the detective novel. This special reality, which Fletcher calls "an idealizing consistency of thematic content"[53] is apparent in the absolutism of Poetic Justice.

As one would expect, certain of these features crop up in myth and fairy tale as well. Poetic Justice is the very criterion philosopher Suzanne Langer uses to define the fairy tale: "The fairy tale, as Plato said, is a story told by nurses to frighten children into obedience; its appeal to the superego is immediate and lasting. It is the poetry of 'poetic justice.' "[54] In a similar vein Vladimir Propp remarks, "In the fairy tale the villain is always punished, or killed in battle, or perishes during pursuit . . . good and evil get their just deserts."[55] The detective can be interpreted as the modern counterpart of the hero of the fairy tale, prince or Knight of the Grail, the modern deliverer from evil.

There is a second kind of order, an external order also portending Poetic Justice, and immanent in the landscape. The argument for Creation as evidence of prior Divine Being is the argument from order, and the landscape of the detective story functions in precisely this way, as a visible guarantor of certain articles of faith. The landscape of the detective story is shaped by its purpose, which is to say, the landscape itself serves an allegorical function. (Again, we must bear in mind that this does not pertain to the thriller, whose purpose and therefore whose milieu, is different.) Allegorical landscape gives the reader touchstones for evil.[56]

What is the landscape of the detective novel? Clearly, it must be an enclosed innocent space, "the great good place," as W.H. Auden terms it; the more innocent the place, the more contradictory the act (or murder). It must be capable of confining its characters in order that they be known to the reader (and to each other) and fall under temporary suspicion; it must be innocent so that the expulsion of the murderer will restore the society to its former state of innocence. For these reasons Auden takes issue with Raymond Chandler, who proclaimed that he wanted to "take the body out of the vicarage garden and give it back to those who are good at it.'' Auden argues:

> If he [Chandler] wishes to write detective stories, i.e., stories where the reader's principal interest is to learn who did it, he could not be more mistaken; for in a society of professional criminals, the only possible motives for desiring to identify the murderer are blackmail or revenge, which both apply to the individual not the group as a whole, and can equally well inspire murder, restoring the society to the previous state of guilt, not innocence. Actually, whatever he may say, I think Mr. Chandler is interested in writing, not detective stories, but serious studies of criminal milieu, the Great Wrong Place . . .[57]

Now this ''great good place,'' this closed society, the walled-in Eden, is easily recognizable as a version of the allegorical ''hortus conclusus,'' or what Fletcher calls '' . . . health [O.E. Häl, whole] the whole body, the untorn garment, the complete Paradise . . . The hortus is closed so that it may prevent disease [in the crime novel, evil] from entering by contagion.''[58] (This analogy between spiritual and bodily health arose before in our discussion of taboo and the scapegoat.) Furthermore, both this innocent milieu and the literal hortus conclusus of medieval allegory effect a divorcement from reality, shutting in and shutting out. This is another reason for the separation of the detective story from reality.

In contrast with this cultivated, serene, innocent garden, akin to that of St. Teresa, stands the forest, the ''wood of error'' of Dante, Bunyan, and Grimm's fairy tales. The forest is not only an archetypal symbol of confusion and danger but frequently suggests enchantment and magical influence inadmissable in detective fiction. Lawrence Alloway, in an article for *Art News* (November 1971), proposes a distinction between landscape painting and pastoral painting which, when applied to the crime novel, freshly illuminates the distinction between the landscapes of the thriller and of the detective novel. Alloway says:

> Pastoral is ubiquitous, a constant in the arts, not merely in the sense of pertaining to shepherds, but as a celebration of human pleasure in what was not man-made . . . Pastoral, in the sense of a permanent

40

idyll, is not the same as landscape painting, which I take to be based on a time and a place . . . [but is] an exceptional reality, a dream-world in which we can find refuge.[59]

"What is not man-made" I take to be the Eden, the innocent milieu, in which we can feel secure because it *is* "permanent." This is also one explanation of why the environment of the detective novel has undergone so few changes; essentially, the world of the detective novel is not an actual place, but an ideal place. The thriller, however, like landscape painting, is tied to a time and a place and is constantly being made contemporaneous (and therefore dated). New and exotic locales may be introduced to provoke interest; equally effective is the visualization of a mundane locale as a wood of error. The detective story, like the pastoral, is the dream world in which we can find refuge; it is a magic place. This equation,

$$\frac{\text{detective story}}{\text{pastoral (garden)}} \quad \text{as} \quad \frac{\text{thriller}}{\text{landscape (wood of error)}}$$

helps us to understand the "unreality" of detective fiction.

The detective novel adopts a pervasively moral view of Nature or, as Jaques Barzun puts it, "It is not the mind of any man, murderer or victim, that matters in our genre, it is the uniformity of Nature and its legibility."[60] Implicit in the notion of idealized nature is the idealized order which Poetic Justice achieves.

The seventeenth-century view of Nature extends the vision of the Garden of Eden. "The whole visible cosmos is an organized world forever deprived of disorder . . . God's Providence banished chaos."[61] For example, Castiglione, in Bk. IV of *The Courtier,* considers all beauty under the aspect of a concept of universal order—beauty is *formosam,* order and harmony above all. A concomitant of this perception of an all-embracing visible order is an order which is expressed as hierarchy, decorum, propriety. This perception of universal ordering is metaphorically expressed in the Great Chain of Being.

This "unreality" (the fantasy of eternal order) is not only indigenous to but also a *goal* of the detective novel. Ross Macdonald and others have attributed the common setting of the detective story—e.g., the vicarage garden, the country house, the steamship, the university—variously to nostalgia, snobbery, or spurious glamor. But I believe these environments are chosen primarily because they comprise small, closed societies, with a given *modus operandi* which may be easily ascertained and in contrast to which the murder will stand out as an aesthetic as well as moral violation. The landscape of the detective novel is the "hortus conclusus" into which the snake has crept.

Diametrically opposed to the landscape of which we have been talking are the modern counterparts of the "wood of error," the cityscape and the wasteland; either "the image of a narrow, restricted space, in which there are too many objects [or people] for clear definition of their value" or "the impression of vast spaces indifferently inhabited, from which life has all but disappeared and in which an enemy or an evil is suggested merely by the range and scope of desolation apprehended."[62] This is the exaggeration which is native to melodrama. Eric Bentley comments: "Melodramatic vision is paranoid: . . . all things, living or dead, are combining to persecute us. Or rather, nothing is dead. Even the landscape has come to life if only to assault us. Perhaps one might sense something of this vision behind Birnam Wood's coming to Dunsinane in Macbeth. . . ."[63]

Similarly Simone Weil interprets the *Iliad* as a "Poem of Force," defining force as that which reduces anyone subjected to it to an object.[64] Twentieth century force has grown to gain its own autonomy; subject and object are both victims. A new concept of force inexplicable not only at the moment of impact, but forever, has resulted from the depersonalization and intrusion of technological and mechanical power, from warfare conducted by remote control, from governmental and bureaucratic agencies so numerous and so bewildering they defeat imaginative conjuration. The sheer scale of force and its distancing cannot be rendered in a human context. As the concept of force changed, so did the concept of the environment. "Modern literature [and the Thriller] is much concerned with the economy of violence and with the spatial figuration it causes. Not only does it alter space—as in the extreme examples of modern war—but space also assumes the character and decor required by both assailant and victim."[65] Both assailant and victim have become part of the landscape; for both assailant and victim,

42

violence fills an empty space. Thus the landscape becomes an exposition of the fear and evil which remain in it. The society is no longer able to be restored to a state of innocence by the expulsion of the criminal, whereas the detective novel, which always contains its force, always provides a solution. Contaminated landscapes occur in Conrad and Dostoevsky, in Eliot and Auden, in Hammet and Chandler, and innumerable other nineteenth and twentieth-century writers. In Graham Greene's "entertainments" this urban, corrupt, seamy, milieu is such a permanent feature that it has been designated "Greeneland."

The surrealist images of urban life and/or the wasteland are not only exploited as moral indices but in turn become agents, so that Frederick Hoffman calls the landscape itself an "assailant." The scene, then, is the objective correlative of what the author wishes us to accept as a state of mind. About *Crime and Punishment* Hoffman declares:

> There is no question that the landscape of Petrograd is an 'assailant,' in the sense that it scenically and atmospherically invites suspicion of its force. . . . Rooms are also images of the uncertainty and the implicit violence of the total scene. His own (Raskolnikov's) is small, filthy, deathly, shaped rather like a coffin. . . . At the police station, he walks down a narrow corridor as in a passageway to a prison or his tomb. In a profound sense, the city is an extension of his crime.[66]

Despite a mechanistic and violent environment, different degrees of faith remain possible to different authors. Hoffman believes there is a divine omniscience operative in Dostoevsky. By contrast the mindless actions of Stevie in Conrad's *The Secret Agent* or Raven in Greene's *This Gun for Hire* illustrate some of the binary oppositions the semiotic method poses—e.g., between the witting and the unwitting act, between performance imaginative and unimaginative, between the act relevant to intention or circumstantial. For Philip Marlowe, the private-eye hero of Raymond Chandler's books, the world is a "wet emptiness," full of violence and inhumanity, yet he preserves his own code of dignity and integrity and walks through the landscape inviolate—an extremely romantic notion no matter how "realistic" the setting.

The thriller, or more specifically that branch of it which we may term the "tough-guy novel," features precisely this sort of daemonic, isolated hero. Although the physical encounters of the hero may be staged to simulate reality, to a great degree they resemble those which befall the hero of legend. Transcending individual story variants, the constant action is the unquestioned victory of the hero over his opponent or opponents. In this respect he resembles more closely the hero of epic than that of tragedy. Obviously, in the case of a serial hero such as Philip Marlowe or the Continental Op, death must always come to the opponent, fulfilling Chandler's own formula of the genre, "tragedy with a happy ending."[67]

In his obsessiveness and almost supernatural prowess, then, the tough-guy hero strongly resembles the daemonic hero of allegory. Fletcher elaborates:

> The hero of romance moves in a world in which the ordinary laws of nature are slightly suspended; prodigies of courage and endurance, unnatural to us, and natural to him, and enchanted weapons, talking animals, terrifying ogres and witches, and talismans of miraculous power violate no rule of probability once the postulates of romance have been established. . . .[68]

It requires little effort to substitute the tough-guy hero of modern romance, whose continued physical well-being in the face of hazard indeed falls just short of miraculous, for Fletcher's daemonic hero of the fairy tale. Ironically, investiture with extraordinary powers is not tantamount to freedom; the tough-guy hero is no less fixed than any other of his allegorical counterparts. Even if we take the novels not as allegorical but accept them as the "realistic" fiction they purport to be, these daemonic "characters" are monstrous in their obsessiveness and remain abstractions, in contrast to the protagonists in mimetic fiction. (It should be added that in spite of their predictable protagonists Hammett and Chandler's quasi-allegorical novels did provide a convenient medium for the presentation of serious themes: the fine-honed individual conscience pitted against a complacent world; the potential danger of ignorance, a theme Greene was to emphasize; the stratification of society; and particularly the "mean streets" of the criminal.)

Perhaps even more significant than either his superhuman powers or obsessive dedication to his role, is the isolation in which the tough-guy hero operates. Again, we can find sources in early narrative. Frye remarks on the common predicament of early Saxon and Nordic epic: "the isolation of the hero is strongly marked."[69] Jung believes a similar predicament, so common in dreams, of "the lonely journey or pilgrimage," achieves the level of archetype as a "journey of relief, renunciation, and atonement."[70]

Wilkie Collins was one of the first to apply the theme of isolation to the newly developing genre, detective fiction. Gavin Lambert considers Collins' favorite theme to be "the isolated man faced with a secret that demands to be unlocked."[71] The same theme found its way into the major works of the nineteenth century. Dostoevsky's central concern in *Crime and Punishment* is with a character, Raskolnikov, who seems to be "a fragment painfully broken off from the main social structure."[72] But it was really the figure of the detective, the discoverer of guilty secrets, who was to carry on the tradition of the isolated hero, searching for "relief, renunciation, and atonement." In sum, the hero is depicted as isolated because he must be lured from his privacy to effect his cure, he must remain professionally detached, separated from any characters who may be implicated in the crime. Moreover, since the detective, with whom the reader identifies, is so isolated, the reader need not involve himself with the more painful feelings of criminal or victim.

In the modern tough-guy thriller, the lone, stalwart detective hero was forced into a different position vis-à-vis his society. In the twentieth century, society no longer offers values which can be depended upon and returned to; the lone hero walks on the mean streets; violence and anarchy are the only constants. But anarchy is exactly the opposite of the ordered world of the detective story with which we commenced, the world which began with order and is restored to order with the expulsion of the criminal. What, then, keeps the Hammett world from becoming sheer anarchy? The answer lies in the simple integrity of the lone detective. The private-eye is all that is interposed between the reader and total anarchy. For that reason, the tough-guy's personal integrity, in the face of the temptations strewn in his path, makes him the world's last hero: "Down these mean streets a man must go who is not himself mean, who is neither tarnished nor afraid," writes Chandler in "The Simple Art of Murder."[73]

In a violent, corrupt world the tough-guy's virtue, which in many earlier fictions would have united him with values of his society, serves only to isolate him further. In fact, by the time of Graham Greene's novels, the isolated hero, the only remaining idealist, has no choice but to be alone. The world has become a place without romantic love, without camaraderie, without the ideals of progress and beneficence which underlay the work of previous centuries. The hero is no longer alone simply because of his heroic responsibilities; he is alone willy-nilly. Loneliness has become an acknowledged part of the human condition.

But what sort of man has the modern hero become? Robert Edenbaum sees him as a distortion of the human:

> He is free of sentiment, of the fear of death, of the temptations of money and sex. He is what Albert Camus calls 'a man without memory,' free of the burdens of the past. . . . The rejection of the fear of death, perhaps the obvious characteristic of the tough guy in general, is but another aspect of the rejection of sentiment. . . . Here the superhuman is so by virtue of being all but non-human.[74]

Is this non-humanity the product of an allegorical formula, or is it evidence that the landscape, as assailant, has succeeded in misshaping the hero (or redeemer) as well as the criminal?

In *The Rebel* Camus claims that this depersonalization is not restricted to the hero:

> The American Novel [the tough-guy novel of the thirties and forties] claims to find its unity in reducing man either to elementals or to his external reactions and behavior. It does not choose feelings or passions to give a detailed description of. . . . It rejects analysis and the search for a fundamental psychological motive that could explain

and recapitulate the behavior of a character. . . . Its technique consists of describing by their outward appearances, in their most casual action, of reproducing without comment everything they say down to their repetitions, and finally by acting as if men were entirely defined by their daily automatisms. On this mechanical level men, in fact, seem exactly alike which explains this peculiar universe in which all the characters are interchangeable, even down to their physical peculiarities. This technique is called realistic only owing to a misapprehension . . . it is perfectly obvious that this fictitious world is not attempting a reproduction, pure and simple, of reality, but the most arbitrary form of stylization. It is born of a mutilation, performed on reality. The unity thus obtained is a degraded unity of human beings and the world. It would seem that for these writers it is the inner life that deprives human actions of unity and that tears people away from one another.[75]

This is the world of Hammett and Chandler, Simenon, Dick Francis, and other writers who produce the "realistic" thriller with a tough-guy hero. These writers base their works on a notion of realism (murder in the streets) which provides the setting for their works. But, as Lionel Trilling points out, "such an identification can be just as arbitrary and limited a view of 'reality' as the more philosophical or genteel perspective it set out to attack."[76]

The crime novel's concern with internal and external order is rendered through the use of a linguistic order, syntactic, rhythmic, imagistic. The daemonic hero has been shown to act under compulsion; it is easy to discern a linguistic counterpart for the motion of the agent. In his study of allegorical tropes and figures, Fletcher discovers exactly the parallels that suit our case. The "steady propulsiveness," as he terms it, of the daemonic hero of romance finds its linguistic parallel in parataxis—i.e., sentences structured so they do not convey degrees of importance or intensity. In parataxis the predication stands alone: "They wept. He ran." Or the predications are joined by conjunctions of equality: "He wept and they ran." This style may be employed for a multiplicity of ends. It is the style of Ecclesiastes, where the homeliness of the detail is given a portentousness by the bare simplicity and dignity of the speech rhythms whose repetitions imply the rhythmic ordering of life's cycles. Faulkner used this style to confer symbolic importance upon rituals of hunting; T.S. Eliot used it in *The Waste Land* to convey the disjointedness of European culture. And it is, of course, the style heavily favored by Hemingway, whose characters underline their heroic stature by the Biblical directness and compression of their paratactic diction. It has been adopted by the tough-guy thriller as the lingua franca of "realism," and though it lends itself easily to self-parody, writers like Hammett and Chandler have used this flat style to contain violent emotions, as in this passage from Hammett's "Fly Paper":

> "I shot his right knee.
> He lurched toward me.
> I shot his left knee.
> He tumbled down."

And:

> Babe liked Sue. Vassos liked Sue. Sue liked Babe. Vassos didn't like that. Jealousy spoiled the Greek's judgment. He kept the speakeasy locked one night when Babe wanted to come in. Babe came in, bringing pieces of the door with him. Vassos got his gun out . . . Babe hit him with the part of the door that had the brass knob on it. Babe and Sue went away from Vassos together.[77]

Here obsession is mirrored in the "steady propulsiveness" of the language, and the short, staccato, unsubordinated sentences give that facsimile of truth which we associate with the short, declarative statement of reportage. There are no lyrical digressions. Indeed, the very flatness of tone underlines the violence; the detachment of the narrator gives his story a credibility which a more emotional presentation would discredit. The author refrains from passing judgment, and even the characters refrain from ordering actions or events subjectively, partaking in what Fletcher calls a "withdrawal of affect." The isolated and self-contained sentences also convey the isolation and self-containment of the agent. Parataxis is, then, the perfect linguistic device for presenting Camus's "wretched automaton": a man described by his actions alone, a man for whom even danger does not provoke emotion, since, as we have seen, he is devoid of any sentiment, even the fear of death.

Myth, Fairytale, And The Crime Novel

The characteristic prose of the tough-guy novel also partakes of the syntactic symmetry of allegory, which Fletcher calls an "archetypal rhythm." This symmetry (used to such effect in spells, curses, and other incantations) produces a hypnotic effect by its repetitions. The ordering of speech becomes a ritual of its own, imbuing the content with an air of unspecified significance. The reader imagines the order of poetry (which Hammett often approaches) as he experiences the poetic power of the syntactic symmetry.

Both parataxis and syntactic symmetry find a place in the thriller; for the detective novel proper probably the most congenial linguistic device is ellipsis. Quintilian says ellipsis occurs "when something is assumed which has not actually been expressed" (*Institutes,* VIII, vi. Sec. 21). Since detective fiction is the enigma *par excellence,* it stands to reason that it will prove the employer, *par excellence,* of ellipsis, which is the stylistic counterpart of the structural device of deliberate retardation. Much is to be inferred that is not implied, or only implied, though the inferential process does not lead us, in the detective novel, to search for symbolic levels of meaning. In other words, induction is subordinated to deduction. But the whole is no more than the sum of its parts; this may be one of the true drawbacks of the conventional detective novel. The syntactic symmetry and parataxis of the thriller, however, can lead us to doubt that the putative meaning is all.

Furthermore, the detective novel makes visual use of synecdoche (synecdoche being, in Quintillian's view, equated with ellipsis), a kind of imagistic shorthand. Thus in the detective novel the deliberate obfuscation of the criminal's identity is often accomplished by offering the reader only partial glimpses of the whole person; the cane, the hat, or whatever, must be construed properly for the reader to follow the plot. Indeed, the ultimate problem of relating the deed to the source is, in itself, a version of synecdoche. We are given part of the man, the deed (i.e., the murder), from which we must construe the whole man (i.e., the identity of the murderer).[78] Of course, in the detective novel we have not only the linguistic pointer to a meaning withheld (ellipsis and synecdoche), we often have a literal coded message as well.

The authorial ordering of compositional elements is an important part of this coding process in allegory. With any composition, the subjective selection and design of the maker individuates it. As Leo Stein defines:

> A work of art is a composition, and its persistent reality as a work of art depends on relations between the elements of this composition. . . . They belong together only in the vision of the artist, and . . . to a closer observer the heterogeneity is overwhelming.[79]

The reader or viewer also has requirements that act collaboratively: "The haphazardness of objects activates our need for tidy arrangements, which drives us to establish connections and link the objects together."[80] In this way, artist and audience circumvent reality.

In a comparison of *Crime and Punishment* and the classic detective story, Cawelti sees that the components are similar—what differs is the arrangement. If in the detective novel, for example, "the elements of threat and chaos become too strong or dominant, the resolution into order will appear artificial and implausible."[81] On the other hand, undue emphasis upon the victim's state of mind would rival the investigative process. Art lies in the disposition of the elements, and where the emphases take place.

"The silences in allegory mean as much as the filled-in spaces because by bridging the gaps between oddly unrelated images we reach the sunken understructure of thought. . . ."[82] (See Illustration 3, Chapter II). In the detective novel these "oddly unrelated images" must continually be grouped and regrouped out of synonymous possibilities; the clues are grouped—e.g., modified and modifier, event and sign of the event expressed by gesture, by object, or some other objective correlative. It is this interpretive process that leads to the final resolution of the plot, the breaking of the code, and consummates the bond between reader and writer.

The detective novel, then, like many allegorical forms, entertains a fondness for ornament. The "manipulation of a texture of 'ornaments,' " Fletcher maintains, "engage[s] the reader in an interpretive activity." Ornament serves also as "dazzle detail," diverting the reader's attention from the "true" meaning of the plot.[83] Clearly, though the subplot or plots of the detective novel help to achieve its deliberate ambiguity, the bedazzlement of its images, of strewn clues, disguises, detail of atmosphere (and the detective novel abounds in detail) correspond to the "ornament" upon which allegory depends.

All these methods of ordering—the stylistic, structural, and thematic manifestations of Poetic Justic—combine to breed that weakness of which all forms of allegory may be accused: a deadening schematization. But as I will show in the following chapters, Dickens, Conrad, and Greene have drawn on the motifs and themes of the crime novel, while transcending the formulaic of allegory with richer, fuller characterization, and the inclusion of love, humor and irony.

Table 1
CHAPTER II

Motif - Index of Folk Literature - by Stith Thompson
June, September 1932 Vol. XIX studies No. 96, 97 - Indiana University Studies,
University of Indiana, Bloomington, Indiana 1932

Subheadings under Chapter D - Transformation
D671   - Transformation, flight - Fugitives transform themselves to escape
           detection by a pursuer
D720   - Disenchantment by removing (destroying) covering of enchanted per-
           son
D1080   - Magic weapons
D1110   - Magic conveyances

Subheadings under Chapter F. - Marvels
F150.2 - Entrance to other world guarded by monsters (or animals)
F200   - Fallen angels become fairies
F610   - Remarkably strong man
F615   - Strong hero sent for wild animals (or other dangerous quest)
G210   - Forms of witches
G400   - Person falls into ogre's power
G410   - Person betrayed into ogre's power
G420   - Capture by ogre
G440   - Abduction by ogre
G500   - Ogre defeated
G510   - Ogre killed, maimed, captured
G520   - Ogre deceived into self-injury

Subheading under Chapter H - Tests
HO   - Identity tests
H10   - Recognition through common knowledge
H30   - Recognition through personal peculiarities
H50   - Recognition through bodily marks or physical attributes
H110   - Recognition through cloth or clothing
H210-239 - Tests of guilt and innocence
H220   - Ordeals
H510   - Tests in guessing
H530   - Riddles
H900-1199 - Tests of prowess, tasks
H960   - Tasks performed through cleverness or intelligence
H1200   - Quest
H1210   - Quest assigned
H1220   - Quest voluntarily undertaken
H1360   - Quest for dangerous criminals
H1400   - Fear tests
H1410   - Fear of staying in frightful place
H1500-1549 - Tests of endurance and survival

Myth, Fairytale, And The Crime Novel

Vol. XXIX - September, December 1934
Studies Nos. 105, 106
Subheadings under Chapter J - Wisdom, Cleverness

J50	- Wisdom (knowledge) acquired from observation
J570	- Wisdom (knowledge) acquired of deliberation
J580	- Wisdom of caution
J620	- Forethought in prevention of other's plans
J640	- Avoidance of others' power
J670	- Forethought in defences against others
J830	- Adaptability to overpowering force
J1050	- Attention to warnings
J1140	- Cleverness in detection of truth
J1180	- Clever means of avoiding legal punishment
J1800	- One thing mistaken for another
J2130	- Foolish disregard of personal danger

Subheadings under Chapter K - Deceptions

K0	- Contest won by deception
K100	- Deceptive bargain
K520	- Death escaped through disguise, shamming, substitution
K600	- Escape by disarming (making pursuit difficult)
K630	- Murder or captor otherwise beguiled
K700	- Capture by deception
K730	- Victim trapped
K750	- Capture by decoy
K870	- Fatal deception by narcotic (intoxicant)
K910	- Murder by strategy
K950	- Various kinds of treacherous murder
K1080	- Persons duped into injuring each other
K1800-1899	- Deception by disguise
K2200-2299	- Villains and traitors

Subheadings under Chapter L - Reversal of Fortune

L110	- Types of unpromising hero

Subheadings under Chapter N - Chance and Fate

N270	- Crime inevitably comes to light
N330	- Accidental killing or death
N340	- Hasty killing or condemnation
N360	- Man unwittingly commits crime
N440	- Valuable secrets learned
N450	- Accidental discovery of crime
N800	- Helpers

Subheadings under Chapter Q - Rewards and Punishments

Q10-99 - Deeds Rewarded
Q200   - Deeds punished
Q211   - Murder punished
Q411   - Death as punishment
Q580   - Punishment fitted to crime

Subheadings under Chapter U - The Nature of Life, or "Thus goes the world"

U10   - Justice and injustice
U1110 - Appearances deceive

Subheadings under Chapter V - Religion

V10   - Magic results produced by sacrifice (scapegoat)

Note 1
CHAPTER II

Oedipus, Freud and the detective novel are brought together in an alliance most gratifying for our purposes. The man who, more than anyone else, gave Oedipus to the nineteenth and twentieth centuries—Sigmund Freud—was himself called a "Great Detective," as Stanley Hyman notes in his book, *The Tangled Bank.*[a] Hyman continues "In the next year, 1899, Freud published 'Screen Memories,' later included in *The Psychopathology of Everyday Life,* in which he goes into case histories (including his own, disguised) and gives some of his dialogue with patients;

> Patient: But I still don't grasp your point.
> Freud: I am coming to it at once.

It sounds rather like Holmes and Watson. The Great Detective was about to appear. . . . A more interesting matter than the book's style (which is, by general agreement much better than Freud thought) is its tone. There are in fact two tones. The first is of Sherlock Holmes, the Great Detective: assured, intolerant, firm, and strong. Of a difference between himself and a patient, Freud remarks: 'Soon afterwards it turned out that I was right.' When a dreamer protests over revealing a delicate circumstance behind the dream, Freud says with all of Holmes's forcefulness, 'Nevertheless I shall have to hear it.' . . . We can hear Conan Doyle's hand in the titles Freud gives the dreams, so like the Holmes cases: The Dream of Irma's Injection, The Dream of the Botanical Monograph; and Doyle as well as Sophocles has had a clear influence on Freud's form of delayed revelation and suspense." (This is the "device of retardation" mentioned in section III.)

---

a.Hyman, Stanley, *The Tangled Bank* (New York: Atheneum Press, 1962) pp. 309, 313.

Note 2
CHAPTER II

The psychiatrist Charles Rycroft has focussed his attention on the detective story and the impulses to which it caters. From his exegesis I have extracted several statements which are relevant outside a purely psychiatric orientation, and many of which bear specifically on points made in this chapter.

"A Detective Story: Psychoanalytic Observations"
by Charles Rycroft
The Psychoanalytic Quarterly, Vol. 26, 1957, pp. 229-245.
Pub. by The Psychoanalytic Quarterly, Inc. N.Y., N.Y.

"If the victim is the parent for whom the reader (the child) had negative oedipal feelings, then the criminal must be a personification of the reader's own unavowed feelings of hostility toward that parent. The reader is not only the detective; he is also the criminal . . . The detective story writer connives with the reader's need to deny his guilt by providing him with ready-made fantasies in which the compulsive question 'whodunit?' is always answered by a self-exonerating 'not I.'

"In the ideal detective story the detective or hero would discover that he himself is the criminal for whom he has been seeking. Such a story, though it is not generally accounted a detective story, does in fact exist and has given its name to the very psychological constellation which endows observations and fantasies of the primal scene (parental sexual intercourse) with such significance. I am referring, of course, to the myth of Oedipus, the cathartic effect of which the typical detective story denies, is openly admitted . . . One reason, I suspect why the detective story so rarely achieves the status of a work of art is that this identification of the reader with the criminal remains denied.

"They [Mannion in *Basil* and Ablewhite in *The Moonstone*] are the scapegoats, the representatives and agents of the heroes' unadmitted impulses, and, as always happens to scapegoats, they both die as an indirect result of the crimes they commit."

Note 3
CHAPTER II

Victims of Duty - Three Plays by Ionesco - Evergreen Originals, Grove Press, New York, 1958, pp. 119-120.

(The subtitle is "A Pseudo-Drama")

Choubert: You're right. Yes, you're right. All the plays that have ever been written, from ancient Greece to the present day, have never really been anything but thrillers. Drama's always been realistic and there's been a detective about. Every play's an investigation brought to a successful conclusion. There's a riddle, and it's solved in the final scene. Sometimes earlier. You seek, and then you find. Might as well give the game away from the start.

Madeleine: You ought to quote examples, you know.

Choubert: I was thinking of the Miracle Play about the woman Our Lady saved from being burned alive. If you forget that bit of divine intervention, which really has nothing to do with it, what's left is a newspaper story about a woman who has her son-in-law murdered by a couple of stray killers for reasons that are unmentioned.

Madeleine: And unmentionable.

Choubert: The police arrive, there's an investigation and the criminal is unmasked. It's a thriller. A naturalistic drama, fit for the theatre of Antoine.

Madeleine: That's it.

Choubert: Come to think of it, there never has been much evolution in the theatre.

Madeleine: Pity.

Choubert: You see, the theatre's a riddle, and the riddle's a thriller. It's always been that way.

Madeleine: What about the classics?

Choubert: Refined detective drama. Just like naturalism.

It is pertinent here to recall Angus Fletcher's opinion that allegory can be "used in the drama whether ancient (*Prometheus Bound*), medieval (the moralities), Renaissance (the auto sacramentales and the masques), or modern (the surrealist drama of Ionesco or Beckett). . . ."

This dramatic dialogue not only discovers the same allegorical relationship between enigma and detective story, but sees likewise their common relationship to tragic drama. We should also bear in mind as we read "If you forget that bit of divine intervention, which really has nothing to do with it," the stricture against excessive use of the supernatural that Aristotle laid down for tragedy, and that the writers of the "classic detective novel" laid down for *it* in the 1920s.

II. Gustave Moreau (1826-1898). *Oedipus and the Sphinx.*
(The Metropolitan Museum of Art, bequest of William B.
Herriman, 1921.)

Odilon Redon (1840-1916). *The Eye like a Strange Balloon Moves towards Infinity,* Plate I from *To Edgar Poe,* 1882. (Collection, The Museum of Modern Art, New York, gift of Peter H. Deitsch.)

ILLUSTRATION 3
CHAPTER II

We are put in mind here of the silent spaces of Giorgio de Chirico's paintings. Subsequent to this observation, I came by chance upon the following passages in Cyril Connolly's *The Evening Colonnade:*

> Chirico's early work presents a closed world of the imagination, already perfect and passing away, a dream of urban apprehension, a haunted inner city of squares and statues, of freight trains and grief-stricken colonnades in the last second before the explosion.[a]

Coincidentally, Gavin Lambert also uses de Chirico in describing the landscape of Simenon's *Maigret at the Crossroads,*

> Empty and isolated as a de Chirico landscape, the setting is of crossroads surrounded by flat countryside, with only three buildings nearby: a garage, an ugly suburban villa, an old country house surrounded by trees.[b]

Jung also corroborates my interpretation of its literary evocations when he chooses de Chirico's work as an example of a style in painting which gives the viewer an intuition of significance beyond what is depicted:

> The feeling that the object was 'more than meets the eye,' which was shared by many artists, found a remarkable expression in the work of Giorgio de Chirico. He was a mystic by temperament, and a tragic seeker who never found what he sought. On his self-portrait (1908) he wrote: Et quid amabo nici quod enigma est ('and what am I to love if not the enigma?'). . . . The city squares of Italy, the towers and objects, are set in an ever-acute perspective, as if they were in a vacuum, illuminated by a merciless, cold light from an unseen source. Antique heads or statues of gods conjure up the classical past.[c]

---

a. London: David, Bruce and Watson, 1973, p. 13.
b. Gavin Lambert *The Dangerous Edge,* p. 181.
c. C.G. Jung *Man and His Symbols* (New York: Dell Publishing Co., 1968), p. 293.

The Mystery and Melancholy of A Street, 1914
Anonymous collection.

CHAPTER II

[1]Angus Fletcher, *Allegory* (Ithaca, N.Y.: Cornell University Press, 1970), p. 5. Curiously, the *moralitas* itself has its counterpart in the final explication of the mystery by the detective, which is a "set piece" of the detective novel.

[2]*Ibid.*, p. 6.

[3]See Fritz Wölchen's *Der Literarische Mord* (Nurnberg, Germany: Nest, 1953) and Jacques Barzun's "Detection and the Literary Art," *The Mystery Writer's Art*, p. 255.

[4]"The Guilty Vicarage," *The Dyer's Hand.* (New York: Random House, 1962), p. 147. Auden is speaking, here, of the genteel "Whodunit" story.

[5]"Narrative Art and Magic" (1932) *Tri-Quarterly Review* No. 25, Fall 1972, p. 213.

[6]Frank Kermode *The Sense of an Ending*, p. 133.

[7]*Anatomy of Criticism*, (Princeton, N.J.: Princeton University Press, 1971), p. 304. Jung, himself, gives this more generalized definition of archetype: "Archetypes may be considered the fundamental elements of the conscious mind, hidden in the depths of the psyche, or, to use another comparison, they are the roots of the mind, sunk not only in the earth in the narrower sense, but in the world in general. . . . They are that portion of the mind through which it is linked to nature." C.G. Jung, as quoted in S. C. Reid, "The Hidden World of Charles Dickens," University of Auckland Bulletin, n. 61, English Series 10 (1962), pp. 22-23. Jung claims also that the archetype is simultaneously an image and an emotion, and the emotion invigorates the image so that it becomes dynamic and has consequences. If an archetype is to serve a literary function, it cannot be left as just a word picture.

[8]Edmund Leach, *Claude Lévi-Strauss* (New York: Viking Press, 1970), p. 70.

[9]C.G. Jung, *Man and His Symbols* (New York: Dell Publishing Co., 1968), p. 123.

[10]*Claude Lévi-Strauss*, p. 56.

[11]Vladimir Propp, *The Morphology of the Folktale,* ed. S. Pirkova-Jakobson, trans. Laurence Scott (Bloomington, Indiana: University of Indiana Research Center in Anthropology, Folklore, and Linguistics, 1958), p. 96.

[12]"The Detective Story as a Historical Source," *The Mystery Writer's Art*, p. 324.

[13]Paulus Henri de Vries, *Poe and After*, (Amsterdam: Drukkerij Bakker, 1956), p. 52.

[14]Robert A. W. Lowndes, "The Contributions of Edgar Allan Poe," *The Mystery Writer's Art*, p. 2.

[15]*Allegory*, p. 207.

[16]"The Guilty Vicarage," p. 158.

[17]*The Dangerous Edge*, p. 53.

[18]*Allegory*, p. 151. The observation has also been made twice by Lord Raglan. "Yet the hero of tradition (vs. history) is usually alone." And, "In almost every folktale there is a future King or Queen who performs a solitary journey," *The Hero* (London: Watts and Co., 1949). p. 125.

[19]E. Dabcovich as quoted by Wolfgang Iser, *The Implied Reader*, (Baltimore: Johns Hopkins Press, 1974), p. 24.

[20]*A Literary Chronicle* (New York: Doubleday, 1950), pp. 338-345.

[21]*The Dangerous Edge*, p. 45.

[22]Jacques Barzun, "From Phédre to Sherlock Holmes," *The Energies of Art*, (New York: Harper and Bros., 1956), p. 305.

[23]Frye, *The Secular Scripture*, p. 54.

[24]Scholes and Kellogg, *The Nature of Narrative*, pp. 236-7.

[25]As quoted in the book-length study of Chandler, *Down These Mean Streets a Man Must Go*, by Phillip Durham, (Chapel Hill, North Carolina: University of North Carolina Press, 1963), p. 1.

[26]Gertrude Stein made a similar observation: "I used to think that a detective story was soothing because the hero being dead, you begin with the corpse you did not have to take him on and so your mind was free to enjoy yourself, of course there is the detection but nobody really believes in detection, that is what makes the detection so soothing." *What Are Masterpieces* (Los Angeles: Conference Press, 1940) pp. 87-8.

[27]*Allegory*, p. 150.

[28]*The Dangerous Edge*, p. 107.

[29]*Man and His Symbols*, p. 261.

[30]*Allegory*, p. 185. The antithesis need not always be that of good or evil, of course; Poe, despite his immersion in German Romanticism, frequently uses the suffering body-ratiocinating mind antithesis; Thoreau the actor-observer doubling.

[31]Donald Richie, "High and Low" *The Mystery Writer's Art*, pp. 177-8.

[32]"Raffles and Miss Blandish," *Collected Essays*, (Garden City, N.Y.: Doubleday, 1945), p. 145.

[33]*The Mortal No*, (Princeton, N.J.: Princeton University Press, 1964), p. 265.

[34]"The Criminal as Hero and Myth," June 23, 1961, p. vi.

[35]"The Detective as Metaphor," *The Mystery Writer's Art*, pp. 288-289.

[36]It is ironic that the detective story itself may effect that lesson. Jacques Barzun sees it as "an alliance of murder and mirth. The laughter is a touch sardonic and must never degenerate into hilarity. The joke of death is upon us. . . ." "Detection and the Literary Art," p. 261.

[37](New York: Harcourt Brace and World, 1957), p. 190.

[38]William Empson locates this figure within the pastoral mode, and traces its development into tragic drama. "It would be interesting to know how far the ideas of pastoral in this wide sense are universal. . . . In my account the ideas

about the Sacrificial Hero as Dying God are mixed up in the brew, and these, whose supreme form is Christianity, mainly belong to Europe and the Mediterranean." *Some Versions of Pastoral*, (London: Chatto and Windus, 1935), p. 21.

[39]*The Hero*, pp. 178-9.

[40]This last observation was made by Harry Levin in his unpublished notes on "Motif," a course offered at Harvard University, Sept.-April 1970.

[41]Immanuel Velikovsky, *Oedipus and Akhnaton*, (New York: Doubleday, 1960), p. 31.

[42]"The Detective Story as a Historical Source," pp. 311-312.

[43]*Ibid.*, p. 323.

[44]*Ibid.*, p. 315.

[45]Stanley Hyman, *Poetry and Criticism*, (New York: Atheneum, 1961), p. 12.

[46]*Allegory*, pp. 100-101.

[47]*Ibid.*, p. 170.

[48]Gavin Lambert, *The Dangerous Edge*, p. xii.

[49]*Allegory*, p. 98.

[50]Julian Symons, *Mortal Consequences* (New York: Harper and Row, 1972) p. 8; Marjorie Nicholson, "The Professor and the Detective," *The Art of the Mystery Story*, ed. Howard Haycraft (New York: Simon and Schuster, 1946), p. 114; Nicholas Blake, "The Detective Story—Why?" *The Art of the Mystery Story*, p. 401.

[51]In his essay, "Raffles and Miss Blandish," *Collected Essays*, pp. 141, 144.

[52]*Allegory*, p. 339.

[53]*Ibid.*, p. 338.

[54]Fletcher, *Allegory*, p. 191, fn. 13. See also Suzanne Langer *Philosophy in a New Key* (N.Y.: Mentor Books, 1942), pp. 147-148.

[55]*The Morphology of the Folktale*, p. 57.

[56]As Angus Fletcher has noticed: "The western scenery in Grey [Zane Grey] is always more than a tacked-up backdrop. It is a paysage moralisé, and Grey's heroes always act in harmony with or in violent contrast to that scenic tapestry. Furthermore, the conflict of the cowboy hero and the bandit villain, as in the detective thriller [here Fletcher mistakenly combines the two forms into a portmanteau word] are drawn to a dualism of good and evil—a defining characteristic of the mode (allegory) from the earliest days of Occidental literature." *Allegory*, p. 6. For an amplification of this point, see the poem *Paysage Moralisé* by W. H. Auden.

[57]W. H. Auden, "The Guilty Vicarage," p. 151.

[58]*Allegory*, pp. 83-4.

[59]"Frankentahaler as Pastoral," p. 68.

[60]"From Phédre to Sherlock Holmes," p. 314.

[61]*Allegory*, p. 129.

[62]*The Mortal No*, p. 156. This description suggests not only literary examples, e.g., Eliot, Kafka, Baudelaire, Auden, but the increasing cinematic use to which such images have been put: *Hiroshima, Mon Amour; The Midnight Cowboy; The Red Desert; The Last Picture Show;* the penthouse glamour of New York City and Hollywood has been replaced by the Wasteland/assailant city, or desolate landscape; both are extremes, but not opposites.

[63]*The Life of the Drama* (New York: Atheneum, 1964), p. 202.

[64]Carolyn Heilbrun offers this paraphrase of Simon Weil's concept of larger environmental "forces" of evil: "During the twentieth century, when the beauty and necessity of life had become less easily discerned, Simone Weil saw that the true hero of the *Iliad* is force. Force is defined as that which turns anybody subjected to it into a object, and Weil makes it perfectly clear that none can escape this fate when involved with force." *Towards a Recognition of Androgyny* (New York: Alfred A. Knopf, 1973), p. 4. Weil's full statement is found in her essay, "The *Iliad* or the Poem of Force," tr. Mary McCarthy (Wallingford, Pennsylvania: Pendle Hill, 1970 reprint ed. of 1940 essay).

[65]*The Mortal No*, p. 193. The alteration of the spatial relationship between assailant and victim has meant the loss of the epic. ". . . Epic should convey . . . a feeling for the human personality in touch and perhaps even in sympathy with his enemies. . . . Part of the tragic dignity of the conflict lies in the fact that the men involved know their enemies well enough to entertain strong personal feelings of hate, respect, and even love for them. Unlike the mechanical wars of the nineteenth century, it is a conflict which elevates and even enhances the personality rather than obliterating it." Robert Louis Stevenson's *Eight Years of Trouble in Samoa*, discussed by Robert Kiely, *Robert Louis Stevenson and the Fiction of Adventure*, (Cambridge, Mass.: Harvard Univ. Press, 1965), p. 231.

[66]Hoffman, *The Mortal No, pp. 191-2.*

[67]The connection I have drawn between folk literature and crime fiction is supported in a review of Chandler's *Raymond Chandler Speaking*: "Refusal to accept the death of the hero is part of the folk-mythical element of crime-fiction." Maurice Richardson, *London Observer*, (Oct. 21, 1973), p. 41.

[68]*Allegory*, pp. 38-9, 50.

[69]*The Secular Scripture*, p. 116.

[70]*Man and His Symbols*, p. 147.

[71]*The Dangerous Edge*, p. 28.

[72]Penelope Gilliatt, "The Current Cinema," *The New Yorker*, (May 26, 1975).

[73]*The Art of The Mystery Story*, p. 237.

[74]"The Poetics of the Private Eye: The Novels of Dashiell Hammett." *The Mystery Writer's Art*, p. 99. Coincidentally, Edenbaum uses the very term "daemonic" in reference to Hammett's Spade, although he gives no evidence of familiarity with the term as used by Fletcher.

But the gradual dilution of the model fashioned by Hammett and Chandler and other writers for *Black Mask* magazine in the 1930s and '40s has resulted in the admission of a vulnerability rigidly denied to the original. This is partly the result of a transposition of the hero from private-eye to public servant (police inspector)—e.g., the novels of Simenon or Freeling, both of whom feature married heroes.

A Common Spring

An interesting sidelight on this is contained in the review of a re-make of the film, "The Long Goodbye," based upon the Raymond Chandler book of the same name. In the London *Observer*, Nov. 25, 1973, the reviewer George Melly compares the new film and the original film made in the 1930s: "By updating Marlowe and his world, he [the director] has demonstrated how American mores have changed, and for the worse. Marlowe represented the heroic ideal, the individual conscience that can't be bought. For him evil was a dragon, something concrete that could be defeated. By contrast, the present Marlowe is presented as a neurotic comic figure"; and the review, entitled, "Chandler—Without the Moralities" clearly acknowledges the allegorical intentions of Chandler himself.

[75] Albert Camus, *The Rebel*, (Vintage Books, N.Y., 1956), pp. 265-6.

[76] As quoted by Cawelti, *Adventure, Mystery, and Romance*, p. 164. The charge of "unreality" has been levied against Chandler by Albert Camus and Jacques Barzun, among others. Writes Barzun, "The tough story was born in the Thirties and shows the Marxist coloring of its birth years. In Chandler's essay ("The Simple Art of Murder") the critique of the classical formula seems to spring not solely from a mistaken demand for realism, but also from a hostility to a solvent way of life. That the well-to-do could be honest, 'genuine,' and lovable apparently was not realistic either. And obviously the reader was to feel morally uplifted by the solemn conclusion describing the true hero-detective:

" 'He must be a complete man and a common man and yet an unusual man. He must be the best man in his world and good enough man for any world. He must be a relatively poor man, or he would not be a detective at all. He will take no man's money dishonestly and no man's insolence without a due and passionate revenge. He is a lonely man and his pride is that you will treat him as a proud man or be very sorry you ever saw him. The story is this man's adventure in search of hidden truth [a Grail Quest variant]. . . . If there were enough like him, the world would be a very safe place to live in, without becoming too dull to be worth living in.'

"Who's the sentimental tale spinner now? after thirty years it makes no difference to our enjoyment of the sagas by Chandler, Ross Macdonald, and others that the eternal Robin Hood should have got mixed up with Marx's angry young men and Tennyson's Galahad, and wound up in self-contradiction," *A Catalogue of Crime*, ed. Jacques Barzun and Wendell Hertig Taylor (New York: Harper & Row, 1971) p. 11. For Camus's attack, see p. 46 of this chapter. Frank MacShane's recent biography, *The Life of Raymond Chandler*, (New York: E. P. Dutton, 1976) also stesses the subjectivity of Chandler's "realism."

John Buchan shows that the origins of the "realistic" tough-guy hero lie in the wish-fulfillment fantasies of fairy tale: "The fairy tale represents a reaction by folk against a dangerous and cruel world; it pictured weakness winning against might, gentleness and courtesy against brutality, brains against mere animal strength. [Viz. Table I, Chapter II, Motifs 110]. In their own life fortitude was a main virtue, but they depicted daring instead." ("The Novel and the Fairy Tale," *English Institute Essays*, II 79, July 1931, p. 6).

[77]Dashiell Hammett, "Fly Paper," *The Big Knockover* ed. Lillian Hellman, (New York: Random House, 1962), p. 33.

[78]This is the point of departure for many of Borges' improvisations on the detective theme.

[79]Leo Stein, *Appreciation: Painting, Poetry, and Prose.* (New York: Crown Publishers, 1947), p. 58.

[80]Iser, *The Implied Reader*, p. 262.

[81]*Adventure, Mystery, and Romance*, p. 108.

[82]*Allegory,* p. 107.

[83]Anton Ehrenzweig, *Psychoanalysis of Artistic Vision and Hearing*, as quoted in *Allegory*, p. 366. n. 8.

CHAPTER III

Dickens and the Crime Novel

Those who have lived before such terms as 'high brow fiction,' 'thrillers,' and 'detective fiction' were invented realize that melodrama is perennial and craving for it is perennial and must be satisfied. If we cannot get this satisfaction out of what publishers present as 'literature,' then we will read—with less and less pretence of concealment—what we call 'thrillers.' But in the golden age of melodramatic literature there was no such distinction. The best novels were thrilling. . . .

T.S. Eliot, "Wilkie Collins and Charles Dickens"

. . . And Dickens has as good a title as Edgar Allan Poe to be called the father of the modern detective story.

Julian Symons, *Charles Dickens*

From the *Sketches by Boz* that Dickens wrote in his early twenties through the last, interrupted book of his career, *The Mystery of Edwin Drood,* Dickens' absorption in the theme of crime and violence, particularly murder, is unmistakable.

Many reasons may be summoned to explain this. There is, for one, the psychological attraction that this theme had for Dickens personally. Many of his contemporaries have attested to this, and many modern critics have inferred it from his work. Thus, one of his colleagues relates that Dickens had ". . . a curious and almost morbid partiality for communing with and entertaining police officers. He seemed always at his ease with these personages, and never tired of questioning them."[1] His excited, even compulsive, public readings of the murder of Nancy by Sikes (*Oliver Twist*), continued against the advice of his physician, reflect more than an author's pride or an actor's flare. Dickens unquestionably identified himself with the piece: "Come early in January, and see a certain friend of yours do the murder from *Oliver Twist*. It is horribly like, I am afraid. I have a vague sensation of being 'wanted' as I walk about the streets," he wrote to a friend. As a boy he read sensation novels and such journals as *Terrific Register;* as a man he contemplated running for the paid position of Metropolitan Magistrate. Wherever he travelled he investigated haunts of crime and sought out the local police force (for example, on his trip to New York).

Edmund Wilson, in his famous essay on Dickens, "The Two Scrooges," advances this explanation:

> For the man of spirit whose childhood has been crushed by the cruelty of organized society, one of two attitudes is natural: that of the criminal or that of the rebel. Charles Dickens, in imagination, was to play the roles of both, and to continue up to his death to put them into all that was passionate in his feeling. . . . He identified himself readily with the thief, and even more readily with the murderer.[2]

Wilson's view of Dickens seems unconvincing to me in its extremity; Dickens' friend and posthumous biographer, John Forster, may come closer to the truth with this analysis:

> . . . 'underneath his exterior of singular precision, method, and strict orderly arrangement in all things . . . [he had] something in common with those eager, somewhat overbearing natures, that rush at existence without heeding the cost of it.' These two sides of his nature correspond to his admiration for the police and his intuitive understanding of the criminal.[3]

Certainly Dickens' partiality for order is manifest in each book; the spiritual good always inhabits a scrubbed and tidy environment—e.g., the ship-shape dwelling of Miss Crisparkle (*The Mystery of Edwin Drood*), the kitchen of Mrs. Nubbles (*The Old Curiosity Shop*), and, of course, that complete coalescence of goodness and good housekeeping, Bleak House. Indeed, perhaps the very tidiness of the puzzle form was in itself an attraction for Dickens, an antidote to his sympathy with the criminal or outcast. His instinct for order enabled him to side with the police. No one of Dickens' murderers goes unpunished; and even villains like Quilp who, though menacing enough, accomplish little, are destroyed. (George Orwell believes Pip's attitude toward Magwitch [*Great Expectations*] is a reflection of Dickens' own; that is, once a man has transgressed the law, he is a permanent outsider.) The desire for order eventuates in the Providential end, one of the strong bonds between Dickens and the detective novel.

The age in which he found himself also served to direct Dickens to the theme of crime and violence, for Dickens' literary antecedents were the waning romance and the Gothic novel, and he cannot be appreciated unless seen as the successor to Scott and Byron, as well as Walpole, Dumas, Sue, Hugo, and Mrs. Radcliffe. His literary inheritance provided him with a multitude of devices and conventions, the most important of which are those used to excite curiosity and suspense. Mrs. Radcliffe, whom Sir Walter Scott judged the best of the Gothic novelists, interrupts her narrative at peaks of interest; alternates plot lines to maintain intensity; and uses a passive protagonist who is the victim of sensational incidents. Almost every device Mrs. Radcliffe used was calculated to instill fear in the reader. "Fear," declares Eric Bentley, "is the most indestructible of obstacles. Therein lies the potential universality of melodrama."[4]

Dickens adopted the interruption, the alternation of plot threads, the passive protagonist. In *Barnaby Rudge* he even adapted the plot of Mrs. Radcliffe's novel *The Italian. The Old Curiosity Shop,* which according to Dickens grew out of a plan for a Gothic short story, exemplifies both the beleaguered passive protagonist and contrast calculated to arouse fear. Dickens confides:

It has always been my fancy to surround the lonely figure of the child with grotesque and wild, but not impossible companions, and to gather about her innocent face and pure intentions associates as strange and uncongenial as the grim objects that are about her bed when her history is first foreshadowed.

When Gashford, the wily secretary to Lord Gordon (*Barnaby Rudge*), discourses upon his ability to manipulate crowds, we incidentally learn something of Dickens' own methods of composition:

Curiosity is, and has been from the creation of the world, a master-passion. To awaken it, to gratify it by slight degrees, and yet leave something always in suspense, is to establish the surest hold that can be had . . . on the unthinking portion of mankind.

In yet another passage in *Barnaby Rudge* Dickens speaks of ". . . that appetite for the marvelous and love of the terrible" which is eternal in man's nature.[5]

Stage melodrama in Dickens' time aimed at the same evocation of fear, and made use of numerous "cliff-hangers."[6] Dickens confessed his indebtedness to the stage:

We behold, with throbbing bosoms, the heroine in the grasp of a proud and ruthless baron: her virtue and her life alike are in danger; drawing forth her dagger to preserve the one at the cost of the other; and just as our expectations are wrought up to the highest pitch, a whistle is heard: and we are straightway transported to the great hall of the castle: where a grey-headed seneschal sings a funny chorus with a funnier body of vassals. . . . "[7]

Not only the practice of plot alternations but all the trappings of melodrama—stolen inheritances, lost heirs, ruined maidens, diabolical villains, denunciatory confrontations—enliven the pages of Dickens. "Furthermore melodrama offers a rite of passage, like ceremonial mysteries in ancient Greece, revelation through initiation and sacrifice, knowledge acquired by secret and violent experience. It [melodrama] returns to myth and even stretches reality to accommodate the occult element of myth."[8]

71

Thus Dickens can fairly be called one of the 'sensation novelists' (in company with Bulwer-Lytton, Charles Reade, Wilkie Collins), all of whom drew on elements of the Gothic novel and stage melodrama: the use of the supernatural (e.g., Krook's death by spontaneous combustion in *Bleak House*), standard fare in the Gothic novel; sentimentality, a stock ingredient of the Victorian novel and the older romance;[9] the trick of disguise (e.g., Datchery in *Edwin Drood,* Bucket in *Bleak House*), a staple of stage melodrama. As a "sensation novelist" (for so Thackeray describes him, labeling *Oliver Twist* and *Barnaby Rudge* "Newgate novels"), Dickens was committed to a type of book which abounds in incident and action. The sensation novel, essentially allegorical and dramatic, eschews psychological dissection of character in favor of presentation through word, gesture, and act. Characters help to implement action, yet remain subordinate to it.

The literary stockpile Dickens found to hand, coupled with his own predilection for the theme of crime, coincided with the most significant growth in the reading public of England since the Renaissance. From 1825 onwards, machinery made printing costs cheaper; Mudie's circulating library was inaugurated. Serial publication was another publishing practice which catered to this audience. Such dissimilar authors as Thackeray, Dickens, Trollope, George Eliot, Reade, Collins, Meredith, Hardy, all brought their novels out in serial form.[10] What effect did serialization have upon the techniques of Dickens? This question has been carefully and intelligently handled by Archibald Coolidge, who examines the conditions imposed by serialization and the particular ways in which Dickens met or circumvented them. Serial publication poses the immediate problem of lapse of interest. Hence the crowding of incident, the multiple plot threads to maintain suspense, already conventional, acquire additional justification. The appeal to fear was a common denominator for this new, wider audience. The habit of thinking in individual installments led to the conception of both characters and incidents as static counters to be moved about the board. Dickens' stock characters and incidents, readily identifiable in eighteenth-century novels of sensibility and terror and in contemporary and later melodrama, are so because of melodrama's polarization of good and evil, compounded by the serial novel's demand for easy-to-recognize heroes and villains. This approach is intensified by Dickens' own concern with presenting a moral vision, and on one level his novels may all be read as allegories.

The formation of the first law enforcement agency in England interested Dickens and influenced his work. Sir Robert Peel had set up the Metropolitan Police Force in London just seven years before Dickens' first books appeared. Dickens parodies the ineffectual system of watchmen and parish-constables in *Barnaby Rudge* (employing a type of law officer familiar from Shakespeare); he ridicules the Bow Street Runners in *Oliver Twist* and *Great Expectations.* The detective was a new figure; crime was rampant and unchecked in Dickens' London; and both in his novels (Inspector Bucket in *Bleak House* is the first detective in English fiction) and in his articles for *Household Words* ("A Detective Police Party," "Three Detective Anecdotes," "On Duty with Inspector Fields," "Down with the Tide") the new policeman is admired as impartial and imperturbable, the father of a long line of such fictional characters. Angus Wilson believes Dickens would have developed Datchery (*The Mystery of Edwin Drood*) into a private detective in order to provide a character study of that occupation, had he lived to complete the novel. "Charles Dickens may be said to have discovered the modern detective," commented a contemporary.[11]

In fine, qualities of temperament, conditions of publication and audience, literary tradition, the new institution of the Metropolitan Police Force, and his compelling concern with morality, all conspired to attach Dickens to the themes of the crime novel. Murder mysteries occur in five of his fifteen novels: *Barnaby Rudge, Martin Chuzzlewit, The Mystery of Edwin Drood, Bleak House* and *Our Mutual Friend.* Most of his other novels contain strong elements of mystification. Is it then justified to see Dickens as a "crime novelist," or "the father of the modern detective novel?"

We cannot label Dickens the progenitor of a literary type; the novel that he and Dumas and Balzac and Collins and Reade wrote was one of human relationship as well as incident. A convincing case, for example, could be made for interpreting *Barnaby Rudge* as a study of the father-son relationship, since this pairing is examined in the parallel combinations of Joe-Mr. Willett, Barnaby-Mr. Rudge, Edward-Mr. Chester. *Bleak House,* in which the public irresponsibility of Chancery is mirrored in the private irresponsibility of Chadbands, Jellybys, Skimpoles, and Turveydrops, abounds in the kind of relationships the crime novel lacks.

In this introductory section, I have repeatedly made use of the term "crime novel" rather than "detective story" and "thriller" because Dickens' novels do not conform strictly to one category or the other, but partake of elements of both the puzzle and adventure. Since both the detective story and the thriller as we know them today are post-Dickensian forms, we certainly cannot speak of Dickens' debt to them. Nor is it profitable or sensible to refer to Dickens as their fountainhead; we have already noted the confluence of sources which led to the evolution of these genres (Chapter I). But it is worth asking in what their similarity consists. What is there in the crime novel that can be fruitfully employed by a major novelist aspiring to a larger vision than the crime novel may contain? Dostoevsky has given one answer, and Kafka another—and Dickens, who influenced both of them, gave the first. Much has been made in recent criticism of the resemblances among these three writers, particularly since critics have paid increasing attention to the dark side of Dickens (possibly as an antidote to his early Pickwickian persona). But the point at which their work converges is that point at which all three authors subsume the crime novel.

Thematic Resemblances

The Dickens novel uses the same folkloric and mythic motifs and archetypes that are integral to the crime novel (see Table 1, Chapter III). In this lies a hidden but profound bond between the two. In fact any resemblance between the novels of Dickens and crime novels is attributable as much to their common relationship

74

to folklore and mythology as to their shared use of mystification, suspense, and the pivotal action of crime. That Dickens thought in these motifs, wrote in these archetypal images, is indisputable. Cinderella, Babes-in-the-Woods, Jack-the-Giant-Killer, all lurk in his work. The prodigality of his output may be partly repsonsible for this literary shorthand; more significantly, the explanation is that Dickens reproduces the authoritative voice of the myth-maker.

Recognizing the folkloric patterns in his novels, Dorothy Van Ghent sees two major themes as informing his work—the crime of parent against child, and the social crime.[12] (These correspond, actually, to the alternating domestic and public plot lines in Dickens, and are linked by symbolic imagery—e.g., dis-ease). We are back at crime. Archibald Coolidge holds that there are three unfailing groups of characters in Dickens: victim, villain, rescuer (who corresponds to detective).[13] We are back at crime again.

Other critics have volunteered different organizational plans—grouping by occupation, for example. Repetition engenders a feeling of familiarity that impels us to identify a pattern; but this takes us only one short step forward. For although we recognize that the detective story has a pattern (i.e., innocence, loss of innocence, restoration of innocence), we have not accounted for its magnetism until we have traced many components of that pattern back to archetypes. The appeal of Dickens has been attributed variously to his comedic effects, the abundance and energy of his invention, his unabashed sentiment, his use of melodramatic apparatus—all of which undoubtedly play a part. But we must also recognize that through the use of folkloric and mythic material, which itself has archetypal references, Dickens strikes very deep, and recalls us not only to our childhood fears, but to nature,[14] and our subconscious. Not only in the use of archetypes, and the creation of mythic worlds for his characters to inhabit, but in the actual selection of these archetypes we discover another link between Dickens and the crime novel. One of his major themes is crime; and it follows necessarily that the archetypal images he chooses to depict it and the archetypal characters who enact it will correspond closely to the archetypes used by the crime novel itself. If we review the themes of Chapter II we find that of the five—Pursuit, The Quest, Identity and Recognition, The Scapegoat, and Poetic Justice—only The Scapegoat is not a major theme in Dickens (although we may find examples of the scapegoat as well—e.g., Esther Summerson in *Bleak House*). I have restricted myself to drawing examples from *Bleak House, The Mystery of Edwin Drood,* and *Barnaby Rudge,* since they reveal a particularly high concentration of the folkloric motifs that are recaptured in crime fiction.

How, then, do these themes, relevant for an explication of the crime novel, apply to Dickens?

I. The Pursuit Theme

No one who has read Dickens can fail to have been struck by the pervasiveness of this theme: Quilp follows Little Nell; Monks follows Oliver Twist; Mr. Dombey follows Carker; Guppy follows Lady Dedlock; Stagg follows Mrs. Rudge; Opium Sal follows John Jasper; this is but a random sampling. Chapter 55 of *Bleak House* is titled "Flight" and Chapter 56, "Pursuit." If we look at the type of incident which crowds the Dickens scene, we find ". . . oppression, murder, rejection, inheritance, imprisonment, marriage, flight, death, obsession, madness, mob violence, illusions, rebellion, renunciation, revelation. . . . The incidents seem to cluster into a pattern which emphasizes being oppressed and escaping."[15] This emerging pattern of oppression and escape is naturally encapsulated in the Pursuit theme.

Often Dickens' characters are pursued by some one with benevolent intentions (e.g., Mr. Brownlow in *Oliver Twist*). Even in such cases, however, suspense and mystery remain, the question merely shifting to "Will he/she reach him/her in time?" But though it never entirely loses that function, Pursuit is not exploited only as a vehicle for suspense. This theme develops from the pursuit for a missing person (e.g., the pursuit of the grandfather by his long-lost brother in *The Old Curiosity Shop*) into a spiritual quest as well. Thus Lady Dedlock's flight from Chesney Wold breaks the deadlock; it is as much a flight to something (literally her lover's grave, symbolically the truth and consequences of her sin) as from Inspector Bucket and Mr. Tulkinghorn. It was by such original developments—e.g., inserting the issue of retribution—that Dickens reopened the formulaic limits of the pursuit theme.

The Quest Theme

"We have identified the central myth of literature, in its narrative aspect, with the quest-myth."[16] In novels built upon a substratum of folkloric and mythic matter, this is conspicuously evident.

Dickens' characters (particularly children) embark upon two types of quests: the quest for their own material destiny (the Dick Whittington story), or the quest for identity (often literal identity, since in the Dickens novel as in the detective novel, the mystery often depends upon false, mistaken, or unsuspected identity). The quest for identity may, as I mentioned, evolve into a spiritual quest, often in the form of a quest for re-entry into a world of innocence (Rosa in *The Mystery of Edwin Drood,* Little Nell and her grandfather in *The Old Curiosity Shop*); this is also the basic movement of the detective novel. Dickens purposely renders the quest theme complicated and arduous, thereby providing scope for incident, variety, and sensation, justifying strange scenes and juxtapositions of people. Like Kafka, Dickens expands the experience into fantasy. The difficult quest corresponds to the obstacle course which the fairy tale hero must run, or the test of integrity or strength of a folk hero like Arthur, often a test of identity as well.

"The quests and myths of the romantic realists (Balzac, Dickens, Gogol) though their materials are profane, are themselves essentially religious in nature."[17] In this regard, Dickens lies very close to the fairy tale and to the detective novel—exercises to exorcise sin. Thematically, then, the quest as we find it in Dickens often takes the form of an allegorical "progress" or "movement toward the ideal," as well as a "progress of adventure." This progress can be either aided or impeded by the allegorical characters encountered along the way. There are devils

(Headstone, Murdstone, Jasper, Fagin, Quilp, Chester) and there are angels (Little Nell, Little Dorrit, Rose Maylie, Esther Summerson). The allegorical names of the characters enable the reader to understand the topography of the quest: Vholes (rat); Mr. Krook (common name for the devil); the Cheeryble Brothers; Esther Summerson (summer's sun); Ada Clare (clear); John Jasper (jasper = opaque, obdurate stone); Crisparkle (water and rebirth); Rosa Budd (the flower in the hortus conclusus); the Barnacles (of the Circumlocution Office).

Place names, as well as character names, are moral indices in the quest, and though having literal references—e.g., London, Rochester—are equivalents of allegorical stations in the progress of the plot. The geography of the Dickens novel is usually polarized between good-country and evil-city, a convention which Dickens revivified with his graphic, personal accounts of London scenes. (Of the country Dickens wrote with the unparticularized admiration of the city man.)

In *Bleak House* the country is the place the good people inhabit (Mr. Jarndyce, the fairy godfather, Esther, Ada, Charley), and it is the symbolic location of order (Esther's keys) and morality. London is fogbound (morally obscure), dusty (the law is dead), and the home of evil men (Krook, Vholes, Smallweed). Mud oozes upon London in the opening scene like some primeval curse. All is dark, forbidding, and threatening. In contrast, Esther's first Bleak House and her second, duplicate home when she is married are scenes of fruitful abundance, the places from which all blessings flow. Sunshine pours through them; gardens surround them. Many rural dwellings in Dickens' books are invested with this atmosphere—the Peggottys' boat-dwelling, the Garlands' cottage, Wemmick's toy castle. We are unconsciously reminded of fairy tale parallels; nothing is missing to delight; in fact, these places are earthly paradises (so that Mr. Jarndyce, an agent of Providence pictured with the light around his head like a halo, is totally unconvincing when cast as a lover). For the country, the garden, is the symbolic Eden. Pip meets Estella three times in the Garden; Ada and Richard walk out in the Garden when they become engaged; Rosa and Edwin meet in the garden; and the Garlands (their very name is suggestive) provide a garden-oasis for Kit. (An ironic jest is made of this in *Martin Chuzzlewit* where General Cyrus Choke sells shares in a hellish American swamp named "Eden.")

The antithetical station to Eden is Hell, displayed in many urban guises in Dickens' novels—e.g., the den of Fagin, the subterranean hiding place of Mr. Rudge, Quilp's warehouse, Newgate Prison. In *Bleak House* it is Tom-All-Alone's, the disease-ridden lodging in which the isolated, forgotten (Hawdon = Nemo = No One) down-and-outers sleep. It serves as the symbolic center of the book. Chesney Wold is the mid-way station of this allegory, its icy habilaments providing appropriate residence for Lady Dedlock's hauteur, and its dampness and decay suggesting the mildewed stain of the past for which she must still atone. It is a symbol of the absence of social responsibility on the part of the aristocracy and of the heartlessness which Dickens identifies with the upper classes.

Through the metaphor of disease, societal ills are exposed by physical ones. The theme of death and decay attaches to people and places; infection is like guilt, levelling all. The spectrum of people, high and low, is shown to be related through their common susceptibility. Thus infection (i.e., Esther's grave illness and Lady Dedlock's death) forges a bond between those two so separated in life. Donald Fanger claims that *Bleak House* (as well as *Our Mutual Friend* and *Little Dorrit*) "will involve detective work, not merely to unravel the mysteries of plot, but more importantly, to lay bare the subterranean network of social relationships."[18]

Dickens himself avers "that it is at least as difficult to stay a moral infection as a physical one; that such a disease will spread with the malignity and rapidity of the plague; that the contagion, when it has once made head, will spare no pursuit or condition. . . ."[19] The metaphor of disease is central to the detective novel, and as W.H. Auden said, the detective's function is to effect a "cure."

For Dickens' characters the outcome of such a "cure" is often equivocal, as in *Bleak House* and *The Mystery of Edwin Drood.* Despite the basic city-country dichotomy operative in *Bleak House,* evil is not successfully dispelled at the end. True, the murderer is punished; some deserving characters, Esther and Woodcourt, are made happy; but too many deaths have occurred, and the atmosphere is too tainted.

> In the single novel, *Bleak House,* there are nine deaths . . . carefully wrought out or worked up to; one by assassination, Mr. Tulkinghorn; one by starvation with phthisis, Jo; one by chagrin, Richard; one by spontaneous combustion, Mr. Krook; one by sorrow, Lady Dedlock's lover; one by remorse, Lady Dedlock, one by insanity, Miss Flite; one by paralysis, Sir Leicester. . . . all these deaths, but one, are inoffensive, or at least, in the world's estimate, respectable persons; and . . . they are all grotesquely either violent or miserable. . . .[20]

All our senses have absorbed the evidence of this pollution, and it remains with us.

Like the detective novel, the early Dickens closes with reinstatement or final security after the pursuit. But Dickens becomes less sanguine. Redemption in *Bleak House* comes not through an outside agency, as in the detective novel and Dickens' early work, but through personal suffering, symbolized by Esther's temporary blindness and disfiguring illness.

Evil in Dickens is often embedded in Victorian materialism, and consequently his allegory relates societal ills to personal flaws. Rex Warner, himself a social allegorist, points out that:

> Of this middle and later period Dickens seems to be using an allegorical method in his analogies of society and to be indicating, as Dostoevsky did, the massive forces of violence and lawlessness which are counterparts of that legitimate selfishness and personal accumulation on which society rests.[21]

(In *Bleak House,* Miss Flite, Jo, Gridley, and Richard Carstone all are victims of public guilt. In other Dickens novels, Little Nell, David Copperfield, and Pip are pitted against the "wicked witches of sullen bureaucracy and greedy industrialism.")[22]

In *The Mystery of Edwin Drood* we have a different variation on the quest theme. Rosa Budd literally lives in the cloister, in the garden of innocence. John Jasper is like a snake, sinuously

80

inserting himself into the environment of the tranquil cathedral town. In this scheme we perceive a replica of the detective novel, with its closed, innocent milieu into which the alien evil gains access. Yet the countryside of Cloisterham, again the scene where good characters reside (Rosa, Miss Twinkleton, Miss Crisparkle, Dean Crisparkle), is also the setting of the graveyard, of images dark and dusty, and even menacing—e.g., the stonemason Durdles burrowing amidst the tombs, the clock in the church steeple (reminiscent of Poe's story, "A Predicament"). True, London contains much that is condemned: the den of opium Sal, the grit and confinement of Miss Twinkleton's apartment, the staleness and restriction of the urban setting. The rosebud droops, and it is significant that it is not until the boat trip upon the open water with Tartar that Rosa refreshes herself. But Cloisterham and London are not entirely distinct. For instance Mr. Grewgious, the fairy godfather of *Edwin Drood,* dwells in the city. Because we do not possess the remainder of the book, we cannot say how this city-country polarity would have continued. Evil had become more omnipresent in Dickens' work, and to use one of his own favorite metaphors, perhaps in this book too, "the shadow would overtake the sun."

For Dickens, as for Dostoevsky, the city is a measure of a character's isolation, and London, like Petersburg, is the breeding place of monstrous visions (e.g., the dreams of John Jasper, Little Nell, Rudge). "One of Dickens' finest images is the great dome of St. Paul's Cathedral, dimly seen above the London fog, as if disconnected from the Life below. The city's desolation, its spiritual depletion, its lack of vital purpose, are his abiding targets."[23] The moral turpitude and confusion of the city serve as the perfect analogy for those of man himself.

We have encountered this equation before in the thriller; the city as agent, as assailant, in which not only the criminal is isolated, but even the detective. In Dickens' fiction the environment is also oppressive, and the classic struggle of the Dickens book is between a passive protagonist and a villain *or* an environment which is an enemy force. We know that Dickens learned the minutiae of the worlds he undertook to present—the criminal, the legal, the mercantile, and so forth. In a way his allegorical London is more frightening because his actual London is so real. This modern animism (i.e., of the city), partly the result of naturalistic observation and description but transcending this, is an extension of a Dickensian trademark. For Dickens achieves some of his most humorous yet horrific effects (the two are related through the link of the grotesque) by animating the inanimate, and vice versa. We feel the uneasy sensation of continuous transition, transmogrification. While it may be humorous to watch a thing become alive, it is always alarming to watch a person become a thing.

In Dickens, the twin magnets of good-country and evil-city or pleasure-country and pain-city compose the binary opposition of the allegory, and the protagonist travels between them on his quest. "It becomes a slow advance, from a start in pain and orphaning, moving between poles of relief and renewed pain toward a final haven."[24] This spiritual progress finds its physical counterpart in the multiplicity of actual journeys which the major protagonists undertake. Inspector Bucket, for example, abducts Esther from the Jarndyce household in the middle of the night, rattling in a carriage along labyrinthine streets, viewing a landscape obscured by fog, until they reach the final haven, Bleak House.

Identity and Recognition Theme

There are two important aspects of this theme to relate to Dickens: first, identity as one of the commonest mysteries in his plots; second, the relationship of identity to structural function. The first aspect, with its stylistic prerequisites of concealment, retardation, and narrative shift, will be discussed further on in this chapter. We may just note in passing that the complicated web of social relationships, fragile yet tensible, which Dickens explores, is uncovered in such a way as to retain maximum surprise while he presents the moral fable. For one brief example we may glance at the scene in which Lady Dedlock changes clothes with Jenny, a poor brickmaker's wife whose child has recently died. The strange clothes serve to disguise the aristocratic fugitive, and as a consequence her daughter, Esther, mistakes her at first sight for Jenny. This device of disguise (shape-shifting), however, not only masks Lady Dedlock's true identity but underlines the childless condition she shares with Jenny. Thus the dénouement is not only the answer to "whodunit?" - but also to "who is it?", a question which lies outside the limits of the detective novel.

The relationship of identity to literary structure is clarified by Vladimir Propp:

> We observe that the actors in the fairy tale perform essentially the same actions as the tale progresses, no matter how different from one another in shape, size, sex and occupation, in nomenclature and other static attributes. This determines the relationship of the constant factors to the variables. The functions of the actors are constants; everything else is a variable.[25]

This analytic tool obtains for the pursuit and quest themes as well. The departure on a quest is a constant. The departing actors, the motivations behind their departure, are variables; their functions are not. In later stages of the quest, obstacles impede the hero's progress; they, too, are essentially the same, but differ in imagery.

When character is primarily a matter of function, the moral progress of allegory operates. Nowhere is Dickens' consciousness of allegorical characterization more explicit than in *Bleak House,* where we see the figure, Allegory, painted upon Mr. Tulkinghorn's ceiling (reminding us of the painted figure of Time in Poe's "The Pit and the Pendulum"). When this blackmailing lawyer is murdered, he lies beneath this figure, with its pointing, accusing finger. Mr. Tulkinghorn plays the amateur detective for his own malicious ends; Inspector Bucket, the professional detective, has a characteristically active forefinger which points and wags and rests against his nose. Bucket's finger is synecdochical for his investigative function. The social and mythic levels of the book are united in such decoration and detail.

The functional criterion is a valuable way of assessing the enormous cast of characters crowded upon the Dickens stage. Dickens' characters are so memorable it may seem odd to refer to them as "stock" or allegorical, but if we reflect further, we find that what is memorable are their eccentricities, tricks of speech or gait, of dress or gesture—with which they have been invested precisely to differentiate them from their stylized fellows. If we strip away the variables, we may reach the essential nature of his characters. We may first remove all those individualizing touches of caricature which obscure the true typicality of the characters. Then, as Archibald Coolidge concludes:

> Newman Noggs in *Nicholas Nickleby,* Pancks in *Little Dorrit,* and Wemmick in *Great Expectations,* are all basically clerks and all basically odd, but they appear different. . . . [Nevertheless] they all perform the same action. . . . Suppose we try substituting Wemmick for Noggs, Bounderby for Smallweed. Can the stories go on as before? Certainly. We can do the same with the members of other groups in any book of Dickens. This interchangeableness shows us that the difference in characters, if any, between members of any one group are almost always ones which are not important to the plot.[26]

Coolidge arrived at this conclusion as a result of his study of the effects of serialization, and the stock characters to which it gives rise. But we can go further than this. This would still leave us with an exhaustive list of lawyers, military or naval men, parsons, businessmen, teachers, servants, professional Christians, and so on. But if we ask, not "What does this man do for a living?" but "What does he do for the plot?" then we may considerably refine and reduce the list. We have already discovered certain stock figures Dickens inherited from melodrama, Gothic novel, and romance: the benevolent guardian-father-rescuer (who corresponds to the detective); the double and devil archetypes (corresponding to the criminal); the lost child archetype (e.g., Esther Summerson). Thus in *The Old Curiosity Shop* we find that "All the good fairies and all the kind magicians, all the just kings and all the gallant princes, with chariots and dragons and armies and navies go after one little child who has strayed into a wood [Babes-in-the-Woods] and find her dead."[27] We discover recurrent archetypal figures and patterns of imagery which can be summarized:

Archetypal Figures

a. the fairy godmother or godfather	(substitute-father, protector) Mr. Brownlow, Mr. Garland, Mr. Grewgious, the Cheeryble brothers, Betsy Trotwood
b. robber barons (villains who persecute hero or heroine)	Ralph Nickleby, Sir Mulbery Hawk, Jonas Chuzzlewit
c. imps and goblins	Deputy, Quilp's boy
d. the harpy or witch	Madame Defarge, Opium Sal
e. animals, real or imaginary, half-human	Mr. Krook's cat, Grip the raven
also conveyed through metaphor	Hortense described as tiger. Gashford described as dog. Hugh described as centaur. Tulkinghorn described as rusty old crow. Grandfather Smallweed described as bird of prey. Rigaud as wild beast.
f. the child	Little Nell, Oliver Twist, Paul Dombey, Pip

Archetypal Imagery[28] and Corresponding Figures

a. human world is community, or hero who represents wish-fulfillment of the reader, archetype of images of symposium, communion, friendship, love (comic vision)	Pickwick Club; David Copperfield and Little Emily; Little Nell and Kit; schoolmaster in *The Old Curiosity Shop*

tyranny or anarchy, individual or isolated man (tragic vision)	Dotheboy's Hall; Oliver's orphanage; mobs in *A Tale of Two Cities;* Magwitch; Rigaud; Miss Flite
animal world is community of domesticated animals, usually a flock of sheep, or a lamb or one of the gentler birds, usually a dove, archetype of pastoral images (comic vision)	Little Nell's canary; Kit's horse; the Trotwood pony
Birds and beasts of prey, wolves, vultures, serpents, dragons and the like (tragic vision)	Vholes; Mrs. Merdle's parrot; Mr. Krook's cat; Grip ("I'm a devil")
vegetable world is garden, grove, park, tree of life, or a rose or lotus archetype of Arcadian images (comic vision), the hortus conclusus	Rosa Budd; Garland's garden; Mr. Boythorn's garden; garden where Pip and Estella meet
sinister forest . . . heath or wilderness, or a tree of death (tragic vision)	Miss Havisham's room; graveyard where Pip meets Magwitch; heath where Rudge meets Edward Chester

Dickens' conception of himself as a moralist, which inclined him to the overtly didactic lessons of fairy and folk tale, also led him to favor allegorical methods of characterization. Consequently, his characters frequently seem like personifications—e.g., the sin of pride, of selfishness (the Steerforths; Martin Chuzzlewit, Jr.), rather than multifaceted personalities. Though there is a goodly amount of dialogue in the Dickens novel, his people soliloquize rather than converse, confirming our original impression of flatness.

Dickens And The Crime Novel

Although Dickens, as a consummate craftsman, worked conscientiously at characterization, devoting space to dialogue and character development, the type of plot he chose made it very difficult for plot to generate character. As in the detective novel, the plot predominates and the people are done unto. Serialization likewise requires idiosyncratic signposts which jog the memory of the reader after an interval has elapsed. (For the same reason, the detective who appears in a series of books—Holmes, Poirot, Nero Wolfe—is supplied with characterizing habits or quirks.) This signpost device also helps us to recall the character's function immediately.

As V.S. Pritchett and others have alleged, Dickens' characters are really solitaries. The note of isolation, even alienation, creeps in continually, for the hero or heroine is usually dispossessed, a looker-on and looker-in. This Romantic strain we recognize in the rebel-hero who dispossesses himself (the thriller), and in the criminal who is dispossessed by society (the detective novel).[29] The criminal (Dickens' Sikes or Rudge) is the most radical example of isolation.

Dickens persists in treating the criminal as a creature apart, whatever magnetism the subject of crime may have exerted upon him. Dickens argues that "criminal intellect" is "perpetually misread, because [we] persist in trying to reconcile it with the average intellect of the average man, instead of identifying it as a horrible wonder apart. . . ."[30] As one would infer from this quotation, Dickens does scorn many of his criminals—e.g., Fagin and Murdstone. But he sometimes suggests a less simplistic view—characters such as Magwitch and Headstone, who have committed deeds which place them "outside society" nevertheless command our compassion. And, as in the classic detective story, the criminal in Dickens is an amateur, with whom the reader can identify more readily than with a professional.

Even the amateur detective, that trademark of the Golden Age of detective fiction, was anticipated by Dickens—e.g., Nadgett in *Martin Chuzzlewit,* Guppy in *Bleak House,* even Jasper, ironically, in *Edwin Drood.* As in the detective novel it is likely to be a detective from outside to whom we transfer our sympathies—for example, Inspector Bucket. The typical passive protagonist of Dickens is more nearly related to the victim of the detective novel and is therefore a difficult character to identify with, but our omnipresent sense of danger makes the rescuer (not always a detective or even the hero) very important. Inspector Bucket exudes power and confidence; this new character, the active detective, solves the crime. It is no wonder he became the popular pattern after Dickens. (In addition, the rescuer or reassurer often serves to bind together the multifarious complications of the Dickens novel.)

Any discussion of the theme of identity in Dickens would be incomplete without reference as well to the prevalence of the "doubling" motif in his work. However, this must be interpreted for what it was, part of the Romantic legacy. The popularity of this motif, which separates good and evil into two discrete externalities, introduced a literary reign of terror in nineteenth century literature, which can be recalled by citing Poe's "William Wilson," Stevenson's *Dr. Jekyll and Mr. Hyde* and *The Student of Prague,* Wilde's *Dorian Gray,* Melville's "Bartleby," Twain's mysterious stranger, Hugo's hunchback, Keller's Henty, Tolstoy's Ivan Ilyich, Carlyle's Teufelsdröckh, Conrad's "The Secret Sharer," Dostoevsky's *The Double.*

The exploration of guilt which preoccupied Dickens (as it did Kafka and Dostoevsky) ensured that he would engage this motif of doubling. How frequently this motif figures in his work: Sidney Carton and Charles Darnay; Jonas Chuzzlewit and Montague Tigg; Bradley Headstone and Rogue Riderhood; John Jasper (internalized); John Harmon (under two names); Nicholas Nickleby and Smike; Estella and Miss Havisham; David Copperfield and Steerforth; Pip and Joe. Variations are played upon the doubling motif by using disguises (Headstone duplicates Riderhood's clothes to make him appear Eugene Wrayburn's murderer); the assumption of a second character which is circumstantial only (Riah); the inversion or doubling of relationships (Bella in *Our Mutual Friend* calls her father her younger brother, Little Nell in *The Old Curiosity Shop* assumes guardianship of her grandfather).

Edmund Wilson sees doubling in Dickens' work as a device that fades from use as he progresses from a conception of good and evil as separate entities to the portrayal of them in combination; Wilson claims that they are syncretic in *Edwin Drood's* John Jasper:

> [*The Mystery of Edwin Drood*] explore[s] the deep entanglement and conflict of the bad and good in one man. The subject of *Edwin Drood* is the subject of Poe's *"William Wilson,"* . . . Dostoevsky's *Crime and Punishment.* . . . Raskolnikov—*raskolnik* means dissenter—combines in his single person the two antisocial types of the deliberate criminal and the rebel, which, since Hugh in *Barnaby Rudge,* Dickens has been keeping distinct.[31]

There seem to me two flaws in this line of reasoning. The first is that while Jasper may be both rebel and criminal, he is not both good and bad, but only superficially respectable and bad. We are given no instance of any virtue which resides in John Jasper: we neither see him act nor intend good toward any person, and he torments Rosa, whom he claims to love. Moreover, his physical appearance casts him as the prototypical villain of melodrama, dark and mustachioed. Dickens is increasingly concerned with hypocrisy, one of the cardinal sins in his creed; and Bradley Headstone, Mr. Pecksniff, and Mr. Fledgley exemplify this same cleavage between outward seeming and inner being. We might add that a growing apprehension of evil is manifest in the change in Dickens' villains: the early ones, such as Ralph Nickleby and the Chuzzlewits are obvious wrongdoers, but in the later Pecksniff, Murdstone, and Dombey, hypocrisy lends evil complexity. It is less easy to discern and more disillusioning to discover. But a facade of respectability is surely not the same as virtue. Thus there is a dualism, but not the sort which Mr. Wilson describes as "the conflict of good and evil in one man."[32] Secondly, a crucial dimension of character is lacking. Despite his multitude of dispossessed characters, Dickens answers only the question of material dispossession. Thus *Edwin Drood* is not a book about the same subject as *Crime and Punishment,* because the criminal act in *Crime and Punishment* is the outcome of an intellectual and psychologically complex struggle on the part of the hero. Indeed, the very word "dissenter" which Mr. Wilson provides as the translation of "raskolnik" connotes more sophisticated and calculated introspection than the Dickens character is capable of. There is no meditation in Dickens, and little psychological complexity. Jasper is one of his more complex villains (Rudge's motive is so paltry as to render him despicable), but he cannot assume heroic proportions. His hypnotic prowess, for instance, is a standby of the villain's trade; his "celestial singing," which Jasper himself terms "devilish," and the basic irony of his position as choirmaster in the cathedral, place him in the direct line of Lewis' *The Monk.* Thus, though we may feel deflection of energy into criminal activity as a waste, we do not feel the waste of potential, the life prevented from fruition, which is one of the losses of tragedy.

In fact, none of Dickens' novels produces a main character of heroic dimension. We are left with misfortune, or a series of misfortunes, not tragedy. Dickens' works also resemble the detective novel in this regard, for the conception of the detective story, in which plot is not generated by character, precludes the murder becoming a tragic act. This too accounts for the difference between *Edwin Drood* and *Crime and Punishment:*

> The fact that we are now in an ironic phase of literature largely accounts for the popularity of the detective story, the formula of how a man-hunter locates a *pharmakos* [scoundrel] and gets rid of him. The detective story begins in the Sherlock Holmes period as the intensification of low mimetic, in the sharpening of attention to details that makes the dullest and most neglected trivia of daily living leap into fateful and mysterious significance. But as we move further away from this we move toward a ritual drama around a corpse in which a wavering finger of social condemnation passes over a group of 'suspects' and finally settles on one. The sense of a victim chosen by lot is very strong, for the case against him is only plausibly manipulated. If it were really inevitable, we should have the tragic irony, as in *Crime and Punishment,* where Raskolnikov's crime is so interwoven with his character that there can be no question of any 'whodunit' mystery.[33]

By contrast, the organist and choirmaster of Cloisterham is of the type Dostoevsky calls "the old villain of melodrama."[34]

Not only is the crime in a formulaic detective tale rarely a function of the criminal's character, but there is also little room for self-discovery or consideration of the criminal personality. The point of the detective story is not self-discovery but the revelation of the identity of another character. Although Collins' novels might have encouraged a different development, in fact individuality came to mean conspicuous aberration for Dickens, and never led to an exploration of a complex, unconventional personality.

Although *Edwin Drood* is the only one of Dickens' novels to focus on a problem of personal rather than societal evil, this only caused Dickens to move still closer to the classic detective novel than to *Crime and Punishment.* He seems here bent on simplification in every sense. He has returned to the use of allegorical stations in the setting (churchyard at Cloisterham, the Thames); there is no longer a vision of London as a symbolic setting to match the Petersburg which served as the objective correlative of Raskolnikov's state of mind in *Crime and Punishment.* Since his book was never completed, no judgment of it can be definitive. But in the portion of it we possess Dickens has simplified his plot lines, reduced the number of characters, rejected the inclusion of a social theme—in short, set himself a different goal. (He may well have been goaded to this change by the appearance of Wilkie Collins' *The Moonstone* between his own *Our Mutual Friend* and *The Mystery of Edwin Drood.*) We have but to compare *Barnaby Rudge* or *Our Mutual Friend* with *Edwin Drood* to remark the compactness of the later book.

Generations of writers have been tempted to invent a "solution" to *The Mystery of Edwin Drood,* and even to compose a plausible remainder for the novel. Obviously this work is eminently intriguing because it was left a fragment—but if *Little Dorrit* or *Nicholas Nickleby* had been left incomplete? Is it not because *Edwin Drood* has succeeded primarily and by Dickens' intention as a mystery story that successive writers are teased into "solving" it? V.S. Pritchett comments:

> When Wilkie Collins wrote *The Moonstone* and Dickens, not to be
> outdone, followed it with *Edwin Drood,* we begin the long career of

murder for murder's sake, murder which illustrates nothing and is there only to stimulate our skill in detection and to distract us with mystery. The sense of guilt is so transformed that we do not seek to expiate it upon the stage (tragedy); we turn upon the murderer and hunt him down. Presently, in our own time, the hunt degenerates into the conundrums of the detective novels which, by a supreme irony, distract us from two world wars.[35]

The Mystery of Edwin Drood, close as it is to the intellectual puzzle form of the detective novel, substitutes a sense of gamesmanship for the tragic sense, the same gamesmanship evident in the depiction of Inspector Bucket in *Bleak House.* The author describes his detective: "From the expression of his face, he might be a famous whist player for a large stake. . . ." And Bucket tells Sir Leicester, "I don't suppose there is a move on the board which would surprise me."[36]

Gamesmanship implies both "playing the game" (i.e., characters abiding by rules), and "keeping score" (i.e., readers becoming spectators). When we consider the effect of the total work upon us, we marvel at the worlds of Dickens' creation, but the key work is "at"; we look *at* the Dickens world, we do not have what Robert Morse calls "a great immediate experience." A serener movement is begotten, as in the detective story or the folktale; and thus, although all three may beget suspenseful or even horrific effects, the total effect is soothing. Northrop Frye writes, "the detective story [is] a ritual game which the powers of law and order always win. . . ."[37] The game distances us from cathartic involvement. T.S. Eliot asks,

What is the difference between *The Frozen Deep* [a melodramatic story by Wilkie Collins] and *Oedipus the King?* It is the difference between coincidence, set without shame or pretense, and fate—which merges into character. It is not necessary for high drama that accident should be eliminated; you can not formulate the proportion of accident that is permissible. But in great drama character is always felt to be—not more important than plot—but somehow integral with it.[38]

Melodrama stresses accident; tragic drama the fatal.

Dickens And The Crime Novel

In spite of melodrama, archetype, and allegory, the Dickens character lives (though, in common with other functional characters, he does not grow). The characters are related both to each other and to the larger sense of these novels through systems of imagery. In *Bleak House,* for example, the contrasts between light and dark, order and disorder are established immediately and maintained throughout the novel. It is cross-referenced with ease-disease[39] (men are "in Chancery" as they are "in Jail" or "in hospital"). There are also parallel and contrasting upward and downward movements: Lady Dedlock falls from prosperity to poverty; Esther rises from poverty to prosperity; great worldly expectations come to naught; spiritual expectations are fulfilled. In *Edwin Drood* much of this symbolism revolves around colors, especially red, and light: rubies, sunset, tigers, blood, fire, weir, sparkling.

Humor (e.g., in the eccentric signposts) also serves to imprint the Dickens character upon memory. And finally, S.C. Reid explains the animation of the actors as deriving from " . . . the deepest mythology of mankind, the personages of myth being presented with a lavishness of minute and general characteristics that rivals the invention of life itself and prevents them from becoming the hollow shapes of folklore. . . ."[40]—or of the detective story, where the identity of villain, victim, and rescuer (the irreducible Dickensian triad) remains the only valid question.

Poetic Justice Theme

> "At the heart of his vision is the mystery of Providence"
> **J. Hillis Miller**

Poetic Justice is a *sine qua non* of the detective novel. Is this not true of Dickens also? The principle of Poetic Justice is convincingly supported in each of his novels by the tremendous emotional momentum which seems to require a superhuman agency for its resolution.

T.S. Eliot finds the distinction between melodrama and classical drama to lie in the fact that melodrama stresses accident, tragic drama,

93

the fatal. In Dickens' work serious drama triumphs over melodrama because accident and coincidence are the visible manifestations of some obscure power beyond human knowledge. ("Outrageous coincidence, when not frivolously used, has no frivolous effect [in melodrama]. It intensifies the effects of paranoia," writes Eric Bentley.)[41] The reader who cavils must have ignored the fairy-tale atmosphere of Dickens' fiction. He achieves an order like the fairy tale (or detective novel) not just of logical arrangement, but of fatality. The sense of foreboding, for instance, which we find in his work, parallels that of the detective novel; we build up to a suspenseful event which will be integrated into the whole, which is part of a design. The order evident in the organization of the detective story, is there in Dickens also, though obscured perhaps by the richness of the texture. It is a moral order.

Are Dickens' villains punished? Uniformly—Quilp, Fagin, Murdstone, Headstone, Rudge, Chester, Ralph Nickleby, Chuzzlewit, Krook, Blandois, Riderhood, Hortense, Sikes, Mme. Defarge—from the whole rogue's gallery there is not one escapee. We are satisfied by the inexorable advance toward a moral conclusion. This progress is precisely the movement toward the ideal, the type of 'progress' to which the detective story really belongs. The reader feels so confident of the eventual imposition of Poetic Justice that the chain of causality is felt to be satisfying. John Holloway believes that the death of Little Nell and Quilp in *The Old Curiosity Shop* seem unrelated "until [the reader] sees the one as in essence punishment for the other. There is a curiously perennial, mythic structure below what personal involvement dictated."[42]

Dickens' villains, though vital and even attractive at times, are quickly deflated for this same reason—the promise of Poetic Justice. They have been constructed to be quickly collapsible as well as portable, their boasts and posturing resembling the braggadocio of fairy-tale villains whom we know to be papier mâché. This is part of the gratification of reading Dickens; besides the galaxy of characters, the humor, the sensationalism, the details of life, there is the warming familiarity of knowing what he and we are about, and it is exactly this, of course, that also makes the detective novel reassuring. This is why Dickens, though a plot novelist, can be re-read without loss of interest, because what is re-enacted for our edification is the ritual triumph of the hero or heroine over the opposing forces of evil.

The alternation and intermingling of plot lines, which is standard Dickensian practice, only reinforces his own theory about the nature of life outside of fiction, for he upheld the inevitability of the amazing. John Forster comments, "His favorite theory [was] the smallness of the world and how things and persons apparently the most unlikely to meet were continually knocking up against each other. . . ."[43] Dickens was not simply convinced of the contiguities of life; he justified the use of coincidence as a *deus ex machina*. He wrote to Bulwer-Lytton in 1860:

> I am not clear, and I have never been clear, respecting the canon of fiction which forbids the interposition of accident in such cases as Madame Defarge's death. Where the accident in such cases is inseparable from the passion and emotion of the character, where it is strictly consistent with the whole design, and arises out of some culminating proceeding on the part of the character which the whole story has led up to, it seems to me to become, as it were, an act of divine justice.[44]

In this intention—to see Providential order executed—Dickens was not alone; the Victorian sensation novelists, Reade, Bulwer-Lytton, and Collins, share this moralistic view.

Into this ordered world the disorder of grotesquerie intrudes. Dickens' grotesques have attracted the widespread attention which their hold upon our imaginations justifies. Frye reminds us that "the word 'grotesque' . . . always carried with it some of its 'grotto' or underworld [double entendre] connections."[45] In Dickens there is also a separable element of surrealism which suggests interesting parallels with the detective novel. For example, here is a paragraph from *Bleak House*.

> The excellent old gentleman being, at these times, a mere clothes-bag with a black skull-cap on the top if it, does not present a very

animated appearance, until he has undergone the two operations at
the hands of his granddaughter, of being shaken up like a great bottle, and poked and punched like a great bolster.[46]

This description of Grandfather Smallweed restored by his granddaughter, Judy (Punch and Judy?) is extracted from scenes of
hatred and non-communication between Smallweed and wife
which rival the Theatre of the Absurd or Cruel. Dickens' surrealism, besides juxtaposing fantasy with brush strokes of
naturalism, animates the inanimate (as we have discussed
elsewhere) and changes proportions, isolating an image (Mrs.
Merdles' bosom is a jewel-stand) before our eyes in either enlarged
or diminished form, presenting distortion with photographic
verisimilitude. His obsessive characters (e.g., Miss Havisham, Miss
Flite, Mr. Micawber) and his daemonic ones, represent another
mode of surrealism, the isolated idea or quality.

In Dickens, however, dislocation is confined to glimpses, or at
most, vignettes. It does not comprise his total aesthetic premise,
nor betoken internal disruption, any more than it does in the
detective novel. The isolated images, the odd concatenations, are
swept up in the end in a tightening pattern, a mythic and coherent
creation, behind which lies the "mystery of Providence."

Thus Inspector Bucket of *Bleak House* is an ordinary person,
neither omniscient nor omnipotent. Dickens did not want Bucket
to dominate the outcome of the plot because he relied upon the
provisions of providence for a satisfactory conclusion to the novel.
For the same reason, even the emphasis upon coincidence and
chance take on a new and different meaning if we interpret them as
manifestations of the workings of Providence.

Structural Resemblances

So powerful are the structural resemblances between Dickens
and the crime novel, that in his essay on the structural components
of what he terms the "mystery novel" Viktor Šklovskij chose *Little Dorrit* as his model,[47] and in his book, *Charles Dickens and the
World of His Novels,* J. Hillis Miller analyzes *Bleak House* as a

"mystery story" on the basis of structural resemblances. The most important I perceive are:

1. the false or misleading solution
2. the device of concealment
3. the alternation of plot lines for the purpose of prolonging suspense
4. the construction of a foreboding atmosphere
5. the artificial assemblage of characters
6. the exegesis

That these are the "givens" of the modern crime novel is obvious enough to require no further demonstration, but if we apply them to the novels of Dickens the methodological kinship between the two will become apparent.

1. In *Edwin Drood, Barnaby Rudge, Little Dorrit,* and *Bleak House,* the false or misleading solution, often effected by the deliberate interpolation of "red herrings," is present. In *The Mystery of Edwin Drood,* for example, we are repeatedly warned of Neville Landless' temper; he is metaphorically described as a tiger; he is the last person to see the victim, Drood, alive; Drood is discovered dead coincidentally upon Neville's embarkation on a walking trip; Neville's background is kept vague so that we may not be reassured by his past behavior; for all these reasons, he can function as a false suspect. The real murderess in *Bleak House,* Hortense, is a minor character whose motivation never emerges strongly (motive itself undergoes concealment through shifts in emphases); circumstantial evidence, on the other hand accumulates against Lady Dedlock, who is innocent of the crime; the scene is further confounded when George, one of the sympathetic characters, is impounded for the same crime. In *Barnaby Rudge* the identity of the true murderer of Reuben Haredale is obfuscated because we are given the erroneous information that the murderer was himself an incidental victim. (It is one of Poe's criticisms of this book that the "red herrings" are inartistic, produced by "undue means," and it is certainly true that we tumble to Rudge's identity immediately. Nevertheless, the device was intended to work.)

97

This device of the false or misleading surmise can be traced back to Mrs. Radcliffe and other predecessors of Dickens. Clearly the false surmise is used to prevent us from seizing upon the true one—in other words, to keep the design of the mystery hidden as the book progresses. Dickens frequently resorts to the device of doubling, which we have discussed earlier, to suggest a likely but incorrect interpretation. Thus John Harmon's temporary identity as Rokesmith constitutes a false plot line in *Our Mutual Friend*. We have seen how a similar grouping and re-grouping around succeeding interpretations of the characters is indispensable for the orchestration of the detective novel itself.

2. Concealment is a necessary condition of any mystery, and is frequently effected by the device of retardation—i.e., the deliberate withholding of information necessary to the puzzle's solution. For example, in *Little Dorrit* the true relationships of the characters are not revealed until the end, thereby forestalling the solution of the mysteries. Julian Symons elaborates:

> For such concealment Dickens uses from the first tricks which resemble remarkably those of the modern detective story writer. He presents characters whose relation to each other is apparently inexplicably strange; the reader's curiosity is aroused by this strangeness, and he reads the book partly with the object of solving a problem. . . .[48]

Sometimes what is concealed is the relative importance of the characters. For example, in *Nicholas Nickleby* and *Oliver Twist* a minor character opens the book, thus creating false expectations. Or the concealment may pertain to the relationship between parts; thus in *Little Dorrit* the first two chapters initiate two different plot lines, Rigaud's and Clennam's, which we follow through the book without knowing how the lines are related.

3. Serialization afforded Dickens the opportunity of alternating his plot lines, a technique we have noted in stage melodrama. The public (or adventure) line and the private, domestic (though also sensational) line are offered seriatim, each breaking off at the strategically suspenseful moment. Either characters or locales common to the two plots link them. (For example, in *Little Dorrit* the characters of separate plot lines move next door to each other.)

These plot lines tend not so much to converge as to intersect each other from time to time. Furthermore, alternation also enabled Dickens to shift his narrative point of view, revealing only what was consistent with the knowledge of each narrator at any given time. One of the basic motions of mystery is this rearrangement of parts, which is a variety of inversion.

Multiple plot lines do not constitute the only multiplicity in Dickens; the exposition of "mysteries" is simultaneously factual and metaphorical, each level supplementing the other. Thus we "understand" *Little Dorrit* when we understand the metaphor of imprisonment. Using the Marshalsea prison as his point of departure, Dickens makes the prison of society his unifying metaphor.

4. Dickens' genius is nowhere more evident than in his power of evoking dread, a certain apprehension of the terrible. All the spectral shapes of his melodramatic imagination, his eye for atmospheric details of weather, his surrealist landscapes, are summoned to this task. We think of the vigil and search for Krook's "body," the trembling tale told by Solomon Daisy at the Maypole Inn, the sound of footsteps upon the Ghost Walk.

Dickens creates his anticipatory shudders in *The Mystery of Edwin Drood* by a variety of effects. We meet Jasper himself, inexplicably interested in Durdles and his discoveries in the vaults of the dead; we see Rosa's instinctive dread of her music master (the good angel intuitively apprehends evil); we notice the scarifying discrepancy between Jasper's public singing and his private croaking. (Indeed we are exposed to a melange of sounds: nutcrackers, Durdle's hammer, Jasper's tuning fork—harmonious music is a touchstone of Dickens' order; when things jangle, beware.) Dickens rhetorically questions the reader, "Why did he [Jasper] move so softly tonight? No outward reason is apparent for it. Can there be any sympathetic reason crouching darkly within him?"[49]

Occasionally Dickens stoops to the had-they-but-known admonition of the Gothic romance, as when Barnaby (*Barnaby Rudge*) and his mother refuse to sell their raven, Grip, and we have Dickens' own assurance that this act will recoil upon them. Usually, however, the foreboding is a "symbolic foreshadowing," such as he planned for the opening scene of *The Old Curiosity Shop* in which Little Nell is surrounded by the shop's bizarre collection. This juxtaposition of innocence and danger immediately pitches the reader into tension.

We cannot maintain that Dickens, like Dostoevsky, was an atmospheric writer, that houses, rooms, names, weather, are all revelatory, are given to the reader to aid his perception, without also acknowledging Dickens' conviction of the mystery at the heart of things, towards which all of these point. We poke out the truth in labyrinths, cellars, attics, alleys, in an atmosphere of chiaroscuro.

5. The collection of characters in one place at one time is a threadbare device of the detective novel, where in order for suspicion to be cast equally over a number of suspects, they must be part of a closed environment, equally accessible and equally plausible. Similarly, Dickens uses the excuse of quarantine in *Little Dorrit;* in *Our Mutual Friend* the characters are gathered together in a boat. (The device, of course, antedates him by far—e.g., the inn of *The Canterbury Tales* or the villa of *The Decameron.*)

6. The dénouement of the detective story is characteristically divulged in an exegesis to a group comprised of the innocent many waiting to be cleared, and occasionally the guilty one waiting to be accused. In just such a setting does Inspector Bucket of *Bleak House* disclose the identity of Hortense. It is necessary to bring people together, initially that they may serve as suspects, and, secondarily, that they may be an audience for the explication of the puzzle (the *moralitas*).

But how does Dickens transcend the formulae of the nineteenth century sensation novel or the crime novel as it has evolved since his day? The most obvious difference between the Dickens novel and the crime novel is that the former also has a social target—the law courts, the poor laws, prison reform, sanitation reform, and so forth. Dickens connects a social level to his plot very dextrously, but the presence of social consciousness removes his novels from pure puzzle or pure adventure. As we have said, the detective novel, with its static sense of social order, is not a novel of ideas, whether philosophical or social. Dickens' books are not novels of ideas in the strict sense, either. The books do not contain discussions of art, literature, sex, philosophy: they do provide an airing-ground for his social ideas, however. *Bleak House,* Edmund Wilson has suggested, belongs to a genre of which Dickens is the sole exponent, "the detective story which is also a social fable."[50]

The second noticeable difference between the crime novel and the Dickens novel is the luxuriousness of space and time we experience in the latter. We are treated to an uncountable number of characters, descriptions of places, things, smells, sights, sounds, plots, humorous disgressions. Years may elapse between encounters with the same character (e.g., Rudge in *Barnaby Rudge*). The thriller, like the picaresque narrative (e.g., Defoe), is less economical in its detail than the puzzle-detective story, but Dickens' liberality of effect would submerge the adventure line of any conventional thriller. And although the thriller may occasionally intersperse domestic scene and adventure (as melodrama did), there is rarely the domestic comedy with which Dickens regularly alternates his action. If the detail of the detective novel must relate to its system of clues, the extra pictorial detail of the thriller helps to create atmosphere. But Dickens indulges in what Orwell calls "rococo detail" for the sheer exuberance of it (for example, the extremely funny description of the dinner served in Mr. Grewgious' chamber by the "flying waiter" in *Edwin Drood*). The point here surely is that Dickens was not that interested in "whodunit," frequently revealing the answer before the conclusion of the book; nor was he interested in the adventure as an end in itself. Rather he wished to consider the *effects* of the deeds. Many of Dickens' novels—e.g., *David Copperfield, Bleak House, Hard Times, Little Dorrit, Great Expectations*—are *bildungsromans* which demand that other questions be asked.

Third, Dickens' novels distribute among several characters those functions reserved for one person in both the thriller and the detective novel. Although we may assert, "Quilp is the villain," or "Fagin is the villain," it is nonetheless true that there are almost always multiple villains, just as there are often multiple heroes.[51] Who is the hero of *Barnaby Rudge?* Joe Willett? Edward Chester? Gabriel Varden? Geoffrey Haredale? Even in *Bleak House,* which boasts a professional detective whose function is crucial, he is not brought onstage until halfway through the book, and cannot be said to be central. We are meant to be in doubt as to the identity of the villain in *The Mystery of Edwin Drood,* but who is the hero? The weak Edwin? The impetuous Neville? The crusty Grewgious? The mysterious Datchery? I do not believe that this ambiguity exists because we possess only a fragment of the story, but because this is the way of Dickens. We are given two camps of people, a "good" camp and a "bad" camp, and the functions of the characters are distributed among the members of each camp. Indeed in *Bleak House* it comes as something of a shock to realize that the French maid, Hortense, is *the* villainess (i.e., the murderer) because we have been presented with an array of villains far more frightening than she. Even her motive seems slight and contrived, whereas Tulkinghorn, Smallweed, Krook, and Vholes are the very incarnations of villainy. So marked is this system of polarization that John Holloway claims the very definition of Dickens' villains is that they are the agents who polarize good and evil.

Multiple villains produce areas of simultaneous danger. Thus in *Bleak House* we are worried about Esther, about Richard (and about Ada because of Richard), about Jo, about George, about Lady Dedlock, thereby distributing the function of the victim also. Sometimes the villains themselves (even those villains who embody social institutions, such as Mr. Honeythunder in *Edwin Drood*) are pallid, unpleasant but inactive, simply moving the plot forward. Smiliarly, although Esther Summerson is the heroine of *Bleak House,* her characterizing traits, goodness and humility, are found in almost equal measure in the characters Ada, Mr. Jarndyce, Caddy Jellyby, and Charley.

Fourth, Dickens' use of coincidence as a device for resolution distinguishes him from the writers of crime fiction. His reliance upon coincidence has often been judged a flaw; I believe he used coincidence as a literary externalization of a conviction rather than as a literary trick. Dickens believed that coincidence revealed the interrelatedness of lives. There is no doubt that a heavy reliance upon coincidence is not "cricket" in the detective novel; and even in the thriller, which allows a more fantastic progress of events, coincidence is usually found in those books which attempt parody of the form (Ian Fleming's novels of espionage) or ironic inversion (Graham Greene's entertainments).[52] The same may be said for the use of the supernatural: outlawed by convention from the novel of detection which prefers ratiocination, it is rarely invoked in the thriller, either. Providential intervention would belittle the extraordinary abilities of the adventurer-hero whose character, as it has evolved, has taken unto itself some of the supernatural capabilities.

Fifth, aware of the problems of unification presented by multiple plots and viewpoints, serial publication, a large cast of characters, and the introduction of social themes, Dickens increasingly turned to poetic, or metaphoric means of shaping a whole. These metaphors operate so consistently within the world of each book that they can contain all the diversity. They convey meaning to us metonymically—e.g., Chancery = fog, confusion *(Bleak House)*, Midlands = fire, damnation (*The Old Curiosity Shop*). The detective story achieves its unity by its singleness of purpose and simplicity of design; the thriller derives a spurious unity from its protagonist who moves through all of its episodes. Dickens could use neither; he did not wish to restrict himself to the singleness of purpose of the detective story, with its unilateral plot line and single episode; and though he borrowed the picaresque, or episodic structure of the thriller, the multiplicity of his plot lines, with their interruptions and see-sawing points of view, did not afford him the single hero. In fact, he managed to give his fiction the organic unity of poetry, overcoming the feeling of adherence to formula which the detective novel and thriller often impart to the reader.

Last, a significant difference between both the thriller and detective story and the Dickens novel is his espousal of the value and efficacy of human love and kindness. The thriller espouses nothing; it dispenses thrills. (It may be adapted for other purposes, but there is nothing in its nature which demands this.) The detective story espouses and upholds law and order. Neither is committed to a humanistic philosophy; the issue of human love and kindness may never enter either.

These, then, are the vital differences I perceive between Dickens and the crime novel, differences not of degree, but of kind. Nevertheless, an intimate relationship exists between Dickens and the crime novel: thematically (via the centrality of the themes of Pursuit, Identity, The Quest, and Poetic Justice) and structurally (via the devices of adventurous progress, concealment, the false surmise, mounting of atmosphere, alternation of plot lines, dramatic disclosures), some features of his work resembling more closely those of the detective novel, some the thriller.

Although superficially R.L. Stevenson's adventure novels seem diluted versions of Conrad, he identified himself with Dickens and, like Dickens, was enticed by the police and mystery novel. In the epilogue to *The Wrecker* he records that he and his collaborator attempted to produce an adventure novel free of "insincerity," "shallowness," something more significant than "a game of chess," only to find that "it had been invented previously by someone else, and was in fact . . . the method of Charles Dickens in his later work."

Incontrovertibly, the allegorical conceptions and archetypal images of the crime novel offer options to the novelist which are continually being renewed. In the next chapter we will examine the ways in which Joseph Conrad shaped to his purposes the flexible and suggestive possibilities of the crime novel.

Table 1

CHAPTER III

Dickensian examples from *Bleak House, Barnaby Rudge,* and *Edwin Drood* applied to Table 1, Chapter II.

Subheadings under Chapter D - Transformation, flight
D671   - Transformation, flight - fugitives transform themselves to escape detection by a pursuer—Lady Dedlock
D1080   - Magic weapons - Jasper's hypnotic powers; magic enchantment of Chancery captures Richard Carstone, Miss Flite, Mr. Gridley

---

Subheadings under Chapter F - Marvels
F610   - Remarkable strong man - Hugh
G210   - Forms of witches - Opium Sal - George falls into Smallweed's power
G400   - Person falls into ogre's power — Richard falls in Vholes's power; Lady Dedlock falls into Tulkinghorn's power
G420   - Abduction by ogre - Emma Haredale and Dolly Varden abducted by Hugh
G510   - Ogre killed, maimed, captured - Mr. Tulkinghorn, Mr. Rudge, Mr. Krook

---

Subheadings under Chapter H - Tests
H30   - Recognition through personal peculiarities - Jasper's self-betrayal under opium
H50   - Recognition through bodily marks or physical attributes - Guppy guesses Esther's true identity because of her resemblance to portrait of Lady Dedlock; Esther feels tug of recognition upon seeing mother
H110   - Recognition through cloth or clothing - Jasper's neckerchief
H220   - Ordeals - Richard's ordeal in Chancery; Mrs. Rudge's persecution by her husband; Ada's suffering because of Richard; Esther's childhood and later illness; Mr. Jarndyce's self-abnegation; Lady Dedlock's ennui
H510   - Tests in guessing - Guppy; Esther; Datchery; Helena; Opium Sal; Mr. Tulkinghorn; Mrs. Bagnold
H900-1109 - Tests of prowess, tasks - Mr. Varden's stand at prison; Barnaby's stand with flag; Jo's symbolic task of keeping London clean (ironic)
H960   - Tasks performed through cleverness or intelligence - Bucket's detection
H1210   - Quest assigned - Bucket's detection
H1220   - Quest voluntarily undertaken - Esther's search for her mother; Mrs. Bagnold's search for Mrs. Rouncewell; Lady Dedlock's search for Hawdon's grave

TABLE 1 - CHAPTER III (con't.)

H140   - Fear of staying in frightful place - Guppy and Jobling in Hawdon's room; Barnaby's fear in London; Jo's fear in Chancery (ironic); Esther's fear in Miss Flite's room

H1500-1549 - Tests of endurance and survival - Barnaby's imprisonment; Jo's "movin' on" (ironic); Emma and Dolly during abduction; Joe Willett in war

---

Subheadings under Chapter J - Wisdom, Cleverness

J50   - Wisdom acquired through observation - John Jarndyce's opinion of Chancery

J580   - Wisdom through caution - George and the Bagnolds

J1180   - Clever means of avoiding legal punishment - Gashford

J1800   - One thing mistaken for another - Jellyby and Turveydrop households

J2130   - Foolish disregard of personal danger - Barnaby (ironic); Edwin; Esther when nursing Charley

---

Subheadings under Chapter K - Deceptions

KO   - Contest won by deception - Chancery

K100   - Deceptive bargain - Mr. Chester and Hugh

K700   - Capture by deception - Bucket arrests George to deceive Hortense

K910   - Murder by strategy - Jasper

K950   - Various kinds of treacherous murder - Jo's murder by society; Richard's murder by bureaucracy

K1080   - Persons duped into injuring each other - Neville and Edwin duped into becoming enemies by Jasper

K1800-K1899 - Deception by disguise - Bucket enters Gridley's room as doctor; Datchery enters Cloisterham under disguise; Lady Dedlock pretends to be Hortense; Lady Dedlock pretends to be Jenny

K2200-K2299 - Villains and traitors - Lord Gordon, Gashford, Denis

---

Subheadings under Chapter N - Chance and Fate

N270   - Crime inevitably comes to light - discovery of Edwin's jewels while Crisparkle swims in weir

N440   - Valuable secrets learned - secrets of will amongst Krook's papers; Jasper's revelations under opium; Esther's interview with mother

N800   - Helpers - Grewgious, Helena, Mr. Varden

TABLE 1 - CHAPTER III (con't.)

Subheadings under Chapter Q - Rewards and Punishments

Q10-99 - Deeds rewarded - Esther's triumph; Joe obtains Dolly; Edward obtains Emma; Charley comes under Esther's protectorship; Woodcourt gains Esther

Q200   - Deeds punished - Chester killed by Haredale; Miggs banished; Tulkinghorn killed

Q211   - Murder punished - Rudge is caught; Jasper intended by Dickens to unmask himself

Q580   - Punishment fitted to crime - Denis the hangman hanged

---

Subheadings under Chapter U - The Nature of Life, or "Thus goes the world"

U1110 - Appearances deceive - the marriage of Sir Leicester and Lady Dedlock, and the gaiety of society; the respectability of Jasper; the respectability of Sir John Chester; the devotion of Gashford

---

N.B. Villain may be a social institution or person standing for social institution.

NOTES
CHAPTER III

[1]Phillip Collins, *Dickens and Crime* (London , N.Y.: Macmillan Co., 1962), p. 216.

[2]Edmund Wilson, *The Wound and the Bow* (Boston, Mass.: Houghton Mifflin, 1941), pp. 15-16.

[3]John Forster, as quoted in Philip Collins, *Dickens and Crime,* p. 216.

[4]*The Life of the Drama,* p. 201.

[5]Charles Dickens, as quoted in Archibald Coolidge, Jr., *Charles Dickens as Serial Novelist* (Ames, Iowa: Iowa State Univ. Press, 1967), pp. 150, 108.

[6]*Jack Sheppard,* an enormously successful "Newgate" melodrama which ran simultaneously at six London theatres, resembles the modern thriller in its evocation of ambivalent identification on the part of the audience.

[7]*Charles Dickens as Serial Novelist,* pp. 100-101.

[8]Gavin Lambert, *The Dangerous Edge,* p. 270.

[9]At the same time Dickens' awareness of the excesses of the romantic sensibility is shown by his satirical creation, Sim Tappertit, in *Barnaby Rudge,* who utters such absurdities as "If I had been a corsair, or a pirate, a brigand, a gen-teel highwayman or patriot—I should have been alright," and "I feel my soul getting into my head."

[10]Or, for that matter, Dostoevsky. "If I wrote a *roman feuilleton* (which I fully acknowledge) then I and I alone am responsible for this. . . . It has happened very often in my literary life that the beginning of a tale or a novel would be already at the printer's and in galley, and the ending would be sitting in my head, though it had to be written without fail by the morrow." Quoted in Donald Fanger, *Dostoevsky and Romantic Realism* (Cambridge, Mass.: Harvard University Press, 1965), p. 177.

[11]Philip Collins, *Dickens and Crime,* p. 97.

[12]*The English Novel: Form and Function* (New York: Rinehart, 1953), p. 134.

[13]*Charles Dickens as Serial Novelist,* p. 60.

[14]Jung writes: "[Archetypes reside in] that portion of the mind through which it is linked to nature." See fn. 7, Chapter II, p. 62.

[15]Archibald Coolidge, *Charles Dickens as Serial Novelist,* p. 55. The same sense of "being oppressed and escaping" is represented by Warrington Winters, in "Dickens and the Psychology of Dreams," (P.M.L.A., LXIII (1948), p. 948) as "the experience of trying to break thralldom . . . the most notable of Dickens' dreams."

[16]Northrop Frye, "The Archetypes of Literature," *Kenyon Review* (Fall 1951), p. 97.

[17]Donald Fanger, *Dostoevsky and Romantic Realism,* p. 262.

[18]*Ibid,* p. 81.

[19]Charles Dickens, as quoted in Richard Baker, *The Drood Murder Case* (Berkeley and Los Angeles: University of California Press, 1951), p. 225.

[20]John Ruskin, as quoted in Donald Fanger, *Dostoevsky and Romantic Realism,* p. 261.

[21]Rex Warner, *The Cult of Power* (London: Bodley Head, 1946), p. 26.

[22]Harry Levin, "Some Meanings of Myth," *Daedalus* (Spring 1959), p. 230. Nonetheless, Dickens does not counsel political revolution. "Dickens' treatment of these apprentices [in *Barnaby Rudge*] is as violently hostile and as ruthlessly satirical as Conrad's treatment of political revolutionaries in *The Secret Agent* or *Under Western Eyes* or as Dostoevsky's of his plotters in *The Devils.*" Angus Wilson, *The World of Charles Dickens* (London: Secker and Warburg, 1970), p. 148.

[23]Mark Spilka, *Dickens and Kafka* (Bloomington, Ind.: Univ. of Indiana Press, 1964), p. 85.

[24]Archibald Coolidge, *Charles Dickens as Serial Novelist,* p. 114.

[25]Vladimir Propp, "Fairy Tale Transformations," in *Readings in Russian Poetics,* ed. Ladislav Matejka and Krystyna Pomorska (Cambridge, Mass.: M.I.T. Press, 1972), p. 99.

[26]Archibald Coolidge, *Charles Dickens as Serial Novelist,* p. 54.

[27]G.K. Chesterton, *Appreciations and Criticisms of the Work of Charles Dickens* (Port Washington, N.Y.: Kennikat Press, 1966), pp. 53-55.

[28]For these particulars of archetypal imagery which I have juxtaposed with examples from Dickens I am indebted to Northrop Frye, "The Archetypes of Literature."

[29]In this, Dickens belongs to the group Fanger calls the "Romantic Realists." Scholes and Kellogg explain the way in which a romantic concern for the individual, held within the bounds of allegorical characterization, became the most appropriate mode for the "social fable," as Edmund Wilson terms Dickens' works: ". . . The great realistic narratives combine the tragic concern for the individual with the comic concern for the society to produce a representation of reality which is a just reflection of actual conditions and at the same time displays tragic and problematic concern for the individual regardless of his place in the social hierarchy. The typical figure of the Theophrastian character is not an individual but a representative of a social deformity, and thus is properly presented comically and held up to a ridicule based on social norms." *The Nature of Narrative,* p. 229. Thus toward the lower classes, Dickens' attitude is ambivalent, sympathetic to the single representative, wary of the group (e.g., the roving bands of unemployed in *The Old Curiosity Shop*).

[30]Quoted in Archibald Coolidge, *Charles Dickens as Serial Novelist,* p. 150.

[31]Edmund Wilson, *The Wound and the Bow,* p. 88.

[32]The belief in the dualistic nature of man, both Godlike and Satanic, which we find in Baudelaire and Dostoevsky is closer to Poe than to Dickens. The romantic paradox of *creative* destructive energy is not Dickensian.

[33]Northrop Frye, *Anatomy of Criticism,* p. 46.

[34]Donald Fanger, *Dostoevsky and Romantic Realism,* p. 140.

[35]V.S. Pritchett, as quoted in Richard Baker, *The Drood Murder Case,* pp. 193-194.

[36]Charles Dickens, *Bleak House* (London: Collins, 1953), p. 658, p. 660.

[37]*The Secular Scripture,* p. 138.

[38]T.S. Eliot, *Selected Essays* (London: Faber and Faber, 1932), p. 467.

[39]As J. Hillis Miller points out, within the first three pages of *Bleak House* we read "a general infection of ill-temper," "pollution," "defiled," and "pestilent." "Dickens' Symbolic Imagery," (Diss., Harvard University, 1952), p. 185.

[40]Stephen C. Reid, "The Hidden World of Charles Dickens," *University of Auckland Bulletin* n. 61 (English Series 10, 1962): 5-47.

[41]*The Life of the Drama,* p. 203.

[42]John Holloway, "Dickens and the Symbol," *Dickens 1970,* ed. Michael Slater (New York: Stein and Day, 1970) p. 60.

[43]*The Life of Charles Dickens* (London: Everyman's Library, Vol. I, 1927), p. 101.

[44]Charles Dickens, as quoted in Walter Phillips, *Dickens, Reade and Collins: Sensation Novelists* (New York: Columbia University Press, 1919) p. 134.

[45]*The Secular Scripture,* p. 133.

[46]Charles Dickens, *Bleak House,* p. 270.

[47]Viktor Šklovskij, "The Mystery novel: Dickens; Little Dorrit," in *Readings in Russian Poetics,* pp. 220-221. I am grateful to Dr. Bayara Aroutouvna of the Dept. of Slavics, Harvard University, for bringing this material to my attention.

[48]Julian Symons, *Charles Dickens,* (London: Arthur Barker, 1951), pp. 78!79.

[49]*The Mystery of Edwin Drood,* (Garden City, New York: Doubleday Dolphin Books, 1961) p. 135.

[50]"The Two Scrooges," *The Wound and the Bow,* p. 38.

[51]These multiple villains are arranged into archetypal categories of devil-villain, Jew-villain, and beast-villain by Lane Lauriat, Jr. "Dickens and the Archetypal Villain" (Diss., Harvard University, 1953).

[52]"The next step is an ironic comedy addressed to people who can realize that murderous violence is less an attack on a virtuous society by a malignant individual than a symptom of that society's own viciousness. Such a comedy would be the kind of intellectualized parody of melodramatic formulas represented by, for instance, the novels of Graham Greene." Northrop Frye, *Anatomy of Criticism,* p. 46. See my Chapter V for further discussion of Greene's comic irony.

CHAPTER IV
Joseph Conrad and the Thriller

The real significance of crime is in its being a breach of faith with the community of mankind.

Joseph Conrad, *Lord Jim*

The best technical work that is being done in the novel today is, perforce, being put into the romances of mystery that pour from all the world's presses. These must progress from paragraph to paragraph until the final effect is got by the last word—must, in fact embody all that technique that poor Conrad laboriously evolved for their benefit.

Ford Madox Ford *"Conrad and the Sea"*

A casual glance at Conrad's fiction reveals such titles as *An Outcast of the Islands, The Rescue, Suspense,* and *The Secret Agent,* and even his books with less sensational titles still make prodigal use of assassination, murder, shipwreck, poisoning, and solitary treks through the jungle. In short, Conrad offers the reader vicarious excitement and escape—the ingredients of the thriller. Such epithets as "thrilling," "suspenseful," "melodramatic" recur frequently in the considerable body of Conrad criticism.[1]

111

A Common Spring

Conrad's work might most readily be compared to that branch of the thriller practiced by Loti, Kipling, and Stevenson, and termed the exotic novel. Certainly there are superficial similarities: the exotic setting, a liberality of adventurous action, and an outcast hero. With Stevenson, for example, we can particularize these similarities further: *The Beach at Falesá* may have been a source for "Heart of Darkness," *Weir of Hermiston* for *Almayer's Folly, Lord Jim* contains features of *The Wrecker,* a scene in "The Dynamiter" anticipates *The Secret Agent,* and *Victory* resembles *The Ebb Tide.*

But the correspondences between Conrad and Stevenson (and the exotic novelists in general) remain superficial. What differentiates the Conradian work from the boy's adventure tale is, first, that it is a novel of ideas (e.g., the challenge of imperialism, the theory of atavism, the interaction between mind and instinct, the impending death of Western European society), and, second, that it is his imprimatur which correlates characters to the forces of destiny, that mythic element in his work which E.M. Forster dubbed "Conrad's further vision." As Conrad himself phrased it in a letter to Stevenson's friend Sidney Colvin, he had been called "a writer of the sea, of the tropics, a descriptive writer," but his real concern had always been with "the ideal value of things, events and people."[2] This concern with the formulation of an ethos, however circuitous, however ambivalent, has no place in the straight adventure novel or exotic novel which offers vicarious escape to the reader, but never penetrates its illusions of escape. Thus, although as Paul Wiley notes, a key doctrine of Ford's and Conrad's impressionism was "to provoke in sedentary readers the feeling of participating vicariously in active human affairs,"[3] we shall see that Conrad was to map the delusions of escape for his characters, and by inference for the reader, just as he mapped the landscape of fear.

Conrad was intrigued by the psychological effects of fear in all its manifestations upon character, and explored the subject in many of his character portraits (e.g., the sailors of the *Narcissus,* Decoud, Nostromo, and Hirsch). But Conrad did not use fear just as *frisson.* The impact of Freudian psychology, the insights of phenomenology, and the modern sense of existential *angst* have given new authenticity to the element of fear as the sensation novelists employed it. Conrad's character Sophia Antovna, one of the revolutionists in *Under Western Eyes,* speaks of this new kind of fear to account for Razumov's conduct: "There are evil moments in every life. A false suggestion enters one's brain, and then fear is born—fear of oneself, fear for oneself."[4]

Thus Conrad does not employ his characters solely as agents of the action: Some develop, some learn about themselves. Character as a determinant of destiny is an issue. In these respects Conrad's protagonists differ markedly from the usual picaresque heroes of the thriller.

We cannot speak of the Conradian hero as if he were a single conception; the early heroes differ greatly from the later ones. Conrad's attitude toward the hero-as-a-man-of-action, that staple of the adventure book, remains ambivalent. "Thinking is no good for the nerve," Conrad admonishes us; hence a mariner-hero, whose reflex responses are a product of training rather than intellection, is exceptionally attractive to Conrad. We learn from Jim of the *Patna* that not only thinking but imagination itself compromises the nerve. On the other hand, Conrad wrote in a letter to Mme. Poradowska, "Nothing is more futile than the mere adventurer."[5] In fact, the adventurous hero of the thriller, toward whom his readers must also entertain ambivalent feelings—compounded of superiority and indignation, attraction and shock—proved the perfect vessel for Conrad's own ambivalence on many subjects (e.g., sex, authority, and the active life). This is not to say that some of Conrad's characters are not allegorical abstractions, defined by their function. Some do take on allegorical roles: the maiden-in-distress, the law-giver, the rescuer, the loyal servant, and so on. In formulaic literature incident is all; character, and therefore passion, are necessarily diminished.

But if Conrad transcended the constrictions of the exotic adventure novel, he did not disdain its devices: this form, like its predecessors, not only appealed to the romantic side of Conrad's nature, but offered him positive advantages. "Whatever its degeneration into facile modes of romance or sensationalism,"

Morton Zabel writes, "[the exotic novel] played its part in relieving the prose imagination of the age of its addiction to fact, science and social realism, and in reasserting the kinship of fiction with poetry. It has a long ancestry, reaching back into fable, parable, and legend."[6] Where fancy leads and allegory ensues, we shall find in Conrad, just as we did in Dickens, motifs of fairy tale and myth, manifesting again their allegorical relationships.

Rather than discarding the thriller, Conrad invested that relatively flexible form with substance. In comparing the Conrad novel to the thrillers of Robert Louis Stevenson, Albert Guérard writes:

> . . . the melodramatic plots [of Stevenson] profess to demand intense moral choices. But only profess the demand. The difference from *Lord Jim* or even *Almayer's Folly* is largely one of subjective involvement. Whereas Conrad exhibits a conflict between judgment and sympathy, between moral repudiation of the rebel or outlaw and strong identification with him, Stevenson shows neither the judgment nor the sympathy. His beachcombers are completed moral ruins, not even on the edge of ruin; they are too distant from their creator.[7]

The thriller can raise many questions which the detective novel cannot, since the latter must concern itself with actual crime, classically the unpardonable crime of murder. The thriller does not even demand an actual crime to precipitate its action; the same sensations may be produced in the reader by exposure to danger, reversal of odds, proximity of the unknown, or promise of escape. Since the "necessary error" which is the plot's center in the Conradian work need not be a crime either (i.e., a punishable offense against society) but may be a marginal, even well-intentioned error of conscience or judgment, the thriller is naturally congenial to Conrad.

From this quintessential difference arise two corollary questions of extreme importance to Conrad: 1. To what extent can the perpetrator of that "necesary error," Conrad's protagonist, be held responsible? (Dickens placed this question in an economic context, Conrad in a social or political one.) 2. How can we adjust the rival claims of private and public allegiance? (This is, for instance, the pivotal question of "The Secret Sharer.") In the detective novel society is the judge, not the offender. In *Under Western Eyes* it would not be too extreme to say that the whole of Russia is the offender.

We may speak of Conrad as a thriller-writer in another sense, unrelated to the exotic romance: as the author of the political thrillers, *Nostromo, Under Western Eyes,* and *The Secret Agent.* We have on every hand in these novels instances of Conrad's modernity: his intuitions of political revolution and a changed social order;[8] his recognition of that spiritual isolation which has become virtually a *sine qua non* of the modern novel; his anticipation of principles of existentialism ("Chance," as Joseph Conrad's Marlow was to argue, might be "the one remaining escape hatch in a modern and closed universe");[9] his psychological probing and self-consciousness; and his surprising grasp of the subordinate position of women in his society.[10] Lionel Trilling sees doubt as a modern cultural donnée, provoking a ceaseless search for "authenticity," and cites "Heart of Darkness" as "the paradigmatic literary expression of the modern concern with authenticity."[11] But Conrad's contemporaneity is nowhere more striking than in his adaptation of the thriller as a vehicle for political expression, anticipating the work of Liam O'Flaherty (*The Informer, The Assassin*), George Orwell (*1984*), Arthur Koestler *(The Yogi and the Commissar),* and F.L. Green *(Music in the Park, Odd Man Out)*:

> *The Secret Agent* (1907) is now recognizable as a pioneer classic in a genre—the tale of political intrigue, espionage, and moral anarchism in modern Europe—which has become a typical mode of fiction in our sinister age of Machtpolitik, scientific violence, and 'international evil.'[12]

Frederick Hoffman, in his book *The Mortal No,* calls *The Secret Agent* "our first novel of violence." Conrad combines, in uneasy union, the novel of manners or decorum (which is kin to the detective story) and the novel of violence (with which the thriller has become associated). Manners, Hoffman maintains, only remain as irony in Conrad's political thrillers. But the failure of the realistic nineteenth-century novel to serve Conrad's vision, reflecting the failure of the closed society upon which it rested and within whose confines its manners could be examined, became the triumph of the twentieth-century novel of violence, to which the thriller gave voice. The inexplicable (ultimately the absurd), the divided self, anarchy, the fragmented society, the insistent presence of destructive force—not one of these is inimical to the tenets of the thriller. The political thriller became, with the Theater of the Absurd, the representative twentieth-century form.

Conrad describes *The Secret Agent* as a "simple tale of the Nineteenth Century," an ironic description of an ironic book which is neither simple nor backward-looking. Still, we must acknowledge the methodological link he felt with Victorian melodrama. Indeed, Ford Madox Ford, Conrad's sometime collaborator and an admirer of *The Secret Agent* (which he termed "one of the best—and certainly the most significant—detective stories ever written"),[13] used Conrad's example to justify his own adaptation of crime story components. Ford testifies to the conscious effort made by the two authors to forge a style which would renew the novel by rendering it capable of treating "modern" themes. Reminiscing about their joint literary efforts Ford says, "In writing a novel we agreed that every word set on paper—every word set on paper— must carry the story forward and that, as the story progressed, the story must be carried forward faster and faster and with more and more intensity. This is called *progression d'effet.*"[14] This is precisely the effect which the thriller desires. Conrad and Ford seized upon this form, rather than the measured pace of the detective novel, because it conveyed the accelerated tempo of modern life.

Although it is the thriller which Conrad found more adaptable, and although it is the thriller form which his fiction most resembles, there are major aspects of his work which lie closer to the detective novel. Such isolated instances as planting the clue of the label in Stevie's overcoat (*The Secret Agent*) or even the inclusion of actual detective characters—Inspector Heat and Councillor Mikulin—are the most obvious examples. But there are less superficial, though more covert, resemblances: the presentation of

Marlow, whose dissecting, rhetorical exegeses and interest in "getting to the bottom of things" cast him as a detective. Zabel discerns what he calls an "analytical principle" which underlies much of modern fiction, not just the detective novel:

> The analytical principle has developed rapidly in the fiction of the past century. It produced in the Nineteenth Century the tale of detection, where a shrouded mystery, false appearance, or inscrutable condition of circumstance, baffling to the eye by reason of deception or accident, was methodically uncovered. From the fables of Poe this device advanced toward social analysis and criticism in Dickens, and thus toward the analysis of moral or ethical concepts as we find them in our time in books like Gide's *The Counterfeiters* or Kafka's *The Trial,* where, by methods varying from the dialectic to the legalistic, the successive husks of intention or consciousness are stripped from actions and personal relationships until the cell of origin is bared. . . .[15]

This is an acute insight; if the scope of the detective novel can be enlarged, perhaps it will be through manipulation of the "analytical principle." It is also an acute insight into Conrad; the freight of sensation, melodrama, sentiment, and exoticism which his novels bear should not blind us to the investigative mode in which so many of them are cast. The mystery is not necessarily in "whodunit?" but in "why?" or "under what circumstances?" or even "what was done?" The mystery may be that of human behavior, for Conrad was a major novelist who addressed himself to the inner workings of events. But the judicious sifting, the searching for clues to behavior, the accumulating of evidence, even that shifting of narration which, while it may function primarily to enhance tension, also refracts new light upon the mystery—all this constitutes a process of detection. Ironically, one of Conrad's characters in *Chance* comments upon the method of the story in which he himself appears:

> This is like one of those Redskin stories where the noble savages carry off a girl and the honest backwoodsman with his incomparable knowledge follows the track and reads the signs of her fate in a footprint here, a broken twig there, a trinket dropped by the way. I have always liked such stories. . . .[16]

As with Poe, the ratiocinative strain competes with the romantic in Conrad, with the mystification that envelops so much of his writing; mystery is obfuscated by mystification, a "secret" confounded with hints of secrecy.[17] This "mystification" F.R. Leavis judges a serious incapacity, marring even so fine a story as "Heart of Darkness":

> Conrad here must stand convicted of borrowing the arts of the magazine-writer (who has borrowed his, shall we say, from Kipling and Poe) in order to impose on his readers and on himself, for thrilled response, a 'significance' that is merely an emotional insistence on the presence of what he can't produce.[18]

The romantic Conrad may mask a division of temperament or an intellectual irresolution; in any case critics have paid scant attention to his analytical presentation, preferring instead the synthetic (mytho-poetical) process in Conrad. His work resembles the detective novel not merely in its investigative procedures, but in the author's infatuation with the problem of justice. Though it is certainly true that the detective novelist is not free to range amongst questions of the relationship of law to justice, or personal vs. public dispensation of justice as Conrad is, the detective novel revolves around a moral question as the Conradian novel does, and as the thriller does not. Thus we might fairly say that Conrad used the components of the thriller but affirmed the values of the detective novel (though sometimes those values are only shown to be deplorably missing). The search for order, the closed community, the issue of punishment and the desire for justice which are inseparable from Conrad's work, are the same elements we recognized as integral to the detective novel. Indeed, it is the clash of these two worlds, the forsaking of the traditional world (the detective story) for the world of survival (the thriller) which constitutes the prototypical Conradian dilemma.

Knowing that Conrad shares the detective novel's use of Poetic Justice and of the analytical principle, in addition to the thriller's use of melodramatic technique, we can focus on the themes he chose these means to purvey.

Joseph Conrad And The Thriller

Thematic Resemblances

Conrad is telling us something very old and terribly true. . . .
Virginia Woolf
The Common Reader, Vol. I

Joseph Conrad's inherent genius is that strange margin of our minds,
where memories gather which are deeper than memories. . . .
John Cowper Powys, "Joseph Conrad,"
*Suspended Judgments: Essays on Books
and Sensations*

Despite the precision of detail with which he invests his stories
and novels, it is not on this surface level of reality that Conrad ad-
dresses us, but through a reality buried in fantasy, reshaped myth,
and fairy tale. This seems at first a contradiction, since the realistic
reproduction of an exotic atmosphere is admittedly part of the appeal of the thriller. Conrad himself is insistent that he wishes
"before all, to make you see"; and his style is undeniably visual,
imagistic; but these images are placed in such a context that it is
their symbolic meaning for which we grope. His themes are most
often expressed through these symbolic images; the fantasy of
which I speak is not the shallow fantasy of mechanically contrived
escape, but the fantasy of trances and dreams. By the fantasy of
dreams I do not mean to suggest "dreaminess," the mistiness or
imprecision E.M. Forster lays at Conrad's door, but rather that
logical illogicality which is the basis both of surrealism and
nightmare, in which shapes (phantasms) are thrust up by the unconscious, or by race memory, and unified into a fantastic picture
or story. The Conradian narrator himself frequently recounts a
tale of thralldom, in which the protagonist resembles nothing so
much as that character in a fairy tale upon whom a spell has been
cast. "It was like a pilgrimage amongst hints for nightmares."[19] It
is from the background of this thralldom, trance, nightmare that
archetypal characters emanate. "Melodrama is the Naturalism of
the dream life,"[20] is another way of understanding nightmare.

Conrad's books are versions of Morality plays ("Each of his
stories is a kind of pilgrim's progress but without God");[21] this,

plus the similitude to the other allegorical forms—myth (Creation, the Fall, Narcissus, have all been discerned in his work); fairy tale (Dorothy Van Ghent interprets *Nostromo* as a fairy tale, working out the correspondences in detail);[22] exemplum (the object of life is the perfection of individual conduct); fable (Guérard claims Conrad's atmosphere is not so much supernatural as preternatural)—create thematic resemblances to the thriller, which itself utilizes these anterior fictions. One can find those archetypal images and figures upon which myth, fairy tale, and folk literature build, as well as the type of image and imagistic order which belong to the dream. A list of such archetypal images and figures follows:

Archetypal Figures

a. the fairy godmother or god-father
(substitute father, protector) Tuan Jim, Captain Anthony, Lingard, Dr. Monygham

b. robber barons (villains who persecute hero or heroine)
De Barral, Gentleman Brown, Willems, Ricardo

c. imps and goblins
Toodles, Stevie

d. the harpy or witch
Madame do S., the Countess, Montero, Tekla

e. animals, real or imaginary, half-human
Wait, Hirsch, Pedro

also conveyed through metaphor "Generally, then, in Joseph Conrad's bestial imagery, the animals of this menagerie define an underworld of desires and actions into which one may fall"
Donkin described as scavenger bird. Fyne described as a terrier; Wait described as a brute. Massey described as bird of prey in "The End of the Tether."

120

(Stanton de Voren Hoffman, "Conrad's Menagerie: Animal Imagery and Theme," *Bucknell Review,* XII, (December 1964), p. 60.

Revolutionists in *Under Western Eyes* described as vultures. Verloc described as fat pig.

"the animal world and its presence as physical animality—represented in the extreme case by gross fatness" (Avrom Fleishman, *Conrad's Politics,* p. 200).

f. the child

Flora described as forsaken elf. Mrs. Gould described as fairylike.

(Paul Wiley associates the maidens-in-distress who are frequently quest-objects with the heroines of the Romantic decline. The maiden-in-distress is, as we remarked in the previous chapter, a favorite of Dickens, and derives ultimately from the Lost Child, or Babes-in-the-Wood archetype. *Conrad's Measure of Man,* p. 144)

Archetypal Imagery

a. human world is a community, or hero who represents wish-fulfillment of the reader—archetype of images of symposium, communion, love (comic vision)

Lingard's Sambir, the ship *Narcissus, Ferndale* (prior to onstage events) Peyrol, Cervoni, Captain and Leggatt in "The Secret Sharer"

b. Tyranny or anarchy, individual or isolated man (tragic vision)

Jim, Heyst, Anthony, Kurtz. Anarchists in *The Secret Agent.* Leggatt, Razumov, Château Borel, St. Petersburg, Costaguana

121

c. sinister forest . . . heath
or wilderness, or tree of death

Forest in *Almayer's Folly* and *An Outcast of the Islands.* "As lonely and unsafe as though he had been in a forest" describes Verloc in *The Secret Agent.* Woods near Greenwich Observatory where Stevie dies. Jungle in *Nostromo.* Wood where Marlow sees African laborers stretch out to lie in "greenish gloom under the trees" ("Heart of Darkness")

"My purpose was to stroll into the shade for a moment; but no sooner within than it seemed to me I had stepped into the gloomy circle of some inferno."[23]

d. water imagery

Serpent-river in "Heart of Darkness." The "destructive element." Storms in *Lord Jim,* "The Nigger of the *Narcissus,*" and "The Secret Sharer." Floods in *An Outcast of the Islands and Almayer's Folly.* All the voyages which take place on the water, and in which the water takes on an aspect of benignity.

"Forthwith a change came over the waters, and the serenity became less brilliant but more profound. The old river in its broad reach rested unruffled at the decline of day, after ages of good service done to the race that peopled its banks, spread out in the tranquil dignity of a waterway leading to the ends of the earth."[24]

e. vegetable world is a garden, grove, park, tree of life, or a rose or lotus archetype of Arcadian images	There is a dearth of Arcadian imagery in Conrad, although Thomas Moser points out that the earmark of the early heroine is garden imagery

Of the five thematic headings (Pursuit, The Quest, Identity and Recognition, The Scapegoat, and Poetic Justice) which we have constructed in order to analyze the crime novel, and around which our discussion of Dickens was organized, those germane to a discussion of Conrad are The Quest, Identity and Recognition, The Scapegoat, and Poetic Justice. (Conrad's investigative mode of advancing the progress of the novel I read as a substitute movement for the thriller Pursuit element which we find in the hunted-man novels of Graham Greene or F.L. Green.) Although the whole of Conrad's work qualifies for consideration from these aspects, I will mainly consider "Heart of Darkness," *The Secret Agent, Chance, Under Western Eyes,* and "The Secret Sharer," representatives of both the political thriller and the romantic adventure.

The Quest

The quest-myth, the basic myth of literature, finds its natural expression in the journeys of the Conradian world. All but two novels *(The Secret Agent* and *Under Western Eyes)* utilize the sea voyage, the sea frequently functioning as a force of destiny. *Lord Jim, Chance,* "The Shadow Line," Heart of Darkness," "The Nigger of the *Narcissus"* all employ the voyage. They are outwardly adventure tales, replete with realistic details of sea, landscape, foreign customs. But though the adventure is external, the quest is internal, a progress. The journey of the picaresque novel, which afforded scope for episodic adventure and is part of the inheritance of the thriller, becomes that more adventurous journey of the spirit which Conrad conducts: Marlow's journey "into the interior" in "Heart of Darkness" or Gould's journey "to the underworld" in *Nostromo.*

Conrad's journeys typically move through darkness to illumination and psychological insight and are thereby related to the quest for identity. Thus the captain in "The Secret Sharer," unsure in his first command, can steer through difficult waters after acknowledging Leggatt as his spiritual brother, can see the way by the grace of Leggatt's hat:

> As in earlier writings like 'The End of the Tether' the motif of vision figures prominently in 'The Secret Sharer'; and from this first reference to the eye staring into space [See Illustration 2, Chapter II] the narrative proceeds to a final concentration of sight on the hat left behind in the water by Leggatt, a 'saving mark for the eyes.'[25]

In "The Shadow Line" the narrator is launched on a journey into darkness by Giles; in *Nostromo* the journey is infernal, down successive rungs of blackness to the illusory promise of the bright silver; Marlow, on his journey into darkest Africa, ironically experiences an illumination; the scene of Razumov's searing confrontation with Nathalie Haldin in which ambiguities are finally reduced to "black and white" is enacted in an anteroom of glaring white punctuated by the black mourning dress of Nathalie, Razumov's black umbrella, and the black and white tiles of the floor, recalling the similar black and white marble hall in *The Arrow of Gold*. Guérard called the Conrad journey a "night journey," an archetypal Jonah adventure, after which solitary and dangerous experience the voyager is changed.

The journey through blackness and the process of interior change which it engenders lead us to qualify, however, the usual fairy tale equation of black with evil. "Darkness" or "blackness" in Conrad is equivocal; it cannot stand simply for primitivism, as in "Heart of Darkness," since the London of *The Secret Agent* is also black, "the devourer of the world's light." The modern city, a concrete jungle, is as much a heart of darkness as the Asian or African jungle. The distinction here lies between atavism and primitivism; Marlow, surveying the Thames estuary, tells his listeners, " 'And this also . . . has been one of the dark places on the earth.' "[26] If the darkness were uninstructive, then it was folly to invade it, an act of absurdity.

"Blackness" or "darkness" may also be related to "the destructive element." When Stein in *Lord Jim* advised men to "submit to the destructive element and with the exertions of your hands and feet in the water make the deep, deep sea keep you up,"[27] he was not advocating the dubious thrills of self-destruction, but a surrender to experience which tests the self and forges identity. Thus experiencing "the destructive element" is part of the quest for identity. The admiration which Marlow feels for Kurtz, despite the cruelty, despotism, and greed which he witnesses in Kurtz' territory, can be explained only if Kurtz is interpreted as a mentor, someone who can speak from the experience of darkness, a Vergil in this underworld. But the darkness cannot be construed as external only; the "heart of darkness" beats in us all as passion and irrationality.

Conrad uses two motifs of the quest theme almost obsessively: the isolation of the hero (literal isolation in the fairy tale, moral in Conrad), and the introduction of hazards and obstacles which test the hero's fidelity or strength or cleverness. Marlow remarks, "the approach to this Kurtz digging for ivory in the wretched bush was beset by as many dangers as though he had been an enchanted princess sleeping in a fabulous castle."[28]

True, it is a condition of any hero, by virtue of that superior authority or excellence that makes him a hero, that he *be isolated;* it is hardly surprising that he be isolated on his quest. But in Conrad isolation is part of every man's existence, not just the hero's. "We live, as we dream—alone. . . ."[29] An important corollary of this is that Conrad's hero can be an allegorical everyman; by stressing the hero's likeness to us rather than his elevation above us, Conrad is free to delineate the hero's limitations, which he does.

The test motif, providing an inescapable crisis towards which the novel or story progresses, is of obvious structural importance to Conrad. For the character it provides a confrontation with his destiny which is not only inescapable but irremediable. The test for Conrad is rarely the epic one of vanquishing a foe; rather its purpose is that of tragedy, to bestow self-knowledge. The soul as well as the body is at risk. Marlow foretells, after the death of Kurtz:

Destiny. My destiny. Droll thing life is—that mysterious arrangement of merciless logic for a futile purpose. The most you can hope from it is some knowledge of yourself—that comes too late—a crop of inextinguishable regrets.[30]

When the hero meets his test in Conrad, as in Hemingway, he meets also his "moment of truth," irrevocably defining and stamping him.[31] Jim's misappraisal of his test, or momentary failure of nerve, turns him into a wanderer, atoning for the same mistake again and again (recalling the myths of Ulysses and of the Wandering Jew). The test offers an opportunity to display endurance—i.e., the ordeal as survival—which ranks high in the Conradian moral schema. "Moral resistance, moral resistance," Razumov repeats to himself in an effort at self-possession. So Captain Anthony of the *Ferndale,* doomed by the gallantry and self-abnegation of his own character, goes his appointed rounds in silent suffering, enacting the isolation and test motifs simultaneously.

Should the test be successfully negotiated, the reward is entry into a fellowship (the ship is a characteristic embodiment of such a fellowship), and hence the test may most properly be described as an initiation. In this it resembles the Grail myth, a major quest myth. Although the community is valued highly by Conrad, initiation need not be into a specially respected order of society; thus Marlow speaks of Kurtz as an "initiate wraith" because he has stepped over the threshold of "Nowhere."

There are many other variations of the test and/or quest theme in Conrad. At times he uses the quest theme in order to satirize its romantic conventions, as in his quixotic (Anthony, Heyst), naive (Gould), or self-deluding (the figures of Château Borel) characters. The test, and/or the quest, may be compromised from within by man's dualistic nature, hermitic and sensual, rational and irrational (dramatized by the device of the doppelgänger and light/dark imagery), or from without by Chance (symbolized by the many images of cataclysm). The gradual shift in Conrad's oeuvre from internal to external betrayal corresponds to the shift in emphasis from the quest theme to that of Poetic Justice, under whose dominion Conrad challenges Chance.

Joseph Conrad And The Thriller

An insistent variation of the quest theme in Conrad is the quest to break thralldom, either one's own or somebody else's, which fuses the familiar bewitchment motif of fairy tale with the equally familiar nightmare of involuntary paralysis or involuntary action. In "Heart of Darkness," Marlow's task, like that of the Prince in "The Sleeping Beauty," is to break the spell that holds Kurtz entranced. Paradoxically, Marlow, in his role as narrator in "Heart of Darkness" and "Youth," endlessly recapitulating his experiences, may be likened to that other teller of tales, Scheherazade in *The Arabian Nights,* a spellbinder. In *The Arrow of Gold,* Rita transfixes George (with the arrow of Cupid?) the first time he beholds her. In *Under Western Eyes* Razumov is told, " 'A curse is an evil spell. . . . And the important, the great problem, is to find the means to break it.' "[32] And E.M.W. Tillyard, who agrees that *Nostromo* is a fairy tale, casts Montero as the evil fairy at the christening feast—i.e., the one who casts a curse, or spell.

The prototypical Conradian situation is that of the hero beleaguered and alone is an isolated spot, threatened by intruders, his will corrupted or betrayed; Conrad found in the spell or enchantment a means of conveying to the reader that state of mind induced by failure of the will. In "Heart of Darkness" Marlow says of his tale:

> It seems to me I am trying to tell you a dream—making a vain attempt, because no relation of a dream can convey the dream-sensation, that commingling of absurdity, surprise, and bewilderment in a tremor of struggling revolt, that notion of being captured by the incredible which is of the very essence of dreams. . . .[33]

What is dramatically realized through this mythological or fairy tale motif may in fact be the Freudian death-wish of the Western world, or the reduction of the human personality to an automaton, or the related visions of the nightmare-cityscape and the extreme isolation of its inhabitants, or even schizophrenic division of personality. These possibilities, released via the mechanism of the motifs of thralldom and the trance, will be developed under subsequent headings as they arise.

127

In Conrad's novels the quest for Eden is no more successful than the quest to break thralldom because it is subject to the same prevailing conditions. The quest for Eden is the most highly developed variation of the quest theme in Conrad,[34] occurring in "Heart of Darkness," "A Smile of Fortune," *Victory, An Outcast of the Islands, Almayer's Folly,* and *Lord Jim.* The *mise en scéne* inevitably connects such books with the exotic romance; yet, unlike the romance, the paradisal vision is not realized. The landscape has more in common with Henri Rousseau than with Jean-Jacques, combining, as it does, primitive beauty with horror, rankness with mystery, luxuriance with disorder (the erotic as well as the exotic). (See Illustration 1, Chapter IV.) Almayer's house is a "garden of death" for his sin of selling love; the small Eden in *An Outcast of the Islands* is violated by Willems, and disorder triumphs; in "A Smile of Fortune" the myth is falsified by the forcible restraint with which Alice is constrained to the garden; Heyst's island is a "false Eden." The quest for Eden fails because man is already corrupt (the very desire for second beginnings which prompts the quest for Eden has its origin in a sense of sin), and because Nature is indifferent.

Thus the Eden which we find is not the hortus conclusus, the innocent, ordered community of the detective novel, but a garden of decay, physical and moral. Conrad is very explicit about this. "Going up that river was like traveling back to the earliest beginnings of the world, when vegetation rioted on the earth and the big trees were kings. An empty stream, a great silence, an impenetrable forest. [But] the air was warm, thick, heavy, sluggish. There was no joy in the brilliance of the sunshine."[35] The forest in *Almayer's Folly* resembles the forest of error in *The Inferno.* Just as frequent as the images of garden decay are other Biblical images of destruction, such as the flood at the conclusion of *An Outcast of the Islands.* In that work, or others such as *Lord Jim* or "The Nigger of the *Narcissus,*" the natural world acts as a foil for man's self-destructive impulses, presaging ruin.[36] Anarchy (disorder) is the impulse to self-destruction. Order is an ideal for Conrad, as it was for Dickens; both men are anti-revolutionary, sharing a distrust of the mob—but for Conrad order remains improbable.

The Arcadian attempt is invariably unsuccessful. We are denied the tame pastoral of Dickens' world, and there is no pole around which the "good people" cluster in community. Jim, for instance, though described by Marlow as capturing "much honor and an Arcadian happiness (I won't say anything about innocence) in the bush . . .,"[37] ultimately goes to his death to atone for a second guilt. (Conrad's pessimism, though, is tempered by a belief in that grace we may acquire through acquitting ourselves commendably.)

So the quest seems, in the Conradian world, to border on the absurd, particularly since it may be initiated by Chance. The allegorical progress is no longer towards the ideal; rather it is the non-progress of a Sisyphus without even the consolation of a Judgment. Essentially the existential hero is a Sisyphus, repeating gestures of a tragic hero in a context whose divorcement from chronicity makes him absurd rather than tragic. Though it is necessary that we undertake the quest, Eden is never forthcoming.

If we do not find in Conrad any place paralleling Dickens' Arcadia, we do meet there a similar vision of Hell in the wasteland-city (though Hell in Conrad has the unfair advantage of being both natural and man-made). Like Dickens' metropolis, it is peopled by grotesques, surreal in its landscape, and irrational in its *modus vivendi*. It is an allegorical projection of the evil which Conrad, like Dickens, saw in the materialism and selfishness of society:

> Then the vision of an enormous town presented itself, of a monstrous town more populous than some continents and in its man-made might as if indifferent to heaven's frowns and smiles; a cruel devourer of the world's light. There was room enough there to place any story, depth enough there for any passion, variety enough there for any setting, darkness enough to bury five millions of lives.[38]

Just as the failure to recapture innocence and to break the evil enchantment point to a failure of Providence, so the vision of Hell, without the counterpoise of Eden, seems to me unmistakably such an indication. I have postponed my discussion of Hell until it can be viewed in relation to Poetic Justice. For it is not one station of the allegorical progress; it is within us, and all around us.

Identity and Recognition

The problem of identity and recognition in Conrad is not, as it commonly is in Dickens, a literal one, concealed by intricacies of plot and itself the subject of secondary plots.[39] The thing which is concealed is not a prize (e.g., a legacy as in Dickens and Collins) but the reverse, a burden, or punishment. Typically, Conrad conceives identity muffled by protective layers which are subsequently stripped off in a Swiftian manner so that the character may stand most completely revealed and alone during his trial. This trial, in turn, offers that extremity in which he discovers his identity. Zabel writes:

> By divesting him or her of the familiar supports and illusory protection of friendship, social privilege or love, by throwing the villain violently out of an accepted relationship with family or society, this crisis suddenly makes him aware of a hostile or unknown world which must be learned anew, conquered or mastered, before survival is possible. Obviously this order of drama has a classic ancestry. It is the oldest mode of tragedy.[40]

Let us assume, then, that Conrad handles the identity and quest themes in such a way as to engage the tragic mode. Does the conception of his heroes accord with this? In some respects, it does. We notice the monumentality of their struggle— his heroes are pitted against an overwhelming Nature, the snowy vastnesses of Russia, the entrapping jungle of Africa. Also, Conrad's personification of destiny as an autonomous force—e.g., the sea—prepares us for an eventual confrontation (just as the dramatic method of the doppelgänger does), thus meeting the requirement that tragedy must not seem accidental. Furthermore, if we adopt the modern view of tragedy as having its origin in character, we have but to look at the flaws in Heyst, Gould, Jim, or many others to find examples.

Yet there is a pervasive irony which undercuts tragedy: the double agent in *Under Western Eyes,* forced into his political position because of the insupportability of the social contract, ironically frequents the park in Geneva presided over by the statue of Jean-

Jacques Rousseau, author of *The Social Contract*. The incongruity of banal Geneva heightens the discrepancy between the struggle and its setting. This same irony, which is employed in such a manner as to distance us from the action (as compared, for example, with Dostoevsky), is but one of a number of related and important factors militating against the tragic effect.

The first is that isolation to which I have already drawn attention. Razumov is described as being ". . . as lonely in the world as a man swimming in the deep sea. He had nothing."[41] When the final layer of protective insulation is removed, Razumov emits this *cri di coeur,* "Who knows what true loneliness is—not the conventional word but the naked terror? To the lonely themselves it wears a mask. The most miserable outcast hugs some memory or some illusion. . . . No human being could bear a steady view of moral solitude without going mad."[42] In this isolation the hero meets a personal trial, but because he is no longer the representative of the community, nor its noblest example, he cannot act symbolically.

Traditionally, whether in a tragedy of fate or character, the position of the hero in his society is such that his actions will vitally affect it, whether he be priest, warrior, king, or private citizen. As Dorothy Van Ghent comments:

> Orestes freed Argos from a tyranny, and Oedipus freed Thebes from a plague. Their guilt and suffering had a constructive social meaning; they had acted for the positive welfare of the citizens; and that social version of their heroism, internal to the dramas in which they appear, is the immediate, literal basis of our appraisal of their heroism.[43]

But the degree to which Conrad has pushed the idea of isolation does not permit this "measure of man." Though there are examples of individuals who have acted for the community, especially in the context of the ship, the hero is most often solitary and can at best act for himself. It is not personal identity but rather the broader state of human affairs which is at issue. The hero cannot act for the community because the bonds between man and his community have been dissolved in the modern world. Winnie's famous statement in *The Secret Agent* that things "don't bear looking into" epitomizes this attitude. The most extreme example of this divergence of interests is in the same novel, in which those who purportedly act for the community actually help to victimize it. (To the extent, however, that he achieves self-realization, it may be said that the Conradian solitary hero does partake of our latter-day conception of tragedy as rooted in character.)

This isolation and loneliness, being, in fact, co-extensive with mortality, is shared by hero and villain alike. It follows, therefore, that for Conrad, unlike Dickens, the criminal is not set in a class apart by virtue of his outcast state but embodies the extremity of the normal condition, just as the hero is not an extraordinary man, but an ordinary man subjected to extraordinary conditions. De Barral, for example, that arch-villain, is disappointingly commonplace, being neither particularly clever nor personally remarkable. The hero, who may himself be a criminal, most often qualifies as the allegorical protagonist of a morality play.

The reduction in stature of the hero raises the second serious objection to his qualification for the tragic role: the allegorical interpretation of character. This approach, which contributes to a "mytho-religious" rather than tragic effect in Conrad's writing, may be seen on the most superficial level in a character such as Toodles, a Dickensian under-secretary. It is also apparent in the conception of such characters as Lingard the law-giver, Archbold the hangman. Thomas Moser considers Conrad's depiction of sailors to be allegorical: "Conrad persuades the reader to admire his simple, faithful, hard-working seamen [e.g., MacWhirr or Singleton] by suggesting that their heroism is of mythical proportions. . . . Perhaps . . . Conrad the psychologist does not quite believe in his moral heroes: his tendency to assign to them more-than-human qualities suggests that they do not exist, are a myth, an ideal." This ideal figure is then pitted against an equally extreme villain—e.g., Ricardo—so that a St. George and the dragon battle may be enacted.[44]

The inarticulate sailor is only one version of the more-than-human hero; Paul Wiley divides the Conradian hero into three basic types: the Hermit, the Incendiary, and the Knight. The captain of the ship, for whom a larger-than-life role is natural, might be cast as Hermit. In *Chance* Conrad explains:

132

The captain of a ship at sea is a remote, inaccessible creature, depending upon nobody, not to be called to account except by powers practically invisible, and so distant that they might be looked upon as supernatural for all that the rest of the crew knew of them as a rule.[45]

Yet in this same novel the captain is powerless (unlike the supernatural hero of the thriller) and will be saved by the intervention of an ordinary sailor cast as a Knight-Detective.

There is a seeming contradiction here in Conrad's conception of the hero as everyman or as superman, heroes of different allegories. This objection may be answered in part by the realization that Conrad's delineation of hero and villain was not uniform; the later heroes are more imaginative; the later villains, more black. Furthermore, as Paul Wiley reminds us, even the adventurer-hero, such as Kurtz or Lingard, is, in Conrad, a severely limited figure. Also, this is a place in which Conrad's ambivalent attitude is apparent.

Thus we hover on the outskirts of tragedy; the scale of forces and the sense of implacable destiny tend toward it. (Conrad himself termed *Under Western Eyes* "tragic".) Yet the reduction to allegorical terms, and the movement in Conrad ever nearer the interpretation of destiny as chance (accident) rather than Providence, both undercut it. Finally, Conrad's use of irony seems to me more comic than tragic in its method; it is employed not as a means of concealing from the actor that which is revealed to the audience, nor of securing the unexpected outcome, but of indicating derision.

If the problem of identity in Conrad focuses on isolation, the problem of recognition centers around community. "A man's real life is that accorded to him in the thoughts of other men by reason of respect or natural love,"[46] says Conrad. This apothegm recognizes the need for a standard of conduct and assigns man a role that is inherently social rather than hermitic. That is, Conrad insists that no man is, finally, alone, because his conduct is judged against a standard of honor which is outside him. In the thriller the honor of the private-eye often stands in contradistinction to the lack of honor in the community, and indeed is one of the signs by

133

which we recognize him. Conrad then is closer here to the values of the detective novel, where the detective is assumed to share sense of honor which, though rarely successful, unites his Conradian hero in his test to the world of proofs and values. Conrad's heroes are never carefree rogues, such as we encounter in the picaresque novel, but are subject to the operative morality of the book in which they appear. His rebels, romantic in their misogyny or misanthropy, nevertheless experience the desire to be reinstated into society; they do not, ultimately, glory in their rebellion:[47]

> And now to work, he [Razumov] says, three weeks after the Haldin affair is past, and immediately thinks of Mikulin and his silence. 'What did it mean? Was he forgotten? Possibly. Then why not remain forgotten—creep in somewhere? Hide. But where? How? With whom? In what hole? And was it forever, or what?'[48]

The contradiction between the desire, even the necessity, for community if man is to survive, and the observable state of man's increasing isolation, constitutes the paramount crisis of identity and recognition in Conrad.

Whenever bonds slacken, the results are disastrous. We can say that Winnie Verloc's murder of her husband is the outcome of the failure of the conjugal bond and of the gross misunderstandings which follow upon that failure. The doomed relationship between Flora and Anthony arises from the abrogation of the paternal bond as well as the bonds of sisterhood and friendship. When the solidarity of the ship's bond is broken in "Falk," cannibalism results. These failures are not the contrived products of plot manipulations. Characters are brought face to face; the opportunity exists for communication and resolution. The lack is in a vital response, not in the lack of occasion. Here, white does not understand black; man, woman; husband, wife; East, West. During his arduous voyage, Marlow yearns to talk with Kurtz with an almost mystical belief in the importance of such an occasion; yet their first encounter is one of physical sparring, and their only communication is finally the vatic distillation, "The horror! The horror!"

The failure of communication is symptomatic of chronic isolation, and often exacerbates a character's sense of detachment, creating a dream- or trance-like state. Marlow explains:

> The idleness of a passenger, my isolation amongst all these men with whom I had no point of contact, the oily and languid sea, the uniform somberness of the coast, seemed to keep me away from the truth of things, within the toil of a mournful and senseless delusion.[49]

In extreme cases this results in a divided self, tantamount to the doppelgänger, although internalized. "He felt, bizarre as it may seem, as though another self, an independent sharer of his mind, has been able to view his whole person very distinctly indeed."[50]

The family unit, the city, and even so large a unit as Western Europe, are seen as inchoate. *Under Western Eyes* and *The Secret Agent* both teach us that safety is but a communal illusion: "anarchy is a moral condition involving everyone."[51] This is mirrored in the isolation and dislocation of images—the fragments of concrete and stone—that comprise a landscape corroborating the disintegration of character.

Alternative possibilities of community are explored in many contexts—that of the ship I have already mentioned. In such a community self-interest demands the fraternal bond which enforces certain regulations for purposes of security. When the individual appoints himself a private judge, as do Nostromo and Kurtz, Lingard and Razumov, he precipitates catastrophe; individual law means anarchy, the very antithesis of the explicit order of the ship. In order to save man from random choices and the transgressions of ego, law must derive from custom and have the sanction of society. Here again Conrad affirms the values of the detective novel and, like the detective novelist, refuses to glorify the outlaw. Thus the conniving patroness of Michaelis in *The Secret Agent* is shown to be an addlepated fool, inadvertently contriving the breakdown of the very system which affords her security. Despite the idealistic goals of the revolutionists in *Under Western Eyes,* their efforts are destined to fail,[52] just as is the autocratic regime which they oppose. Conrad writes:

The ferocity and imbecility of an autocratic rule rejecting all legality and in fact basing itself upon complete moral anarchism provokes the no less imbecile and atrocious answer of a purely Utopian revolutionism encompassing destruction by the first means to hand, in the strange conviction that a fundamental change of hearts must follow the downfall of any given human institution. These people are unable to see that all they can effect is merely a change of names. The oppressors and the oppressed are all Russians together; and the world is brought once more face to face with the truth of the saying that the tiger cannot change his stripes nor the leopard his spots.[53]

The final stage of dissolution of the Western civil contract is reached in *The Secret Agent,* in which the idea of community is completely inverted, and community is based upon guilty complicity rather than "respect or natural love." Stevie clearly illustrates this inversion; his ability to express tenderness sets him apart from the rest of the characters as much as his handicap.

Conrad does not polemicize or even formulate a political or social doctrine which will ensure his ideal of order. Nor does he seem to find a panacea in any particular type of individual—the adventurer-hero (Kurtz), the idealist (Gould), the hermit (Falk), the rebel (Razumov), the revolutionary (Haldin), the anarchist (Michaelis). None provides a viable answer. The desideratum seems to lie in the smallest possible unit of love and sympathy, moving outward towards a solidarity of mankind, assuming importance in proportion to the demonstrable failure of both instinct and authority, and in the face of the coldness of the cosmic world. In both *Under Western Eyes* and *The Secret Agent,* Conrad opts for the personal bond.

The emphasis upon the idea of community is in itself a diagnosis of the sickness of society, where the outcast, the fugitive, and the betrayer within the gates are always lurking. In both the Dickens novel and the detective novel, disease (evil) must be diagnosed and excised before the continuance of society can be assured; in the detective novel this is accomplished by the detective, who is a magus figure, capable of determining the hidden locus of disease—the murderer.[54] In Dickens, the restoration to communal health is sometimes effected by private philanthropy, sometimes by muckraking, sometimes by Providence. (It is no accident that Esther's husband in *Bleak House* is a physician; how ironic, by comparison, is the medicine man Ossipon in *The Secret Agent*.)

With few exceptions (possibly Peyrol or Powell) there is no corresponding character in Conrad, despite his preoccupation with the same metaphor of disease. Because the hero is prevented from acting for the community, because the figure of the rescuer (detective) or guardian is crippled by self-interest or self-division, the health of the community is not restored. Finally, in *The Secret Agent* we find that the guilty Professor is left unmolested at the conclusion of the book. He remains at large to spread his pestilence. ("He passed on unsuspected and deadly, like a pest in the street full of men.")[55] Furthermore, the infection itself is no longer easily localized and excised. As A. Alvarez writes, there is an "awareness of a ubiquitous, arbitrary death . . . which descends like a medieval plague on the just and unjust alike, without warning or reason—[which] is, I think, central to our experience of the twentieth century."[56] Death is more horrible because it is arbitrary. Because of the guilty complicity of the police, Inspector Heat (the detective in *The Secret Agent*) not only does not restore health (innocence) to the community but is part of its affliction.

No one in Conrad is left to fulfill this role: any potential hero is rendered unacceptable to the reader—in *The Secret Agent* "fool," "madman," "idiot." There is an ultimate fusion of the madness and absurdity of the public world and the anarchic personalities of the characters. The role magus, rescuer, benevolent guardian, father, posits an omniscience and omnipotence which are secular versions of Providence, exemplified by the "revelation" which the detective provides. Thus, in a view which questions Providence, it is not to be wondered that a secular viceroy is missing.

The Doppelgänger - (Identity and Recognition, continued)

Though the literary use of the doppelgänger bourgeoned during the Romantic period, it may be traced back ultimately to folk literature, particularly that branch of it which deals with magic and the possibilities of enchantment and thralldom. The motif of the doppelgänger, then, both connects Conrad with prior narratives employing these same archetypal motifs and conveys to the reader that modern sense of thralldom to the self. In this regard, the author offers an ethos sharply differentiated from that of the detective novel, in which evil is embodied in an outsider who is expelled, thereby removing the danger. In Conrad, the "enemy within the gates" can be in everyone and may not be expelled; doom may be ordained.

In the thriller proper the doppelgänger is used most commonly to add complexity of plot and to provide a Gothic *frisson*. For Dickens, the doppelgänger was part of the Romantic legacy and a convenient tool for the externalization of evil, the traditional allegorical function assigned to it. For Hoffmann and for Dostoevsky, and for Conrad too, doubling had the primary function of illuminating human psychology. With the twentieth century awareness of the internal split between conscious and unconscious, the doppelgänger theme acquires the authority of a diagnosis.

What a profusion of guises doubling assumes in Conrad's work! The doppelgänger may be an apparition—Haldin in *Under Western Eyes,* Leggatt in "The Secret Sharer," Burns in "The Shadow Line." It may be a doubling of function—both Razumov in *Under Western Eyes* and Verloc in *The Secret Agent* are double agents. It may be the twin horrors of revolution and autocracy in Russia—"the old despotism and the new Utopianism are complementary forms of moral anarchy."[57] In "Heart of Darkness" Africa itself is doubled—both attractive and repellent. Again in *Nostromo* we are presented with the Hobson's choice of the reigning corrupt government of Costaguana or the cruel and greedy band of insurgents under Sotillo. I have also previously alluded to the dualism of Nature—beautiful yet suffocating, exotic yet rotting. Finally, R.W. Stallman characterizes the Conradian plot itself as double: "The plot is a double conflict, external and internal; the one a conflict between an estranged individual and his hostile universe, the other a clash between an isolated soul and his ethical or aesthetic conscience."[58]

138

Conrad used the double mainly to objectify "a side of the self we sympathize with and yet condemn," an essential schism in man.[59] This duality is firmly rooted in Conrad's conception of identity, of selfhood. He writes in a letter to Mme. Poradowska:

> But you are afraid of yourself; of the inescapable being who is forever at your side—master and slave, victim and executioner—who suffers and causes suffering. That's how it is! One must drag the ball and chain of one's selfhood to the end. It is the price one pays for the devilish and divine privilege of thought. . . .

We stand convicted of being ourselves; and this selfhood, an inescapable destiny in itself, binds character to fatality and allows it to be read as destiny:

> The doppelgänger becomes part of the drama of character and self-determination when Jim delivers his long monologues to Marlow; when Flora bares her soul to Marlow, Mrs. Fyne or Captain Anthony; when Razumov writes his entries in his diary and disburdens his soul to the language-teacher and finally to Nathalie Haldin herself; when Decoud or Gould ruminate their secret histories, these people are really carrying out the drama of their divided natures, objectifying under the compulsion which psychoanalysts have seized upon as therapeutic necessity their souls' dilemmas and thus trying to save themselves from madness. But the divided man—the face and the mask, the soul and its shadow—figures even more concretely than this in Conrad's dramatic method. The rival character—sometimes a villain, sometimes a friend or lover, sometimes a fellow-fugitive like the 'secret sharer' in the story of that name—serve the hero as a transferred embodiment of his other self.[60]

The recognition of division offers a plausible explanation for the dearth of straightforward villains in Conrad;[61] they are either heroes *manqué* or doubles—Gentleman Brown and Jim, Razumov and Haldin, Heyst and Jones (as Heyst conquers the weakness in himself, Jones "inexplicably" drops dead). The knowledge that this character, whom we may save or betray, is actually a projection of ourselves is the knowledge at which both Razumov and the Captain in "The Secret Sharer" arrive. "All a man can betray is his conscience," Razumov summarizes. Betrayal of the "other" self leads to self-punishment, whereas acknowledgment leads to reward ("The Secret Sharer"). When the captain exclaims, "If he [Archbold of the *Sephora*] had only known how afraid I was of his putting my feeling of identity with the other to the test!",[62] he is dramatizing the test motif through the doppelgänger.

Conrad demonstrates, by means of the doppelgänger, his belief in the necessity for a balance between freedom and order. He reminds us of the constant threat of irrationality which is the outcome of unbridled freedom. The double may be the secret side of us in which fear or guilt resides and which we cannot shrug off (Wait, Nostromo), that "ball and chain," as Conrad calls it. Or, the doppelgänger may represent a different, but not necessarily unacceptable nature—for example, the split between the ascetic and the sensualist (Heyst, Anthony).

The creation of a double who is not the incarnation of evil, but upon whom we must look as upon our other self, invites the question: What is the correct attitude toward such a brother? Once we have acknowledged him, we cannot dismiss this brother as we would a criminal; we must investigate with judicious attention his scene and his action. We see that Jim's crime (*Lord Jim*) was begotten of an overly sensitive imagination rather than the deliberate intention of wrongdoing. We see that Leggatt's crime ("The Secret Sharer") was a by-product of his natural instinct and occurred accidentally in the execution of his duty. (Conversely, Archbold, Leggatt's captain, is depicted unsympathetically; he never questions the relevance of the law, and his actions are mechanistic.) Furthermore, isolation connects the hero and villain, ordinary and extraordinary, the two selves.

For all these reasons, the doppelgänger becomes, in Conrad's hands, not only a mechanism by which we may delve into the psyche, but one means by which Conrad may approach tragedy. That is to say, we can both identify with the hero and suffer with him, thereby creating the necessary conditions for catharsis. In this way, Conrad's use of the doppelgänger diverges sharply from that of the crime novel; for in detective fiction we identify with the instrument of justice, and in the thriller, though we may identify with the rogue, his invincibility precludes our necessary suffering.

There remains for discussion that special use of the doppelgänger which we meet in *The Secret Agent*. This allegory of the destruction of the Western world is like a Chinese box, secret hidden within secret. Everything is dark, hidden—the home, the shop, the motives, the allegiances. The book makes its points by confounding expectation, extending the paradox between the respectable and the criminal.[63] The guilty complicity which is the most devastating secret of all finds its expression in the doubling of Inspector Heat, the detective, and Mr. Verloc, the agent. Conrad himself pointed up this identification by requesting that, when the novel was adapted for the stage, the two characters resemble each other physically. In a larger sense, the police and the criminals together form a secret society and uphold a compact. For this reason they both fear the Professor, who recognizes no compact. Heat himself is continually thrown off balance by this deviation; he cannot cope with someone who is outside the system: "The mind of Chief Inspector Heat was inaccessible to ideas of revolt. But his thieves were not rebels." [Note the use of 'his.'] And later:

> 'You don't know who you're talking to,' said Chief Inspector Heat, firmly. 'If I were to lay hands on you [the Professor] now I would be no better than yourself.'
> 'Ah! The game!' [The Professor answers][64]

The Professor is operating within the mores of the thriller; he does not abide by rules; the Inspector is operating within the context of the detective story. Heat meditates, "Catching thieves was another matter altogether. It had that quality of seriousness belonging to every form of open sport where the best man wins under perfectly comprehensible rules. There were no rules for dealing with anarchists."[65]

The warning that there are spheres of life and conduct which are incomprehensible and unpredictable to those subscribing to codes, that the world of the thriller is overtaking the world of the detective novel, is found in many of Conrad's works—e.g., *An Outcast of the Islands* (Lingard's inability to deal with Willems), *Under Western Eyes*, "Heart of Darkness." Marlow, who comes from a world of codes is shocked by Kurtz and the natives who surround him:

He had taken a high seat amongst the devils of the land—I mean literally. You can't understand. How could you?—with solid pavements under your feet, surrounded by kind neighbors ready to cheer you or fall on you, stepping delicately between the butcher and the policeman, in holy terror of scandal and gallows and lunatic asylums—how can you imagine what particular regions of the first ages a man's untrammeled feet may take him by way of solitude—utter solitude, without a policeman—by way of silence—utter silence, where no warning voice of a kind neighbor can be heard whispering of public opinion? These little things make all the great difference.[66]

In all Conrad's works, the vital perception is that of latent political and moral anarchy—a world in which the values of the detective novel have ceased to obtain. A new dimension has been introduced into the contest—a clash between the assumptions of the detective novel and those of the thriller. The Professor's dictum, "No God, no master," renders Inspector Heat absurd, and the anarchist himself is a prefiguration of that cult of violence which leads to a belief in the absurd. Tragedy gives way to the absurd.

The world of the Professor is one in which even the thriller-hero is obsolete. As Frederick Hoffman has observed:

> The forms which explain, fulfill or maintain man's irrational impulses are adequate only in a world in which the status quo is assumed [i.e. the world of the detective novel]. Violence can be tolerated if it is seen in a humanly limited context.[67]

In the twentieth century the sheer scale of violence (symbolized by Hiroshima) has made the irrational the status quo. In his recent book about suicide, *The Savage God,* A. Alvarez quotes a noted psychiatrist, Dr. Robert Jay Lifton, as saying, "After Hiroshima we can envisage no war-linked chivalry, certainly no glory. Indeed, we can see no relationship—not even a distinction—between victimizer and victim—only a sharing in a species annihilation."[68] The relationship, the tension, implicit in the personal experience of the chase has been subverted to irrational destruction on the one hand, and guilty passivity on the other. This is why the pursuit element, which normally plays an important part in a tale of this sort, is minimal in Conrad. The "insane will"—and Heat terms the

Professor a "lunatic"—is inadmissible in the detective story, to which motive is crucial. The acts committed by a lunatic are not only irrational in themselves but preclude him from functioning as a suitable adversary. Certainly the bond between pursued and pursuer as I discussed it in the context of the thriller can no longer exist when, as Dr. Lifton says, "We can see no relationship—not even a distinction—between victimizer and victim. . . ." This lack of distinction, also a symptom of loss of community, is revealed in the following conversation between Razumov and Councillor Mikulin (*Under Western Eyes*):

> 'Good-bye, Mr. Razumov. An understanding between intelligent men is always a satisfactory occurrence. Is it not? And, of course, these rebel gentlement have not the monopoly of intelligence.'

> 'I presume I shall not be wanted any more?' Razumov brought out that question while his hand was still being grasped. Councillor Mikulin released it slowly.

> 'That, Mr. Razumov,' he said with great earnestness, 'is as it may be. God alone knows the future. Buy you may rest assured that I never thought of having you watched. You are a young man of great independence. Yes. You are going away free as air, but you will end by coming back to us.'

> 'I! I!' Razumov exlaimed in an appalled murmer of protest. 'What for?' he added feebly. 'Yes! You yourself, Kirylo Sidorovitch,' the high police functionary insisted in a low severe tone of conviction. 'You will be coming back to us. Some of our greatest minds do that in the end.'

> 'Our greatest minds,' repeated Razumov in a dazed voice.

> 'Yes, indeed! Our greatest minds . . . good-bye.'[69]

This dialogue cannot fail to recall the similar exchange between Raskolnikov and Porfiry in *Crime and Punishment* which exemplifies one function of the doppelgänger: asserting the psychological truth that we need the touchstone of others to maintain our identity. But in *Under Western Eyes* the relationship is

143

more one-sided: Razumov has no other identity than that he gleans from Councillor Mikulin's understanding of his sensibility.

In the world of the Professor there is no relationship, only "species annihilation." *The Secret Agent* deserves to be called "our first novel of violence."

The Scapegoat

Although this theme is not relevant enough to Conrad's fiction to merit extended consideration, a few remarks can be made before proceeding to a consideration of Poetic Justice.

As a consequence of the modern ineffectuality of both the quest for identity and the recognition of community, the individual is diminished. The traditional hero who by ritual means insures the well-being of the society, or having successfully passed tests, achieves self-recognition and fulfills his own identity, may no longer be able to undertake his role. A self-designated scapegoat, rather than one cast for the role in the *dramatis personae,* becomes a possible alternative. Thus Alvarez views the suicidal artist of the twentieth-century society as a scapegoat figure, murdering himself as previous victims were murdered by others. The continual urge to experiment, to dwell nearer and nearer the edge, is a symbolic subjection to the "destructive element" which the artist, in his role as seer, undertakes for the community. So Alvarez chooses the line Stein utters in *Lord Jim,* "In the destructive element immerse," as the motto of the twentieth-century artist, and Stephen Spender used "The Destructive Element" as the title for his book appraising the post-World War II climate of literature.[70]

Adam Gillon discusses the role of the scapegoat figure in the Conrad canon in an article entitled "Conrad's Archetypal Jew," which interprets Hirsch of *Nostromo* as a scapegoat figure. Although both Decoud and Nostromo had wished to kill Hirsch, they cannot do so because they identify themselves with the Jew as a hunted figure. Hirsch evokes compassion in Nostromo when he sees the Jew's tortured body hanging from the roof; the dead man, suspended in a posture of crucifixion, becomes a symbolic warning to Nostromo. Hirsch, then, becomes a scapegoat to his tormenter Sotillo.

Stephen C. Reid, one of the critics who adopts a mythic interpretation of "Heart of Darkness," believes that Kurtz may be
identified with Frazer's god-king, a figure sacrificed to insure fertility. Kurtz' refusal to accept this ritual leads to the "unspeakable
rites," which Reid construes as sacrificial murder.

A curious variation upon this theme is Lionel Trilling's view of
Kurtz in the story. He says, "For Marlow, nevertheless, Kurtz is a
hero of the spirit whom he cherishes as Theseus at Colonus
cherished Oedipus: he sinned for all mankind."[71] By juxtaposing
these two characters, Kurtz and Oedipus, Trilling underlines once
more the mythological foundations of "Heart of Darkness" and
the criminal's function as a variant of scapegoat.

Poetic Justice

> Was there, under heaven, such a thing as justice?
> **Joseph Conrad,** *An Outcast of the Islands*

The poetic justice which informs the moral outlook of the detective story and fairy tale is missing in Conrad, in spite of his
palpable belief in order and hierarchy, his concern with justice and
morality. The dream-like quest, and the dream-like method of narrative advancement, do not here accompany the implicit idealizing
motion of allegory. Conrad's novels examine a world in which
man is limited and Providence is absent. ("There are suggestions
at times that he felt a certain resentment against a Providence that
had abandoned mankind and the world to a fallen state.")[72] Reality is conveyed in negative terms as a lack of cohesion and/or
reason, and therefore images of disunity and irrationality
predominate. In this world, anarchy and destruction challenge
justice.

In practice, this means that the conclusions of many Conrad
novels are equivocal, or at most permit Pyrrhic victories. Can we
say that Lingard triumphed over Willems? Can we say that Jim's
atonement imparted posthumous meaning to his life? Why did
Captain Anthony accidentally die after being saved for his union
with Flora? The final negation of Poetic Justice comes with the

gratuitous deaths of Winnie and Stevie in *The Secret Agent,* while the malefactor is left to operate. Kingsley Widmer suggests that the extreme of Conrad's irony is the triumph of evil over evil, indeed the ultimate doubling.[73]

The absence of Providence explains, too, the profusion of images of cataclysms in these stories and novels: the storm in *An Outcast of the Islands* and "Typhoon," the explosion of Stevie in *The Secret Agent.* These are not instances of divine retribution but, quite the contrary, are the physical counterparts of the mental agitation of the characters. Darkness, which Conrad uses to denote danger and irrationality, often seems to brood over both land and sea as if the light of Heaven were extinguished. This is not the scarifying blackness of the Gothic novel but a physical representation of the void.

If Providence will not, or cannot, execute justice, should man appoint himself surrogate? Conrad answers this question negatively in every context in which it arises. Haldin, for example, is forced to assume the role of judge and then assassin because Providence has failed to intercede in the political events of Russia, but he sets in motion an overwhelming chain of events and counter-events which, lacking omniscience, he could not anticipate. Lingard fails when he assumes this judgmental role with Willems, as does Razumov with Victor. Man's nature disqualifies him for such a role; for Conrad, neither God nor man suffices.

The meaninglessness of such a world, in which we must reckon both on the lack of Providence and on improvident mankind, and can oppose to both only the pitifully weak ties of ethical union, is depicted by the grotesque and the surreal.

The element of the grotesque is interpolated into the narrative by techniques for displaying physical and moral disproportion and dehumanization; these we have already met in Dickens. A character in Conrad may be introduced as eccentric in appearance:

> He looked like a harlequin. His clothes had been made of some stuff that was brown holland, probably, but it was covered with bright patches, blue, red, and yellow—patches on the back, patches on the front, patches on elbows, and knees; colored binding around his jacket, scarlet edging at the bottom of his trousers. . . .[74]

146

Characters may be visualized as bestial, or there may be an enormous disparity between their attitudes and their actions or intentions. The domestic activity of the Verlocs, for example, suggests an intimacy which is non-existent. Mrs. Verloc's murder weapon, a kitchen knife, provides its own ironic comment on the Verlocs' domestic scene. Finally, the characters can suggest the inhuman, the inorganic, by their machine-like movement, which by implication transform them into puppets or automata:

> The slim one got up and walked straight at me—still knitting with downcast eyes—and only just as I began to think of getting out of her way, as you would for a somnanbulist, stood still and looked up. Her dress was plain as an umbrella-cover, and she turned round without a word and preceded me into a waiting-room.[75]

Mrs. Verloc, moving in a trance after the shock of Stevie's death, mechanically goes through the motions of housekeeping while in a state of extreme emotional upheaval. This discrepancy between external semblance and internal emotion is symbolized by the discrepancy between time felt (after she murders Verloc) and actual time, so that she is amazed to find that the kitchen clock registers the passage of but a few minutes.

Conrad, like Dickens, also achieves his grotesque effects by making analogies of opposites, animating the inanimate (e.g., ". . . the contorted mangroves . . . seemed to writhe at us in the extremity of impotent pain"), or by separating a part from the whole ("And the legs inside them [the trousers] did not, as a general rule seem of much account either," or "A door opened, a white-haired secretarial head, but bearing a compassionate expression, appeared and a skinny forefinger beckoned me. . . .")[76]

The element of grotesquerie belongs to that Conradian vision of the world in which divine intercession rarely restores balance. Man's intercession, as we have seen, is of dubious value either because he is maimed or impotent or because he lacks the sanction of community; we rarely see the gesture of disinterested beneficent intervention which is the *raison d'être* for so many Dickens characters. Conrad's humor, which inclines to wry commentary and irony, rarely creates characters whose grotesquerie seems the spillover of comic exuberance. In sum, the comedic effect which tempers the horrific in Dickens is missing, and this too is a reflection of the absence of Poetic Justice.

The equivocation, the Pyrrhic victory, manifested by the grotesque, may be an index of Conrad's modernity. Thomas Mann's essay on Conrad confirms this:

> Essentially, the striking feature of modern art is that it has ceased to recognize the categories of tragic and comic or the dramatic classifications, tragedy and comedy. It sees life as a tragi-comedy, with the result that the grotesque is its most genuine style—to the extent, indeed, that today that is the only guise in which the sublime may appear.[77]

Thus, personal anarchy, the isolation of the self, and the absence of communal bonds, may all be expressed by means of the grotesque—the individual doesn't fit. Social anarchy and the lack of external order are expressed through the surreal; the composition of the whole does not fit together.

In his book *The Dehumanization of Art,* Ortega y Gasset says that surrealism alters the hierarchy of the importance of things; the small things are made large, and vice versa.[78] The obvious result of this alteration of perspective and juxtaposition of images is that the physical order is perceived as irrational. The expected order of things is changed and with it our perception of reality. Jung quotes Max Ernst's version of surrealism in the visual arts: "The association of a sewing machine and an umbrella on a surgical table is a familiar example, which has now become classical, of the phenomenon discovered by the surrealists that the association of two (or more) apparently alien elements on a plane alien to both is the most potent ignition of poetry."[79] Cawelti applies this to literature in his discussion of parataxic sentence structure in the "realistic" novels of Hammett and Chandler: "[This] stylistic combination [can] exemplify utterly fantastic events described in merely emotionless, lucidly descriptive vernacular prose [and] has a surrealistic flavor, like those paintings by Dali where flaming giraffes and melting watches are rendered with the most carefully drawn 'realistic' detail."[80] Despite the seemingly emotionless quality of this juxtaposition, its impulse is a "metaphysical anxiety," writes the surrealist artist, Mario Marini, and "as soon as art has to express fear, it must of itself depart from the classical idea [of order]."[81]

Thus surrealism provides an apt expression of Conrad's perception of the lack of hierarchical order in his society: "The irrationality of the social order, represented by the irrationality of London Streets and house numbers, is crystallized in the confusion of the landscape of the city and related to the greater absurdities of society by Verloc's acceptance of it [in *The Secret Agent*]."[82] The passage to which Fleishman refers is a description of a walk taken by Mr. Verloc to the Embassy:

> . . . before reaching Knightsbridge, Mr. Verloc took a turn to the left out of the busy main throughfare, uproarious with the traffic of swaying omnibuses and trotting vans [note animation of the inanimate], and Mr. Verloc, steady like a rock—a soft kind of rock—[dehumanization through analogy with inanimate, and surrealistic oxymoron as with Dali's watches] marched not along a street which could with every propriety be described as private. In its breadth, emptiness, and extent it had the majesty of inorganic nature, of matter that never dies. The only reminder of mortality was a doctor's brougham arrested in august solitude close to the curbstone. The polished knockers of the doors gleamed as far as the eye could reach, the clean windows shone with a dark opaque lustre. And all was still [Note use of silence to convey pernicious isolation]. But a milk-cart rattled moisily across a distant perspective; a butcher boy, driving with the noble recklessness of a charioteer at Olympic Games, dashed around the corner sitting high above a pair of red wheels. . . . A thick police constable, looking a stranger to every emotion, as if he, too, were part of inorganic nature [dehumanization], surging apparently out of a lamp-post [surrealism, altered perspective], took not the slightest notice of Mr. Verloc [irony ʀ faulty perception]. With a turn to the left Mr. Verloc pursued his way along a narrow street by the side of a yellow wall which, for some inscrutable reason, had No. 1. Chesham Square written on it in black letters. Chesham Square was at least sixty yards away [irrationality] and Mr. Verloc, cosmopolitan enough not to be deceived by London's topographical mysteries, held on steadily, without a sign of suprise or indignation. At last, with business-like persistency [equation of respectable and criminal], he reached the Square, and made diagonally for the number 10.[83]

This vision of irrationality, so Dickensian in tone, nevertheless fulfills conditions which Mario Praz describes as indicative of the modern visual and literary modality of perception: "The elements of that reality [a new reality] were implicit in the life of the twentieth century—the intense isolation of anyone and anything, the simple gratuity of existence, the fantastic inventiveness."[84] This "intense isolation" reaches its imagistic apogee in the following passage, in which men and things are rendered so insubstantial and unreal that, like Peter Pan from Never-Never Land, they do not even cast shadows. (The passage also illustrates the manner in which Conrad evokes the moral taint both of the man, Verloc, and of the city, London, by means of images of blood—i.e., bloodshot and rust,—which in turn connote guilt, all the more arresting for being set in a mock-pastoral):

> And a peculiarly London sun—against which nothing could be said except that it looked bloodshot—glorified all this by its stare. It hung at a moderate elevation above Hyde Park Corner with an air of punctual and benign vigilance. The very pavement under Mr. Verloc's feet had an old-gold tinge in that diffused light, in which neither wall, nor tree, nor beast, nor man cast a shadow. Mr. Verloc was going westward through a town without shadows in an atmosphere of powdered old gold. There were red, coppery gleams on the roofs of houses, on the corners of walls, on the panels of carriages, on the very coats of the horses, and on the broad back of Mr. Verloc's overcoat, where they produced a dull effect of rustiness.[85]

Ortega y Gasset sees surrealism as satisfying the urge to elude reality. Insofar as it creates a subjective and new composition, it resembles the order of the dream; indeed Salvador Dali, the surrealist painter, claims that surrealism is based upon dream psychology.[86] We have seen that Conrad repeatedly invokes the dream state or entranced character. His dreams materialize either as nightmare (in which case the surrealistic effect may be macabre—e.g., Leavis alludes to "the slow-motion macabre of the cab-journey to the almshouse")[87]—or trance (in which case the effect is that of thralldom). The dream-variant of thralldom is an aspect of surrealism since it, too, offers the opportunity for escape from reality and from responsibility for actions.

150

Thus, from "Heart of Darkness":

> They were everyday words—the familiar vague sounds exchanged on every waking day of life. But what of that? They had behind them, to my mind, the terrific suggestiveness of words heard in dreams, of phrases spoken in nightmares. (p. 56)

> It is strange how I accepted this unforseen partnership, this choice of nightmares forced upon me in the tenebrous land invaded by these mean and greedy phantoms. (p. 57)

> I did not betray Mr. Kurtz—it was ordered that I should never betray him—it was written that I should be loyal to the nightmare of my choice. (p. 54)

And from *Under Western Eyes:*

> 'I have been unconscious as I walked, it's a positive fact,' said Razumov to himself in wonder. (p.195)

> That [flinging the package out of the railway car window] had been a waking act: and then the dream had him again: Prussia, Saxony Wurtemberg, faces, sights, words—all a dream, observed with an angry compelled attention. Zurich, Geneva,—still a dream minutely followed, wearing one into harsh laughter, to fury, to death—with the fear of awakening at the end. (p. 266)

Finally, as we noted with Dickens, we may be presented with a version of surrealism in the person of an obsessed character who isolates an idea or quality to the exclusion of all others. In Conrad examples such as the Professor (*The Secret Agent*), Haldin (*Under Western Eyes*), or Kurtz ("Heart of Darkness") may be cited.

Surrealism and grotesquerie both reflect the absence of Poetic Justice, violating the expected order of things and events, and inhibiting resolution. The violation of the expected order of things eventually becomes so frequent that it is incorporated into the ritual. This evolution can be traced through the classics of Western literature. Shakespeare's Hamlet declares, "The time is out of joint," signifying a synthesis between the individual act and society; he must wait only for a propitious time. The nineteenth-century novel *Crime and Punishment,* however, presents a world where *"things* are in disarray." Raskolnikov must find not the propitious moment but the propitious act. Despite this larger sense of disorder, a communal order is retained in Dostoevsky's *Crime and Punishment:* "We are . . . still within a world governed by a solicitous omniscience," Frederick Hoffman writes.[88] Dostoevsky's fictions conform to what Kermode calls "schematic expectations"; they are structured so as not to confound the reader's expectation of what will constitute the *peripeteia.*[89]

Conrad's novels oscillate between a presentation of an ordered world governed by that providential justice which had remained valid for centuries before him and the adumbration of a more anarchic world such as the modern thriller describes. By the time we reach contemporary narrative, a breakdown of traditional mores in the society is reflected in corresponding values of the thriller, which has always been more latently anarchic than the detective novel. Because he is caught between the deterioration of one tradition and the emergence of a new one, Conrad is understandably ambivalent about the success of the Quest, the resolutions of Poetic Justice.

In some books, *Lord Jim,* for one, Conrad seems to accept human responsibility as activating the vengeance of destiny; in others, like *Chance,* he does not. In *Under Western Eyes* justice is treated ironically. Following the purgation of his double confession and physical suffering, Razumov is reinstated as a sage of the Russian wilderness, deaf as Tiresias was blind. We recall here Thomas Moser's apt tag quoted earlier—"His [Conrad's] books are a kind of pilgrim's progress (but without God)." In *The Secret Agent,* Conrad's most extreme vision of irrationality, the question of justice hinges upon whether justice can survive the absurd. "Was there, under heaven, such a thing as justice?" is itself a paradoxical question: if "under heaven," then can we doubt the existence of justice? This question, as we shall see in Chapter V, is the crux of Graham Greene's explorations.

Structural Resemblances

Features of the spy story, the adventure, the mystery, or detective novel may be discerned in Conrad's work, though no one branch of the crime novel is a structural paradigm for him. Conrad adopts the following structural features, many of which were made popular in nineteenth-century melodrama:

1. the creation of a sinister atmosphere
2. the use of suspense
3. the confrontation between the forces of good and evil
4. the interview
5. the *peripeteia*
6. the use of sensation

Conrad's work blends an impressionistic with a realistic style: his conceptions of hero and villain change; settings from the Congo to Geneva enliven his scene. All these variables make generalization even more suspect than usual; some of these points, but not all, appear in each work. "The Secret Sharer" and *The Secret Agent,* for instance, resemble the detective novel in their strict economy of dialogue and structure; *Nostromo,* on the other hand, which is less detective novel than thriller, does not display the same tautness of form and relevance of detail.

1. Atmosphere

We have already spoken of the grotesque and the surreal in Conrad's writing: both of these contribute to a sinister atmosphere. The sinister in Conrad is a conflation of two aspects: a realistic and precise rendering of specific locales (the Malay lands and waters, Africa, London), and a poetic or symbolic method of description, frequently dependent upon abstract nouns with emotional connotations, repetition, certain long, loose polysyllables, and what Leavis has termed "adjectival insistence." The latter method works as an incremental refrain carried from novel to novel—for example, the images of tropical foliage and blackness.

Conrad heightens tension by the implication of concealed evil or danger, as melodrama did before him. The menace, far from being diluted by the realistic and precise rendering of detail, is achieved partly as a result of it, since specificity renders more credible that which is vague or unusual. The quotidian is joined to the horrific in striking visual juxtaposition. These two aspects, roughly the denotative and the connotative, may correspond to Conrad's belief that life is composed of a surface, conventonal reality and a secret, hidden reality buried underneath:

> When you have to attend to things of that sort, to the mere incidents of the surface, the reality—the reality, I tell you—fades. The inner truth is hidden—luckily, luckily. But I felt it all the same: I felt often its mysterious stillness watching me.[90]

Conrad imparts his abiding sense of isolation through an enveloping silence which surrounds the actors. "The sense of something deathlike or evil manifesting itself in an atmosphere of stillness of secrecy, like that in the silence of Hervey's house in 'The Return'. . . ."[91] This stillness too becomes a refrain. After Razumov has confessed to the revolutionists, and Nikita has deafened him by blows to his ears, we find the following description:

> He fell forward, and at once rolled over and over helplessly, going down the short slope together with the rush of running rain water. He came to rest in the roadway of the street at the bottom, lying on his back, with a great flash of lightning over his face—a vivid, silent flash of lightning which blinded him utterly. He picked himself up, and put his arm over his eyes to recover his sight. Not a sound reached him from anywhere, and he began to walk, staggering, down a long, empty street. The lightning waved and darted round him its silent flames, the water of the deluge fell, ran, leaped, drove—noiseless like the drift of mist. In this unearthly stillness his footsteps fell silent on the pavement, while a dumb wind drove him on and on, like a lost mortal in a phantom world ravaged by a soundless thunderstorm. God only knows where his noiseless feet took him to that night, here and there, and back again, without pause or rest.[92]

2. Suspense

Suspense, a feature common to the mystery novel and the thriller, may be the product of a variety of tactics. For example,

Joseph Conrad And The Thriller

Conrad uses the device of retardation in "Heart of Darkness" when Marlow does not at first perceive what objects decorate the fence around Kurtz' home. The narrator describes them as "round carved balls" and mistakes them for architectural detail, so that the delayed truth that they are human skulls acquires even more force, striking him like a "blow." This device of retardation is actually a type of inversion (the inversion of time). Conrad relies on many other inversions of the natural order for a suspenseful effect—alternation of narrators (inversion of time and space), multiple plot lines (inversions of space), the plot within a plot or action within action (characteristic of the Dickensian novel as well), and inversions of meaning. In *The Secret Agent,* for example, to convey his detestation of the void, Conrad uses such potentially substantial words as "circle," "silence," and "secret," for their most pejorative connotations. Verloc is the non-agent of a non-secret. Words are often used ironically also—for example, the word "pilgrim" in "Heart of Darkness" is used to describe the brutish passengers, the name "Razumov" which means "man of reason" is used to describe one who repeatedly refers to himself as "impelled," and "driven."

Alternating the narrative voice serves to deflect the progress of the narrative, thereby aiding digression and concealment, but is more particularly useful for purposes of moral refraction. *Under Western Eyes* presents a varied moral perspective by refracting the image of consciousness. The first half of the book is based on Razumov's diary, transposed and relayed to the reader by a third person, the language-teacher; the second half of the book is told in the first person. The effect is that of an image reflected in a mirror in another mirror, and the different and partial truths are more analogous to the gradual disclosures of the detective novel than to the direct confrontations of the thriller.

It is interesting that Conrad does not alternate domestic and public scene in order to shift narrators or plot lines as did Dickens and the Victorian stage melodramatists. In *Chance,* in "The Secret Sharer," and in *The Secret Agent,* the personal and public coincide; domesticity becomes tinged with irrationality and horror. There remain traces of alternation in *Under Western Eyes* in some

155

scenes which Nathalie and Mrs. Haldin share, but there, too, the balance is not regained (another manifestation of the loss of Arcadia).

The dénouement of the formulaic crime novel winds up various narrative strands into a skein. *Chance* does resemble the novels of Dickens and Collins in the tightness of the design imposed upon it and the deftness with which the loose strands are caught up at the end. But in *The Secret Agent,* the book which more than any other puts forward Conrad's view of the disintegration of the individual and society, the characters' lives are presented as parallel lines or strands that can never converge.

In addition, the *progression d'effet* which Conrad and Ford shaped is the style *nonpareil* for the creation of suspense, since it combines a slow accumulation of detail with an impression of momentum. In Chapter II I called attention to the "dazzle detail" of detective fiction, and in Chapter III to the "rococo detail" of Dickens. The mounting emotional tension in Conrad coupled with the actual attenuation of the narration forces the reader to share the protagonist's strain.

The various ways in which progress is deflected intensify, in the manner of melodrama, the suspenseful effect and may well devolve upon that sensation of fear which, paradoxically, contains pleasure (see Note 1, Chapter IV). This should be distinguished from that exploration of fear which Conrad undertakes in the character of Winnie Verloc, for example, or in any of his other psychological portraits.

3. The confrontation between the forces of good and evil

Although the allegorical opposition of good and evil is a premise of the detective novel, the dramatic confrontation is more characteristic of melodrama and its cognate form, the thriller. In both of these, two characters embodying good and evil encounter one another in a struggle which is often physical. The melodramatic confrontation is a scene most congenial to Conrad, relying on a conception of character which is heavily allegorical. *Under Western Eyes* turns upon confrontations between Razumov and Nathalie, Razumov and Haldin, Razumov and the revolutionists.

4. The interview

The obverse of the direct confrontation is the interview, a familiar procedure of the detective novel. In fact, Ross Macdonald characterizes his detective hero as "less a doer, than a questioner."[93] Surprisingly, despite the sensational bent of *The Secret Agent* it is structured around the interview, which lends it the unity it possesses. There are a total of seventeen interviews, three of them long. Each affords a glimpse of the secret life which runs underneath the surface of the novel's action. In *Under Western Eyes* Conrad features interviews between Razumov and Tekla, Razumov and Sophia, and especially between Razumov and the language-teacher, in which the latter attempts to "sound out" the former, only to hear discords he cannot fathom.

A more idiosyncratic method of evoking the thrills of melodrama than the evocation of doom or suspense is Conrad's inimitable use of irony, which often tinges the interview. Leavis says of "Heart of Darkness":

> The irony lies in the association of her [the Intended's] innocent nobility, her purity of idealizing faith, with the unspeakable corruption of Kurtz; and it is developed . . . with a thrilled insistence that recalls the melodramatic intensities of Edgar Allan Poe.[94]

During the course of Marlow's interview with the Intended, the vocabulary is strikingly similar to that of melodrama and is redeemed from banality only by the consciousness of that irony: "A chill grip on my heart," "silence . . . silence," "I stopped in a fright!", "heart-broken," "the dark was repeating then in a persistent whisper all around us, in a whisper that seemed to swell menacingly, like the first whisper of a rising wind," "my heart stood still."[95] Furthermore, the melodramatic tone of the language is accented by the punctuation: exclamation points, dots, and dashes, suggestive of hesitation and suppressed excitement.

5. The *peripeteia*

Conrad uses the sudden *peripeteia* which marks (or disfigures) melodrama, but rescues it from sentimentality by filtering it through an impartial observer who tells it in retrospect. Thus it is from Marlow's lips, not from the mouth of one of the participants, that we hear how Powell dashed the cup of poison from his Captain's hand, and it is from Captain Mitchell that we hear of the nick-of-time reversal in *Nostromo*. Lionel Trilling interprets "Heart of Darkness" as having *peripeteia* at its center. "The stunning *peripeteia* of the story is the revelation that Kurtz, having gone alone to collect ivory far up the Congo River, has become the chief and virtually the god of a local tribe, his rule being remarkable for its cruelty."[96]

6. The use of sensation

Conrad generously infuses his stories and novels with sensational incident, but it does not become an end in itself, as it does in the adventure story or thriller. Thus the death of Hirsch in *Nostromo* is, on the most obvious level, a by-product of the curse upon the mine. More important, it is the occasion for one of Conrad's studies on the subject of fear; an indictment of the attempt to buy justice (just as *Almayer's Folly* is an indictment of the attempt to buy love); and another instance of the choice between evils, in this case between the already corrupt government of Costaguana and Sotillo's insurgents.

In the previous sections of this chapter I have remarked that elements of tragedy and irony lift the work of Conrad above the level of melodrama, adventure, or romance. To these we can add Conrad's ability to make of his fiction a forum for ideas that have an existence outside the pages of his books (e.g., imperialism, the validity of the Rousseauistic ideal, the dangers of revolutionary ardor, and so on). But above all, it is the hegemony of the moral purpose, sometimes accompanied by a didacticism reminiscent of Dickens, that is responsible for the reluctance we feel to compare him with those forms which are usually designated "entertainments."

We might say with some justification that *Under Western Eyes* and *The Secret Agent* are spy novels, for espionage is the occupation of the central characters as well as a number of subordinate characters in both books. Yet Julian Symons demurs from so classifying them in his own book *Mortal Consequences.* Symons states, "Conrad's novels seem distinct in spirit from both detective and spy stories," and decides that the reason they cannot be considered spy stories is that Conrad uses this activity to illustrate the evil of revolution.[97] This conclusion is easily verified. In the usual spy novel the ethos is fashioned by expediency; it is a "we" and "them" dialectic. Any particular action is judged, not by any *a priori* standard, but by an *a posteriori* standard of effectiveness. In both *The Secret Agent* and *Under Western Eyes,* that ethos is rejected as simplistic. Zabel writes, "Conrad had already [1908] fixed upon the police spy and agent provacateur as a radical symptom of the whole sinister machinery of European and Russian corruption."[98]

Certainly the most explicit connection between Conrad and the crime novel is his extension of the thriller into a new type, the political thriller. As I have already pointed out, this opened an eminently fruitful vein for a succession of authors seeking to depict the political events of this century in a fictional way. As Conrad has shaped it, the political thriller bears witness to his reluctant indictment of the social contract, his frustration at discerning unheeded dangers, his observation of the disparity between public and private interest.

Conrad's work shares with the crime novel (both detective and thriller) many thematic elements—The Quest, Identity and Recognition, The Scapegoat, and Poetic Justice—which are ancient, harking back to myth, fairy tale, and folk literature, but which he has been able to fashion to modern postures—while still retaining those archetypal images which are rooted in our imagination and which link him with the tradition of narrative literature. Two examples are his emphasis upon loneliness within the identity theme (later taken up by Graham Greene) and his notion that the paradisal vision is insupportable. Similarly, he has taken those structural elements which arose in the eighteenth and nineteenth centuries—suspense, confrontation, foreboding—and used them superlatively to convey the modern sense of crisis, of exigency, of doubt.

159

A Common Spring

In his unremitting search for a purposive world, in his assessment of the heroic potential of various types, in his depiction of the divided self, Conrad succeeds not in spite of, but with the help of the thematic and structural components of the crime novel.

Note 1
CHAPTER IV

The Writer and Psychoanalysis

by Edmund Bergler, M.D.

Doubleday and Co., 1950, Garden City, N.Y., pp. 156-170

"Reader Participation in the Whodunit"

"Basically, every detective story contains the father-son conflict, symbolized, perpetuated, and projected ad infinitum. This is visible in the problem itself ('. . . the detective story is at bottom one thing only: a conflict of wits between criminal and sleuth'), furthermore, in the aggression toward the official police, and last but not least, in the respectful Watson. On different levels the old fight stemming from childhood is perpetuated; the child is victorious—hence the detective outsmarts the criminal and the offical police."

Dr. Bergler sees the desire for such material as stemming from positive oedipus in women, negative oedipus in men. (Negative oedipus is defined as "unconscious libidinous attachment of the child to the parent of the same sex.") The components of the reader's attraction he itemizes as: 1) Enjoyment of passivity of being overwhelmed (identification with victim); 2) Enjoyment of uncanniness (the uncanny is produced when some impression revives repressed infantile complexes, or when the primitive beliefs we have surmounted seem once more to be confirmed); this enjoyment of the uncanny is tantamount to the "terror" which is one component of the catharsis of tragedy. Dr. Bergler himself notes that both the mystery story and the fairy story produce fear. 3) Voyeuristic enjoyment of the forbidden.

I. Henri Rousseau, *The Dream.* (The Museum of Modern Art, gift of Nelson A. Rockefeller.)

162

Notes

CHAPTER IV

[1]As Carolyn Heilbrun points out, "As recently as 1939, the prominent critic David Daiches reluctantly dismissed Conrad as a writer of adventure stories." *Towards A Recognition of Androgony,* p. 171.

[2]Georges-Jean Aubry, *The Sea-Dreamer: A Definitive Biography of Joseph Conrad,* (Garden City, N.Y.: Doubleday, 1957) p. 273.

[3]Paul Wiley, *Novelist of Three Worlds: Ford Madox Ford* (Syracuse, N.Y.: Syraucuse University Press, 1962), p. 58.

[4]Joseph Conrad, *Under Western Eyes* (Garden City, New York: Doubleday Anchor, 1963) p. 319.

[5]As quoted by Paul Wiley in *Conrad's Measure of Man* (Madison, Wisconsin: University of Wisconsin Press, 1954), p. 42.

[6]Morton Dauwen Zabel, "Conrad: The Terms of Response," *Craft and Character in Modern Fiction* (New York: Viking Press, 1957), p. 170.

[7]Albert Guérard, *Conrad the Novelist* (Cambridge, Mass.: Harvard University Press, 1958), p. 88.

[8]Twenty years prior, Henry James had broached this subject in *The Princess Casamassima.*

[9]Robert Kiely, *Robert Louis Stevenson and the Fiction of Adventure* (Cambridge, Mass.: Harvard University Press, 1965), p. 25.

[10]Because of the dearth of happy and unfrustrated relationships between men and women in Conrad's fiction, and the ease with which women may be divided into two categories [La Belle Dame Sans Merci and The Sleeping Beauty], his treatment of the inequality of women has been largely overlooked. In Flora De Barral we are given an excellent portrayal of the dependent, passive position which women occupied, and even the energetic Mrs. Fyne can teach her female disciples no better lesson than survival through wiliness and obstinacy. (Joseph Conrad, *Chance*)

[11]*Sincerity and Authenticity* (Cambridge, Mass.: Harvard University Press, 1972), p. 117.

[12]*Craft and Character in Modern Fiction,* p. 188.

[13]As quoted in *Novelist of Three Worlds,* p. 52.

[14]Ford Madox Ford, *Joseph Conrad* (New York: Octagon Books, 1965), p. 225.

[15]*Craft and Character in Modern Fiction,* p. 219.

[16]Joseph Conrad, *Chance* (Garden City, New York: Doubleday, Page & Co., 1914), p. 325.

[17]Of special interest in view of our consideration of Conrad vis-à-vis the crime novel, is the following description of Poe, which seems remarkably applicable to Conrad: ". . . Poe lived simultaneously in two worlds, one of which he explicitly

described as 'grotesque and arabesque,' the other 'ratiocinative.' In the first of these worlds all truth is symbolic and is apprehended intuitively; in the second, truth is a pattern of facts knowable to persons with keen physical senses and acutely deductive minds. Poe's heroes, thus, tend to be either mystical lunatics [leading to Dostoevsky] or detectives [leading to Conan Doyle]." Terrence Hipolito, "On the Two Poes," *Mystery and Detection Annual,* 1972, ed. Donald Adams, (Pasadena, California: Castle Press, 1972, p. 15.

[18]F.R. Leavis, "Joseph Conrad," *The Great Tradition* (Garden City, New York: Doubleday Anchor, 1954), p. 219.

[19]Joseph Conrad, "Heart of Darkness," *Great Short Works of Joseph Conrad* (New York: Harper and Row, 1966), p. 223.

[20]Eric Bentley, *The Life of the Drama,* p. 205.

[21]Thomas Moser, *Joseph Conrad* (Cambridge, Mass.: Harvard University Press 1957), p. 15.

[22]In her "Introduction," *Nostromo* (New York: Holt, Rinehart and Winston, 1961), pp. vii-xxv, she sums up the novel as the story of a stranger knight coming to a wasteland, rehabilitating it, but not living happily ever after.

[23]"Heart of Darkness," p. 225.

[24]*Ibid.,* p. 212.

[25]*Conrad's Measure of Man,* p. 95.

[26]"Heart of Darkness," p. 213. Variations on the atavism/primitivism theme run through the work of Stevenson and of Graham Greene, and provide co - respondences between these two writers and Conrad. Greene's treatment of the primitive will be discussed in the succeeding chapter; of Stevenson, one may briefly refer to Archie in *Weir of Hermiston,* who "travels backward in search of himself." *Robert Louis Stevenson and the Fiction of Adventure,* p. 258.

[27]Joseph Conrad, *Lord Jim,* (New York: Modern Library, Random House, 1931), p. 141.

[28]"Heart of Darkness," p. 254.

[29]*Ibid.,* p. 237.

[30]*Ibid.,* p. 284.

[31]Morton Zabel suggests that the rigor of Conrad's own undertakings, the seaman's life and then the life of letters, may have been responsible for this emphasis.

[32]*Under Western Eyes,* p. 164.

[33]"Heart of Darkness," p. 237.

[34]I am indebted to *Conrad's Measure of Man* for my introduction to this conception.

[35]"Heart of Darkness," p. 244.

[36]It is interesting here to compare these images with similar images of flood and primeval cataclysms in Charles Dickens' *Bleak House.*

[37]Joseph Conrad, *Lord Jim,* p. 175.

[38]Joseph Conrad, *The Secret Agent* (Garden City, New York: Doubleday Anchor, 1953), p. 11. This can be compared with Mark Spilka's similar vision of

Joseph Conrad And The Thriller

Dickens' London quoted in Chapter III: "One of Dickens' finest images is the great dome of St. Paul's Cathedral, dimly seen above the London fog, as if disconnected from Life below. The city's desolation, its spiritual depletion, its lack of vital purpose, are his abiding targets." And with a description of Conan Doyle's London: "The prevalence of monsters is the most striking feature of these years. Glaring, snarling, smoking, they erupt with the force of unconscious images. When Conan Doyle describes the labor of fueling up the blue-gap monster [London], dozens of people rolling boulders into the cave—the metaphor is unmistakeable." Clearly this corresponds to Fletcher's daemonic world. *The Dangerous Edge,* p. 51.

[39]There are a few exceptions to this rule—e.g., *The Rescue.*

[40]*Craft and Character in Modern Fiction,* p. 158.

[41]As quoted in Morton Zabel's "Introduction," *Under Western Eyes,* p. xli.

[42]*Under Western Eyes,* p. 31.

[43]*The Art of Joseph Conrad: A Critical Symposium,* ed. R.W. Stallman (East Lansing, Michigan: Michigan State University Press, 1960), p. 144.

[44]*Joseph Conrad,* pp. 17-19. Moser further suggests that Conrad's villains are based upon schoolboy adventure stories, stage melodrama, and ballad, with traces of Satanism and the Jew-devil.

Since writing this, I have come across a passage in Lionel Trilling's *Sincerity and Authenticity,* p. 111, which bears on this. Trilling reminds us that there is substantial precedent in English literature for making the hero a naval man, and thus what seemed to be the outcome of Conrad's own experience should also be read as customary: ". . . for the English themselves gave the seafaring profession a special place in their imagination of the moral life, not unexpected in an island people. The sailing officer was admired as exemplar of a professional code which prescribed an uncompromising commitment to duty, a continuous concentration of the personal energies upon some impersonal end, the subordination of the self to some general good. It was the officer's response to the imperatives of this code that made for the singleness of mind and the openness of soul imputed to him. Not least among the traits which inspired respect was his ability to meet the practical demands of an exigent trade, his technical competence painfully acquired through an apprenticeship which began in his boyhood. Gentleman though he was, he worked." Another spokesman of this tradition was Jane Austen, whose preference for the naval hero is only matched by her fondness for the clergyman. Jane Austen and Joseph Conrad also share a respect for the work-ethic, which combines the virtue of dutifulness with avoidance of idleness. Both, I believe, saw idleness as a vacuum into which disorder would rush. Conrad, for example, seems to hold the sin of sloth against revolutionists as much as their political doctrine. Indeed, one begins to wonder whether Conrad's rapport with England was not based, at least partially, upon the fact that he found there a belief in duty, practicality, and its imaginative model in the life at sea which matched his own. (Dickens' Tartar in *The Mystery of Edwin Drood* is another prototypical naval worthy.)

[45]*Chance,* p. 302.

165

⁴⁶As quoted in Avrom Fleishman's *Conrad's Politics* (Baltimore, Maryland: Johns Hopkins University Press, 1967), p. 227.

⁴⁷The views of the Romantic decline may lie behind Conrad's appreciation of the passion of destructive energy; as he asserts in *A Personal Record,* it can even be creative. But he never makes the short step from there to the credo that crime is an art, which we find in the Romantic decline.

⁴⁸*Under Western Eyes,* p. 254.

⁴⁹"Heart of Darkness," p. 222.

⁵⁰*Under Western Eyes,* p. 194.

⁵¹John Hagan, Jr., "The Design of Conrad's *The Secret Agent,*" *Journal of English Literary History,* XXII (June 1955), p. 155. The political events that inspired this view have been amply documented: the assassination of Plehve, the Tsarist tyranny, the forming of the Socialist Revolutionary Party in Russia, as well as assassination attempts upon rulers in Spain, Italy, the Phoenix Park murders, the Haymarket riots, are but a sampling of the radical socialism and anarchism that Conrad feared and whose strength he intuited.

⁵²The Château Borel, which is the spiritual center of the revolutionists' activities, is treated ironically. Madame de S., its resident spirit, is a macabre eccentric reminiscent of Dickens' Miss Havisham, and the idealistic vision supposedly generated in this establishment in actual fact encompasses exploitation of the servants.

⁵³Joseph Conrad, "Introduction," *Under Western Eyes,* p. lxi.

⁵⁴This metaphor runs like a leit-motif through modern literature, e.g., Thomas Mann's *The Magic Mountain,* Albert Camus's *The Plague,* Jean-Paul Sartre's *La Nausée.*

⁵⁵Joseph Conrad, *The Secret Agent,* p. 253.

⁵⁶A. Alvarez, *The Savage God: A Study of Suicide* (New York: Random House, 1972), p. 243.

⁵⁷Joseph Conrad, "Introduction," *Under Western Eyes,* p. lxi.

⁵⁸R.W. Stallman, "Life, Art and The Secret Sharer," *Forms of Modern Fiction,* ed. William Van O'Connor (Minneapolis, Minnesota: University of Minnesota Press, 1948), p. 238.

⁵⁹*Conrad the Novelist,* p. 32. Conrad was an admirer of Baudelaire, whose passion for Poe's versions of the doppelgänger in thriller form should be recalled here.

⁶⁰As quoted in *Craft and Character in Modern Fiction,* pp. 164-165.

⁶¹The exception that proves the rule is Ricardo in *Victory.*

⁶²"The Secret Sharer," *Great Short Works of Joseph Conrad* (New York: Harper and Row, 1967), p. 388.

⁶³This is the method of the *Dreigroschenoper,* as discussed in Chapter II.

⁶⁴*The Secret Agent,* p. 85.

⁶⁵*Ibid.,* p. 90.

⁶⁶"Heart of Darkness," p. 261.

⁶⁷Frederick Hoffman, *The Mortal No,* p. 40.

[68]p. 244.

[69]p. 249.

[70]*The Savage God*, p. 240; *Lord Jim*, p. 214. In a similar vein, William Empson views the artist-outcast-criminal-tragic hero as the offspring of the Romantic *Weltanschauung.* "It is clear that the view of the poet as outcast and unacknowledged legislator, equally strong in Byron and Shelley, puts him exactly in the position of the mythical tragic hero; . . . it keeps an idea that crimes are the fate of the artist merely because of his greatness, and that to commit hubris is only to admit that one is a tragic demigod." *Some Versions of Pastoral,* pp. 207-8.

[71]*Sincerity and Authenticity*, p. 108.

[72]*Conrad's Measure of Man*, p. 19.

[73]Kingsley Widmer, "Conrad's Pyrrhic Victory," *Twentieth Century Literature,* V. (October, 1959), p. 123.

[74]"Heart of Darkness," p. 265.

[75]*Ibid.,* p. 218.

[76]*Ibid.,* p. 223; *The Secret Agent,* p. 18; "Heart of Darkness," p. 218.

[77]Thomas Mann, "Conrad's Secret Agent," *Joseph Conrad: A Critical Symposium,* p. 231.

[78]*The Dehumanization of Art* (Princeton, N.J.: Princeton University Press) p. 35.

[79]*Man and His Symbols*, p. 298.

[80]*Adventure, Mystery, and Romance*, p. 166.

[81]*Man and His Symbols*, p. 314.

[82]*Conrad's Politics*, pp. 198-9. Fleishman analyzes in detail both the fragmentation and transmutation into inorganic matter which the whole novel treats.

[83]*The Secret Agent*, pp. 25-26.

[84]Mario Praz, *Mnemosyne* (Bollingen Series, Princeton Univ. Press, Princeton, N.J., 1970), p. 210.

[85]*The Secret Agent*, p. 23.

[86]*Mnemosyne,* pp. 198-9.

[87]*The Great Tradition*, p. 254.

[88]Hoffman, *The Mortal No,* p. 191.

[89]*The Sense of an Ending*, p. 19.

[90]"Heart of Darkness," p. 244.

[91]*Conrad's Measure of Man*, p. 211.

[92]*Under Western Eyes*, p. 311.

[93]*On Crime Writing* (Santa Barbara, California: Capra Press, 1973), p. 24.

[94]*The Great Tradition*, p. 221.

[95]"Heart of Darkness," pp. 289-292.

[96]*Sincerity and Authenticity*, p. 107.

[97]*Mortal Consequences,* pp. 234-5.

[98]*Craft and Character in Modern Fiction*, p. 196.

CHAPTER V

GRAHAM GREENE AND THE MODERN THRILLER

Introduction

What we have written is not a story of detection
Of crime and punishment, but of sin and expiation.
T.S. Eliot, *The Family Reunion*

The wonder is not that it [the world] is so bad but that any good
should be left in it.
Rider Haggard, *King Solomon's Mines*

Joseph Conrad was one of Graham Greene's literary progenitors. By his own testimony, Greene had to struggle to shake off Conrad's "heavy hypnotic" style.[1] He shared with Conrad an interest in the split self and in the efficacy of suffering, and he belonged, like Conrad, to a neo-Romanticism which inclined toward the exotic. Greene makes specific reference to "the heart of darkness," and he alludes to Conrad's *Prefaces,* to *Victory* and *Nostromo.* Though he deprecates the handling of evil in *The Secret Agent* as "cruder than Jamesian evil,"[2] *Under Western Eyes* and *The Secret Agent* showed him a way to modernize the thriller.

Individual mannerisms may be traced from the later to the earlier novelist, but in an overall sense we may say that Greene was impressed by Conrad's presentation of both the visible world and its moral sense. If Conrad was, as Greene expressed it, "busy with the interpretation of a few moral ideas," so was Greene himself. Greene admired Conrad for forcing choice upon his characters and stressing the responsibility which such choice incurs (a theme Greene was to develop mainly in relation to the religious impulse). He was convinced that the Conradian concern with the "importance of the human act,"[3] the conviction that human behavior is purposeful, must ultimately derive from a religious sense.

Greene's contention is that all major writers have obsessions, not least of all himself. "Every creative writer worth our consideration, every writer who can be called in the wide eighteenth century use of the term, a poet, is a victim: a man given over to obsessions. . . . The obsession is perhaps detected in the symbols the author uses."[4] Greene's obsessions have been summarized: "the divided mind; . . . the idea of pity; . . . [and] the terror of life, the ground of all obsessions, . . . rendered through the somber general picture of a fallen world."[5]

Greene reconstitutes allegory in his thrillers. He was to turn to actual stage drama later in his career (in the 1950s, '60s, and '70s), but from the beginning (1920s) he writes a Morality within his entertainments and novels. This automatically raises certain difficulties. George Orwell argues that the novel is essentially Protestant, its well-being predicated upon the individual response and free election of its characters. But Greene's obsessions turn characters into dominant ideas. Greene's use of religious determinism, then, required a literary compromise; O'Faolain faults Greene: "All of [his] novels are as subject to the tyranny of the last page as a railway train to its destination."[6] As we noted in Chapter II, one of the pitfalls of the allegorical mode is a deadening schematization of plot and stylization of character.

Green does attempt some psychological probing in *It's a Battlefield* and varying degrees of political probing in novels such as *The Comedians, The Quiet American,* and *The Honorary Consul* (though of a simplistic sort). Even in *The Power and the Glory,* assuredly not a "political" novel, we are presented with the conflation of the respectable citizen and the criminal (remarked before in *Dreigroschenoper*) as part of the up-dating of the thriller, its politicizing. In Tabasco the faces of law and order are the faces of corruption, while the faces of the accused are honest.[7] But the "unsolvable mystery" for Greene can only be the relation of man to God, not that of man to the state or man to man (which is the mystery of the human heart, as distinguished from the human condition). When we finish reading a representative nineteenth-century novel such as *Vanity Fair,* we do not inquire whether the protagonist, in this case Becky Sharp, is damned; it is the temporal fate of the character which absorbs us. The fiction of Greene, on the other hand, deliberately provokes the question of judgment. Because of this *weltanschaung,* Greene's allegory is the allegory of evil and Hell, upon which his vision of Heaven is dependent:

> Enlarge your Hell;
> Preserve it in repair;
> Only a splendid Hell
> Makes Heaven fair.[8]

The seminal myths for Greene are the Day of Judgment, the Crucifixion, and the Garden of Gethsemane.

Besides Conrad, Greene's literary preferences run to Hardy, Dickens, and James, in all of whom he singles out a preoccupation with evil. In his essay on James it is the damned characters who receive attention: Kate Croy and Merton Densher, the Prince and Charlotte, Peter Quint and Miss Jessel, Mme. Merle and Gilbert Osmond. "A sense of evil religious in its intensity"[9] is Greene's verdict upon James. Greene's own avowed purpose was to restore to the English novel that religious dimension missing since James' death. Greene rationalizes the use of coincidence in Dickens as necessary compensation for the weight of evil; indeed, Greene interprets Dickens as a Manichean, a label which in turn was to be affixed to him. Greene approves of James' villains because in his view they possessed "the sense of supernatural evil."[10] Greene's interpretation of evil as spiritual perversion prevents him from accepting the sexual or economic snares depicted by Fielding or Defoe as proper illustrations of evil.

He discovered this same conviction of evil in another branch of fiction. Morton Zabel writes:

> . . . it appeared that there was another order of talent that had conditioned Greene's own imagination from its earliest workings. He responded to it in the adventure tales of John Buchan ('Now I saw how thin is the protection of civilization') and Conan Doyle ('think of the sense of horror which hangs over the laurelled drive of Upper Norwood and behind the curtains of Lower Camberwell . . .'), but its mark had been laid upon him long before he encountered these writers: in childhood when 'all books are books of divination.' Its masters then were the literary heroes of his boyhood: Rider Haggard, Percy Westerman, Captain Brereton, or Stanley Weyman. But vividly as these ignited his imagination, much as *King Solomon's Mines* 'influenced the future,' it 'could not finally satisfy'; its characters were too much 'like Platonic ideals; they were not life as one had already begun to know it.'[11]

Life as he had already begun to know it he found in a now obscure book called *The Viper of Milan* by Marjorie Bowen. "It was," Greene says, "as if I had been supplied once for all with a subject." Here for the first time he learned that while "goodness has only once found a perfect incarnation in a human body and never will again," evil "can always find a home there"; that there is a sense of doom "that lies over success" (his own work portrays failure sympathetically, sometimes heroically); "perfect evil walks the world where perfect good can never walk again." And he acknowledges that it was Miss Bowen's Italianate melodrama that "gave me my pattern—religion might explain it in other terms, but the pattern was there."[12]

Thus Greene recognized his pattern, hugged his obsessions, and seized upon his vehicle, the thriller. "I had found what I wanted to express, my fixation if you like, could best be expressed in the melodramatic, the contemporary and the Catholic" (which he made melodramatic).[13] The deliberateness of his choice is apparent: "If you excite your audience first, you can put over what you will of horror, suffering, truth."[14]

Though Greene found much in Marjorie Bowen, Anthony Hope, and such writers to attract him, he was sensitive early on (roughly after this third book) to the need for tempering their romanticism. Stevenson's romantic flair may have appealed to him, but he seems to have been more impressed by the sense of evil and the use of the doppelgänger. Despite his wholehearted admiration for Conrad, he condemns *Lord Jim* as "false and romantic,"[15] since it is built upon the premise, which he rejects out of hand, that events shape lives. Greene rejected, too, the atmospheric effects of Conrad; Greene does not paint his pictures evocatively, but constructs them from repeated details—e.g., the laterite roads, the sweat on the blotter. In *A Burnt-Out Case,* his most recent African novel, "the heart of darkness" is as much a geographical as a spiritual attribution, and the tone is not portentous but gently mocking. Greene sees absurdity even in situations where other writers stress danger.

Greene came to view romanticism as an attitude of mind and style greatly to be deplored, preferring instead a comic irony. In *The Ministry of Fear,* his narrator voices Greene's own skepticism:

> Over there among the unknown tribes a woman was giving birth, two people were seeing each other for the first time by the light of the lamp; everything in that darkness was of such importance that their errand could not equal it—this violent superficial chase, this cardboard adventure hurtling at forty-five miles an hour along the edge of the profound natural common experience of men. Rowe felt a longing to get into that world . . . the longing was like the first stirring of maturity.[16]

Rowe's romantic, schoolboy-adventure-story outlook ends in a pistol shot in a lavatory, just as Alden Pyle's romantic conception of his country leads to his murder in *The Quiet American.* Greene's comic irony is captured in the epigraph he chooses from Santayana for *Stamboul Train:* "Everything in nature is lyrical in its ideal essence, tragic in its fate, and comic in its existence."

Of an earlier book, *Rumour at Nightfall,* later suppressed by Greene, Allott and Farris state:

> Greene's reversal of all the values of the conventional 'revolutionary'
> romance is evident both in his characters and in the ordering of his
> plot. There is something mean and egotistical about most of the con-
> spirators: . . . Opposed to them is Demassener, the dictator. Instead
> of the usual man of blood and iron, Greene depicts an aging man,
> tired and courteous, who hates freedom because 'freedom means
> freedom for the animal in man'. . . .[17]

The traditional romantic sympathy with revolution is reversed in
Rumour at Nightfall; what is retained that is romantic is a
weltschmerz which ripened into eschatology.

Thus Greene proved alert to the hazards, both stylistic and idea-
tional, of the convention he adopted, the thriller. For example, he
scaled down violence and horror so that they would not lose their
impact; as Zabel understood, ". . . the modern thriller is permitted
its prodigies of contrivance and hecatombs of death at the cost of
becoming a bore."[18] Greene discarded the superman hero (preferring to explore the limits of human capability), incidentally placing
less strain upon the reader's credulity.

Although the detective novel was in its Golden Age when Greene
began writing entertainments, he found it uncongenial for his purposes. He dismissed the ambience of the country house (Auden's
"great good place"), which was the natural milieu of these
novels, as an exercise in nostalgia. (See Note 1, Chapter V, ex-
cerpts from Raymond Williams' *The Country and the City* and
Cyril Connolly's *The Evening Colonnade*.) Thus, Arthur Rowe in
The Ministry of Fear reflects that the "Edwardian security of his
childhood with its silver teapots and croquet lawns has vanished;
. . . lady novelists describe it over and over in 'books of the
month,' but it's not there any more."[19] (But this is not simply a
case of *O tempora! O mores!* It reflects Greene's rejection of the
pastoral as a glimpse of the eternal.)

The thriller, on the other hand, is a story of action, and this provided a pattern of reduction which appeals to Greene's search for
the simplicities, "life before we went astray." "It [the thriller]
reaches our understanding at subconscious levels [through the use
of archetypal symbols and actions] while its narrative reduces the
complexities of contemporary existence to a more comprehensible

form."[20] The thriller thus becomes a tool for clearing the underbrush of confusion, personal and societal. Though the detective story also offers a pattern of reduction, Greene faults it for "intellectual childishness"; its mysteries guarantee resolution, its clever traps are papier mâché hurdles. Furthermore, it fails to take into account any irony in the dispensation of justice, or any agency which shelters such irony. Most importantly, for Greene the detective novel's "search for exact truth" does not make sense at a secular level; it is only a prelude, a kind of Ignatian exercise to reach the truth that embraces God. Greene feels, "murder, if you are going to take it seriously at all, is a religious subject"[21]—far from the gamesmanship of the detective story. The stricture that life is sacred (i.e., belongs to God to be taken) is such a cultural donnée in the Judeo-Christian tradition that it spills over, for example, into the censure of suicide, the taking of one's own life, not just murder, the taking of another's.

The jeopardy to life inherent in the adventures of the thriller is retained and fully exploited by Greene. Furthermore, in his expert hands the ambiguities and contradictions of existence are not omitted, as they are in most thrillers, but they are also submitted to God's inscrutable mystery, mystery consigned to mystery.

The tempo of Greene's narratives rejects the leisurely style of the Golden Age detective novel and substitutes what Robert Graves calls the "tense graphic cinematic style," (see Note 1, Chapter I) easily traced to Greene's professional involvement with the cinema. His adaptation of cinéma vérité transposed the odd angle of vision, the detached but probing eye, and the swift conveyance of emotion through imagery from the screen to the written page. The Greenean novel and cinéma vérité share (with W.H. Auden) an inordinate fondness for taxonomy, derived perhaps from the prevalence of the "reportage" style in the 1930s. The selective catalogue of the cinematic or "reportage" style offers the opportunity to manipulate details so that they confirm Greene's pattern. Though the pattern is not that of the detective novel, it is just as invariable.

Greene has written much journalism, but he has never written a documentary novel. What Greene gives us, in fact, is not a documentary but the simulacra of documentary realism; he is not interested in investigating the criminal milieu. And he is cut off from actuality not by a sense of the innocence of the great good place (the detective novel), but by a conviction of the guilt of the great bad place (Greeneland). *"Son actualite consiste à être inactuel,"* comments Mauriac.[22] The thriller is admirably suited to the fabrication of Greeneland. Not only is it an allegorical form, but its particular atmosphere—compounded of fear, distrust, suspicion, and betrayal—is identical to the signs of the "great aboriginal calamity"—i.e., the fallen world.

Coincidentally, in creating this world for the purpose of exploring two questions which preoccupied him, "What is justice?" and "What is innocence?", Greene at the same time created an image of our modern public world and became its able historian, earning himself the title, "the Auden of the modern thriller."[23] Greene was prescient enough to know that "today our world seems peculiarly susceptible to brutality . . . at times as though our whole planet had swung into the fog belt of melodrama."[24] In *The Ministry of Fear* he comments that the stuff of melodrama—spies, motor car chases, murder, violence—are now the observable phenomena of everyday existence. Melodrama is no longer paranoia, no longer even exaggeration.

Thus Greene's private appreciation of evil fuses with the public; each corroborates the other. By placing the problem of guilt at the center of modern moral sensibility, Greene was able to revivify fustian melodrama by eliminating the rigor and propriety and decorum. Morton Zabel writes:

> Where once—in James, Conrad, Dostoevsky, in Dickens, Defoe and the Elizabethans—it was society, state, kingdom, world or the universe itself that supplied the presiding order of law and justice, it was now the isolated, betrayed, but finally indestructible integrity of the human life that must furnish the measure.[25]

Now Greene must face "the whole barbarism"; we are all guilty of the crime that is the modern world; individual crime seems refreshingly manageable. Bram Stoker and Edgar Wallace seem appallingly innocent.

Whereas the detective story aims by its resolution to restore innocence to the many by affixing guilt to the one, Greene insists on the guilt of the many. We all "dunit." Ironically, this general indictment accounts for a meagre sense of community. This communal guilt was apparent to Northrop Frye when he called the Greene novel:

> . . . an ironic comedy addressed to people who can realize that murderous violence is less an attack on a virtuous society by a malignant individual than a symptom of that society's own viciousness. Such a comedy would be the kind of intellectualized parody of melodramatic formulas represented by, for instance, the novels of Graham Greene.[26]

In addition to the guilt we bear for "the crime that is the modern world" we are all implicated in Newman's "great aboriginal calamity."[27] Greene has changed the terms by which the allegorical battle between good and evil must be interpreted, from secular (the detective novel) to sacramental (the thriller infused with his personal message). Greene may be said to have transmuted original fear (the impulse of the detective novel) to the more specifically Christian doctrine of original sin. This shift is the whole point of his novel *Brighton Rock*. His view is fundamentally opposed to the detective novel, which depends for its solution upon ratiocination and the agents of secular justice and is content with temporal issues. Greene's solutions depend upon the irrational (faith) and the sacred (Grace). The line between hero and villain is blurred, and we are all equally in need of Grace.

The metaphor of the battlefield (made explicit in his title *It's a Battlefield*) is absolutely central to Greene's perception of life, and provides an excellent illustration of how his fiction functions both on a temporal and eternal level. The battlefield is, first, the scene of the spiritual war between good and evil, part of the same Christian tradition to which Milton and Spenser belong. For this reason the seediness which characterizes the Greenean milieu is not simply the by-product of current social conditions but is the visible sign of Godlessness, of man abandoned. It is ubiquitous; the battlefield is everywhere. "The world is all of a piece of course; it is engaged everywhere in the same subterranean struggle . . . there is not peace anywhere where there is life; but there are quiet and active sectors of the line.''[28] And in *Brighton Rock* we find the line, ''It lay there always, the ravaged and disputed territory between the two eternities.''[29] W.H. Auden, who also has been fascinated by many of these words and their conjurations—maps, frontiers, quislings, betrayals, smuggling, alignments—himself reverts to the battlefield metaphor to explain Greene's work: the narratives of Greeneland intrigue us ''because each of us is a creature at war with himself.''[30] Even as the vocabulary of war has become all too familiar to any twentieth-century adult, the battlefield metaphor speaks on an allegorical level to the universality of man's divided state. Evil within and evil without. The metaphor of the battlefield analogizes not only the human condition *sub specie aeternitatis,* but also man's temporal condition in the twentieth century; it is the world which was emerging in *Under Western Eyes* and *The Secret Agent.*

Greene's battlefield was not simply metaphorical; the violence of the thriller was another aspect of popular fiction Greene adapted. But violence was to be more than a device. In an essay on Henry James, Greene defines the problem he set for himself:

> The novel by its nature is dramatic, but it need not be melodramatic, and James's problem was to admit violence without becoming violent. He mustn't let violence lend the tone (that is melodrama): violence must draw its tone from all the rest of life; it must be subdued, and it must not, above all, be sudden and inexplicable.[31]

Greene has testified to the inescapable connection he sees between violence and evil in the larger, for him supernatural, sense. ''Violence comes to us more easily because it was so long expected—not only by the political sense, but by the moral sense—the world we lived in could not have ended any other way.''[32] Even in the entertainments, saturated as they are with violence, the action is less important than the moral. Greene maintains that not action is the telling component but the character's feelings, his moral outlook, of which the event is merely the inevitable expression. One of Greene's critics elaborates on the relative importance of action and morality:

But the thriller is more than action; it is a set of patterns and conventions as firmly established as those of classical tragedy. It is not surprising, then, to find in novels episodes of violence that are so formal as to be almost allegorical: the killing of Hale, the gas-mask scene in *This Gun for Hire,* the two deaths of Harry Lime, the murder of Else in *The Confidential Agent.* In this imagined world the action that matters is the eternal spiritual war between good and evil, and the novels are the legends of the battlefield.[33]

The awareness of incipient violence leads to an awareness of how thin the veneer of civilization is. The physical world is perceived as a stage-set waiting for the violent act; a blow is as expected a means of communication upon this stage as a word. The veneer of civilization consists not just of manners and buildings and talk, but intellection. Consequently—"There is a touch of nostalgia in the pleasure we take in gangster novels, in characters who have so agreeably simplified their emotions that they have begun living again at the level below the cerebral. . . . It is not, of course, that one wishes to stay at that level, but when one sees to what peril of extinction centuries of cerebration have brought us, one sometimes has a curiosity to discover if one can at what point one went astray." The fascination which Africa and Mexico, Haiti and Vietnam (the "uncivilized") exert upon Greene he attributes to their capacity to "satisfy temporarily the nostalgia for something lost"; they are part of the re-tracing, the search for simplicities, the quest for origins. Then, too, there is the undeniable connection which the outsider assumes between the primitive and the exertion of spontaneous violence, on the part of both man and nature. How quickly the efforts of man vanish from sight—the jungle, the desert obliterate the house of Tench (*The Power and the Glory*), the British club (*The Heart of the Matter*). The immutable dark core of human nature can also be presented in a geographical context: "They [i.e., the primitives] are not after all, so far from the central darkness," writes Greene.[34]

Violence is also, paradoxically, a touchstone of the mercy of God. "If we wish to make clear the mercy of God to the eyes of unbelievers, it is necessary that one see it from the view-point of the most degraded."[35] Hence the narrative point of view is frequently that of the hustler, the con man, the spy, the inhabitants of a Greeneland laced with violent action.

Finally, violence provides for Greene personally an antidote to the ennui which, by his own admission, plagued him all his life. From the Russian roulette which he played as an adolescent to the ceaseless peregrinations of his adult life, the desire to escape from ennui accounts for the insistence upon narrative action. In his story "Before the Attack," Greene describes himself as a "voyeur of violence."[36] As an author, this led him to impose the melodramatic upon routine existence, because the routine remained inert for him. Even in a supposedly "domestic" novel such as *The End of the Affair* the approach is melodramatic, as we shall see later.

In sum, violence is the climax, the symbolic act, the anticipated result of sin, the act of release toward which our political and moral life tends. It has the additional merit for Greene of being an act undertaken without cerebration and therefore of disclosing something essential about man's nature; it is spontaneous and vital (as enacted by the child and the primitive) in contrast to the limp rationalizations of Western Europe. In his essay "The Bombing Raid" Greene asserts that "action has a moral simplicity which thought lacks."[37] Bentley realizes, "it is as children and dreamers . . . as neurotics and savages too—that we enjoy melodrama."[38]

In the fairy tale Greene discovered another allegorical mode upon whose moral simplicities he could draw; in *A Burnt-Out Case* he encases a discrete fairy tale in his larger narrative. The world of the fairy tale is the child's world, and, like that of the primitive, it relies upon terror and magic to explain mystery; its systems of rewards and punishments are schematized into something meaningful; it posits supernatural powers; it appeals to a level below the cerebral. The primitive society is close to the child's vision; it could be argued with some justification, for example, that the Babes-in-the-Wood myth is central to both states, childhood and primitivism. (The unknown, uncharted areas of Africa serve Greene as a metaphor for both.) Greene writes:

> In childhood we live under the brightness of immortality—heaven is
> near and actual as the seaside. Behind the complicated details of the

179

world stand the simplicities: God is good, the grown-up man or woman knows the answers to every question, there is such a thing as truth, and justice is as measured and faultless as a clock. Our heroes are simple: they are brave, they tell the truth, they are good swordsmen and they are never in the long run easily defeated. That is why no later books satisfy us like those which were read to us in childhood—for those promised a world of great simplicity of which we knew the rules, but later books are complicated and contradictory with experience: they are formed out of our contradictory memories—of the V.C. in the police-court dock, of the faked income-tax returns, the sins in corners, and the hollow voice of men we despise talking to us of courage and purity. The little duke is dead and betrayed and forgotten: we cannot recognize the villain and we suspect the hero and the world is a small cramped place.[39]

The primitive or childlike acceptance of magic, of secret sacraments, is an aspect of Western religion Greene would wish to reinstate, seeing in it a less insipid, less abstract response. "We are too apt to minimize the magic element in Christianity—the man raised from the dead, the devils cast out, the water turned into wine."[40] Magic is power; in Africa Greene recaptures that childhood notion of Power which has not replaced the supernatural explanation with the scientific or materialistic one. (Hence, another reason the thriller is more viable for Greene than the detective novel is that the supernatural is acceptable in the former but not in the latter.) Neither good nor evil but Power is the ancient link between magic and religion. This Power has been translated into traditional narrative, Scholes and Kellogg state: "Sacred myth is the link between magic and religion."[41] But whereas the magic of myth and fairy tale, like that of the detective story, intercedes to marshal the forces of good, magic in the Greenean context is limited to intercession of Grace.

Thematic Resemblances

Our five themes—Pursuit, The Quest, Identity and Recognition, The Scapegoat, and Poetic Justice—are all germane to a discussion of Graham Greene. The theme of Identity and Recognition is divided into its separate components: Identity, Doppelgänger, and

Recognition. The Doppelgänger and The Scapegoat are developed more fully than in any of the authors we have previously considered. The logical outcome of Greene's insistence both upon damnation and upon the burden of moral responsibility is a supererogatory identity—the scapegoat; this identity is central to his message and finds its prototype in the figure of Christ.

I. Pursuit

Greene's novels, termed "novels of pursuit" by Roy Fuller, might equally be called "novels of betrayal" or "novels of pity," but there is no gainsaying the fact that Greene's dynamic is pursuit: Raven is pursued in *This Gun for Hire*; D. In *The Confidential Agent*; Hale and Pinkie in *Brighton Rock*; Dr. Czinner in *Orient Express*; Jones in *The Comedians*; Harry Lime in *The Third Man*; Arthur Rowe in *The Ministry of Fear*; the whiskey-priest in *The Power and the Glory*; Andrews in *The Man Within*; Sarah in *The End of the Affair*. But no mere recital of instances can do justice to the centrality of this theme; it is not just a *modus operandi* for Greene the fiction writer, but a *modus vivendi* for his characters.

This pursuit theme derives, first, from Greene's inclination toward the picaresque; like Dickens, he rhythmically alternates pursuit and encounter. These encounters often serve as impediments to the narrative just as they do in fairy tales and in the Morality *Everyman*. The pursuit theme also enables Greene to satisfy his feeling that the ordinary must be enlivened to be made believable: the pursued figure is propelled dramatically across the commonplace background of other lives. Finally, the pursuit theme has acquired a special contemporaneity; the once singular outlaw has become an everyman in our day. Greene shares with Ignazio Silone (*Bread and Wine*) the vision of the political outlaw hounded by government powers; with T.S. Eliot (*The Family Reunion*) the vision of the psychological outlaw pursued by the Eumenides of conscience; with the existentialists the philosophical outlaw, Alice-Through-the-Looking-Glass in a murderously senseless world (e.g., Wormold).[42]

181

In Greene this theme of pursuit, so common in the thriller, goes through new permutations and combinations. Chases reverse, and chases occur within chases. There is the chase conducted simultaneously by and for the character: the first section of *The Confidential Agent* is entitled "The Hunted," the second "The Hunter"—both refer to the same man. In *The Heart of the Matter* Scobie, in his public position as policeman, is a pursuer, but in his private life he is the quarry of love. As the devil pursued Christ into the wilderness to tempt him, Scobie is afraid love tempts him to damnation. Raven, D., Arthur Rowe, are all transformed from hunted to hunter when some vulnerable aspect of their natures is touched. "In both *The Confidential Agent* and *This Gun for Hire* a preoccupation with treachery and a deep emotional upset at an encounter with unselfishness and decency forces the man into the role of an avenging angel."[43] In the thriller, it is rare to find a motive which generates plot action other than self-protection or preservation. But in Greene's entertainments, as well as his novels, events may inspire characters to step out of their roles.

Another of Greene's variations on the theme of pursuit is the character pursued by two destinies, that of the body and that of the soul, the pursuit by the hounds of power and the pursuit by the Hound of Heaven. The secular, or natural, is relatively easy to depict; the supernatural must be implied in the words and thoughts of the pursued. In the later Catholic novels, such as *The Heart of the Matter* and *The End of the Affair,* these two levels are made explicit, but even in the earlier books the religious level is hinted at. Often the secular and the sacred pursuit lines are intertwined so as to enhance each other. Just so, Sarah, in *The End of the Affair,* strikes a bargain with God of which the reader and the other characters are equally ignorant. Her conduct is inexplicable, mysterious, motiveless, subjecting her to the pursuit of the private detective. Simultaneously, Smythe, who represents the rationalist position, pursues non-God. Often the tension of Greene's books devolves upon the unpredictable outcome of concurrent lines of pursuit.

The natural level of the chase produces the hunted man, the supernatural level the haunted man, and these are frequently combined. While Pinkie is pursuing Hale, he is pursuing his own damnation; while Sarah is being pursued by Parkis, she is pursuing her own salvation. Perhaps the best example is the whiskey-priest in *The Power and the Glory,* who is chased simultaneously by the police and by his own spiritual destiny. Francis Kunkel explains:

> The pursuit conducted by the Lieutenant has not the universal im-
> plications to be found in the one conducted by God. Whereas the
> priest is the object of the Lieutenant's search and the locale is Com-
> munist Mexico, the human soul is God's object and the locale is the
> world. The divine pursuit results in metaphysical alchemy: the place,
> the central character, and the central act . . . are all turned into sym-
> bols. Tabasco represents the world as it has existed since the fall of
> Adam; a place where order has been shattered by original sin and a
> people, in consequence, whose minds have been unawakened and in-
> clined towards evil; the Priest represents the search for Everyman
> and the search for the human soul.[44]

Another variation of the pursuit theme is opened up by Greene's dismissal of the simplicistic We-Them formula of the thriller (which consequently elicits a more complex response from the reader). Though Dickens was fascinated by the criminal, for him such a man remained a specimen apart from other men; in Conrad we begin to see some adumbration of the blurring of roles. For Greene this became a major theme. In certain cases—for example, those of Raven and Jim Drover—blame is laid partly at the door of society; this may displace both the earlier "villain ingrato" of melodrama and the moral exclusivity of the detective novel. The villain may be no more than a *poseur,* living by his wits, like Jones in *The Comedians.* The police in *The Power and the Glory* are not caricatures of vicious officialdom; the revolutionaries are not more admirable than the dictator in *Rumour at Nightfall.* Rather than relying on the formulaic, inevitable pursuit of the bad by the good, Greene allows alternatives to be pitted against each other (Ida Arnold against Rose in *Brighton Rock,* the police Lieutenant against the whiskey-priest in *The Power and the Glory*).

The hunt, or pursuit, is very closely tied to the theme of Poetic Justice in Greene's work. Derek Traversi writes:

> Life—or so Greene's characters seem continually tempted to argue—hunts down the isolated victim, worms out of him his most shameful and closely guarded secrets, visits upon him, through his own baffled and inferior emotions, the consequences of his own intimate weakness; and once 'life' has been in some obscure way equated with the operations of destiny, the only possible defence is a gesture of propitiation, the adherence to a rite which is itself imposed upon the individual as something incomprehensible and alien.[45]

(Hence Greene's insistence upon the ritualistic and magical aspects of religion.) Thus the author hunts down his characters in order to demonstrate the workings of providence and providential justice; the motive for pursuit (*and* flight) is often expiation.

By conducting his chase through an innocent milieu (recalling James' "the horrible and sinister embroidered on the very type of the normal and easy")—e.g., the holiday seaside at Brighton, the church fête grounds in *The Ministry of Fear*—Greene achieves an effect equivalent to that of the detective novelist when he places his murder in the least likely place. The juxtaposition, *ipso facto,* increases the suspense by subjecting bystanders to a danger of which they are unaware.

II. The Quest

The Greenean quest resembles most closely the type of the Grail quest—i.e., the search for something once possessed and now lost, specifically something sacramental. Following the picaresque tradition, Greene's characters look for satisfaction outside the establishment. It is not a quest made by necessity, but a movement toward the ideal. However gropingly or reluctantly undertaken, it differs from the Kafkaesque quest in that it is not imposed.

As with Conrad and Dickens, the quest is realized through the journey motif,[46] and Greene's non-fiction (*The Lawless Roads, Journey Without Maps*) illustrates this as well as his fiction (*The Quiet American, The Heart of the Matter, A Burnt-Out Case*). These journeys, in keeping with the tradition of the fairy tale, and again like those of Dickens and Conrad, are solitary, and the traveler is beset by obstacles. Of the nameless priest in *The Power*

184

and the Glory (whose very namelessness signifies that he is Everyman) Karl Patten writes, ". . . in short, like Christian in *The Pilgrim's Progress,* he travels an unknown way, continually meeting portions of his own character, God-ordained obstructions or revelations which eventually help him to his death and salvation."[47] The journey of the priest is a spiritual journey but it is figured forth in his many actual journeyings across the symbolic landscape of Mexico. Greene externalizes the journey, as in the Grail quest (from which all such "treasure quests" as *Treasure Island* surely derive), with the use of maps (a ritual of space) since the journey is actually a movement toward the ideal, an idyll which exists outside time.[48]

By the time *The Quiet American* appeared (1955), however, the early glamour of travel to far-off places (as captured in the title *Orient Express*) had been replaced by a fear of exploration: Fowler's sensation is that strange territory is too near, just across the plank. Here Greene allies himself with Camus's view that the traveler is a mutilated man, the opposite of the reconciled man. Such a rootless creature (alone and afraid in a world he never made) Greene explores in the characters of Brown (*The Comedians*), Wilson (*The Heart of the Matter*), and Querry, who in *A Burnt-Out Case,* seeks solace for his mutilated soul amongst the mutilated bodies of the leprosarium. Thus maps acquire additional significance, marking as they do the changing landmarks, colors, and boundaries which represent moral confusion.

In a sense the Grail quest is partially a search for that lost happiness which tinges Greene's prose with melancholic nostalgia. "Nous étions herureux," Deo Gratias confides to Querry about his childhood at Pendélé.[49] This remembrance of something lost, something connected with our origins before we went astray, is a common memory of that idyllic place in which the fairy tale transpires. It is toward this that Greene directs his allegory. But though he seems to be perpetually searching for the hortus conclusus, he never finds it; Hell is all too oppressively around us. Greene writes:

> The curious wastelands one sometimes saw from trains, the cratered
> ground around Wolverhampton under a cindery sky with a few

cottages grouped like stones among rubbish: those acres of abandoned cars at Slough; the dingy fortune-tellers on the first floor above
the cheap permanent waves in a Brighton back street: they all
demanded violence, like the rooms in a dream where one knows that
something will presently happen—a door flies open or a window
catch gives and lets the end in.[50]

This is why the glimpse of hell in Conan Doyle and John Buchan
interested him so much; he enlarged that glimpse into a vision of
Greeneland.

Ugliness is hellish, but paradoxically also endearing. It is beauty
which is suspect to Greene, a distraction, a facade, unreal. (Thus
we shall find in the next theme, Identity and Recognition, that
Greene's protagonists are most appealing in the light of their
defects or failure.) Hell is essential to Greene, since by his own admission one cannot give up one's grasp of Hell without
simultaneously losing one's intuition of Heaven. Greene's Hell
envelops us verbally through his use of dehumanizing categoriza-
tion, repetition, and his own stylistic mannerism of the threefold
phrase, a sort of dying cadence, suggesting hopelessness. (For example, "he had been slowly broken in by parents, by
schoolmasters, by strangers in the street.")[51] Nothing numinous
shows. This is a world of spiritual emptiness, of man abandoned
by God. Greene's Hell exists in the mind and therefore can exist
anywhere, in that bastion of bourgeois suburbia, Berkhamsted, or
in the great emptinesses of Africa and Mexico, with their burning
heat, buzzards, and flies. From the crowded facelessness of London slums to the literal desert, there are neither romantic views of
the city nor romantic prospects of nature.

Garden images do exist in Greene, but rarely can they be read as
glimpses of the sought-after Eden. For instance, the garden in the
opening scene of *The Ministry of Fear* is full of hidden traps for
Rowe, who burrows blindly, like a mole in a garden laid with
mole-traps. Gwenn Boardman writes about the opening scene of
the church fête in the garden:

Feeling himself both an intruder and an exile, Rowe pays his shilling
'joyfully,' with a child's excitement; he finds himself in the forgotten

world of dreams and romantic distortion. The childhood that Rowe discovers is as terrifying as the childhood of Greene's dreams and memories and as filled with unexplained incidents as the racial childhood of Liberia. Hints of magic are ironically fulfilled: Rowe's 'fairy-tale' wish that he could mislay the events of the past twenty years becomes a fear-filled reality. Stumbling through a 'magic' door in the fortune-teller's tent, and speaking the magic words that guard the secret to the treasure . . . Rowe finds that the world takes 'a strange turn, away from innocence.'[52]

Greene hints again at a religious meaning in the garden of innocence, the apple trees, the magic island. He calls one section of *The Ministry of Fear,* "The Happy Man: Conversations in Arcady." But Arcady is a deception; cruelty and squalor thrive in the nursing home which, at first sunlit and floral, seemed the antithesis of the dark world of London bomb shelters. Rowe is not permitted newspapers in the nursing home; even the illusion of life is bought by filtering reality. Finally Rowe comes to wonder if the nursing home has more reality than "the conception of Hell presented by sympathetic theologians—a place without inhabitants which existed simply as a warning."[53] The deception of Arcady is a taste of Hell. Because original fear, which could be assuaged by Utopian visions or other fictional consolations, is transmuted by Greene to original sin, the pastoral dream cannot be reinstated in this post-lapsarian state.

As a consequence, innocence is a suspect virtue to Greene. It exists at the price of compassion, suffering, even of observation. "Point me out the happy man and I will point you out either extreme egotism, evil—or else an absolute ignorance," he warns us.[54] The nostalgia for childhood is in part nostalgia for *justifiable* innocence. The child is natural victim to the man and, as such, the child represents an innocence which succumbs inevitably to the adult awareness of evil. The experienced Fowler of *The Quiet American,* rather than the idealistic Pyle, is the character towards whom the reader's sympathies are blatantly directed—Fowler does not ignorantly, unsuspectingly, injure others.

The converse of this ignorant or egotistical innocence is the assumption of responsibility for others, the acceptance of the complications and commitments of love and pity. This burden is so great as to make Rowe and Scobie and others who accept it yearn for the peace that only death can bring. Only in Querry is this yearning commingled with *contemptus mundi* (although more probably with *akedeia*). Energy is equated with false heartiness, with Ida Arnold. Greene's hero, worlds away from any *joie de vivre,* longs to be quit of "the battlefield," while valiantly staying the course. (His foreseeable end is that of the scapegoat.)

Similarly the idealist, personified in a character such as the Presidential Candidate (*The Comedians*), fails because his quest is the mistaken one of trying to establish a utopia on earth. The significance that Greene attaches to this idea the reader overhears in Scobie's musings in *The Heart of the Matter*:

> 'Why,' Scobie wondered, swerving the car to avoid a dead pye-dog, 'do I love this place so much? Is it because here human nature hasn't had time to disguise itself? Nobody there could talk about a heaven on earth. Heaven remained rigidly in its proper place on the other side of death, and on this side flourished the injustices, the cruelties, the meanness that elsewhere people so cleverly hushed up.[55]

The counterweight to Hell is not utopia, but Heaven. The idealist's innocence is mistaken, and therefore dangerous. Querry wryly notes, "God preserve us from all innocence. At least the guilty know that they're about."[56]

The garden image arises again in the guise of the nurturing potting shed. Andrews finds refuge there while on the run; in the garden in which Rowe finds himself there is a lavatory "like a potting shed." And in his drama *The Potting Shed,* which expands this image to major proportions, Anne Callifer's dream of a lion that licks her hand recalls for us the prophecies of Isaiah and paintings of The Peaceable Kingdom. The invocation of the Edenic myth is an invocation of the idealized 'once upon a time' time which has been overlaid by the myth of the Fall. In his short story "Under the Garden," Greene composes a legend in which Javitt, guardian of a treasure in the garden, keeps the rites of faith like an ancient oracle. As Greene had written thirty years before in *Orient Express,* "We have been for a thousand years in the wilderness of the Christian world, where only the secret treasure is safe."[57] Here we come again upon the subterranean, Delphic image; if there is a garden, a glimpse of Heaven held in fee in perpetuity, it is fed by hidden springs. "There lives the dearest freshness deep down things."[58]

For Greene the quest inevitably founders on the betrayal which he sees as an omnipresent function of the human condition. "He wondered where the inevitable Judas was sitting now. . . ."[59] Greene himself refers to "the Judas complex"—i.e., his theory that the cruelties and betrayals of adult life are conceived in childhood: "In the lost childhood of Judas/Christ was betrayed."[60] Anne betrays Raven; Conrad betrays Jim; Scobie betrays Ali; Wilson betrays Scobie; Sarah betrays her husband; the mestizo betrays the priest; Parkinson betrays Querry; Dr. Plarr betrays Fortnum. This litany of betrayal (which could be amplified with examples from the whole range of his work) is made all the more poignant by Greene's conception of Judas as a degraded figure of God, not unlike Milton's (and his own) conception of Satan. "I know—from experience—how much beauty Satan carried down with him when he fell. Nobody ever said that fallen angels were the ugly ones. Oh, no, they were just as quick and light. . . ."[61] But Greene himself betrays the quest theme by failing to create men who can overcome their radical corruption. The thriller hero, or the epic hero, is toppled; Greene sniffs suspiciously at heroics and chooses Oliver over Roland (*Chanson de Roland*). His characters can be saved only by Grace (and even that is complicated by Greene's Jansenist sympathies), not by deeds. Virtue, in both its older and more modern meanings, is downgraded. The only commodity worth having is faith, but even that does not insure election. The only quest left intact in Greene's fiction is the quest for expiation. The success of the quest seems at best providential; at worst, capricious.

III. Identity and Recognition

Greene admired Shakespeare for achieving "the perfect dialectical tension"[62] between the Morality (i.e., the drama of abstraction) and the play of character. In his own fiction Greene's characterization is enriched by his ear for dialogue, his eye for details, which turn backdrops into backgrounds from which his characters emerge and then retreat. Nevertheless, Greene's medieval imagination frequently reverts to an Everyman hero and Morality stage conventions: Padre José, the married priest in *The Power and the Glory,* is torn between his seductive angel and his demon child; Scobie's soul is the object of a contest between Yusef and Ali (*The Heart of the Matter*).

But Greene's conception of Everyman is much closer to a hero *manqué*—e.g., Jones, Andrews, the whiskey-priest, Rivas, Padre José. Far removed from the superman or larger-than-life hero of the thriller, these men are smaller-than-life, and have none of the *certitudo salutis* of the medieval Morality figure. At times Greene's comic irony results in a parodic turn, for example in the persons of Brown and Querry. The hero *manqué* of *The Comedians,* Jones, a pseudo-Ché Guevara with flat feet, literally cannot run from his martyrdom. Greene's heroes differ also from the hero of the detective novel who, by annexing the magical qualities of the magus, effects a resolution.

Furthermore, the detective novel understands its world through ratiocination, whereas Greene's world does not yield up its secrets to reason. Sean O'Faolain writes:

> One constant coercion that follows from his treatment of mankind is that their power of intelligent thought is gravely impaired. . . . Nearly all his people are forced to act violently, and to come to disaster.[63]

This is another manifestation of Greene's anti-humanist bias; skeptical of man's dignity and free will, he depicts a creature continually seduced or coerced into sin. We remarked in Chapter III that the ". . . criminal act in *Crime and Punishment* is the outcome of an intellectually and psychologically complex struggle on the part of the protagonist." Pinkie, Raven, even Conrad Drover, are unfit for such a struggle; their struggles already seem more complex than is consistent with their characters. While Dostoevsky demonstrates that criminality may be an assertion of individual intellect in a struggle toward identity and recognition, Greene's fiction does not address itself to this relationship or to the intellectual quest.

Morton Zabel argues that melodrama is a traditional tool for exploring the concealed passages of human nature. Assuredly Greene explores evasion, panic, and fear (even the fear of God)—they pollute the very air of Greeneland—but his characters do not achieve self-mastery; they flounder in the bottomless irrationality which is the source of melodrama. Even those characters who are meant to feel their Gracelessness and desire its opposite—Sarah, Scobie, Querry—cannot reason their way to change. Rationality is not accepted as a step toward spiritual fulfillment. Sarah (*The End of the Affair*) expressly rejects the rational solution represented by Smythe. As O'Faolain charges, for Greene intellection seems to be at odds with faith. Even in those later novels (e.g., *The Comedians, The Honorary Consul*) which temper the bleakness of Greene's earlier outlook, violence and brutality abound; "the dignity of reason" is little in evidence. Thus an impatient reader may feel that the characters forfeit intelligent choices, that Scobie, for example, muddles things hopelessly; this is the view of Sean O'Faolain.

R.W.B. Lewis, on the other hand, maintains that Scobie achieves heroic, and finally tragic, stature. And clearly Pinkie (*Brighton Rock*) is driven and damned; he seems not even to inhabit the "real" world of Brighton but to be pursued by Furies through some private Hell, like Walter in *The Family Reunion*. R.W.B. Lewis explains:

> Evil is fertile and is always heard from again; every move Pinkie makes—from the killing of Hale, through the further necessitated murders and the detested courtship and marriage, to the climax in which, like Oedipus, he blinds himself (with vitriol)—has a compulsive inevitability, the more dreadful since it seems rooted neither in private temperament nor social background.[64]

This is the inevitability of tragedy, not the accident of melodrama.

Though Greene's heroes may impart an impression of passivity, an anti-heroic spirit of *laissez-faire* (Querry, like a French *farceur*, dies at the hands of an irate, but mistaken, husband), this

191

interpretation is mistaken. Fatalism, in Scobie and Querry, is an expression of faith, of leaving destiny to Providence; the anti-heroic posture, a by-product of the longing for peace. "In Thy will is my peace. . . ." The adventure-lust which, like insatiable Don Juanism, demands new conquests perpetually, is drained away by this desire for peace. In *The Honorary Consul,* the erstwhile priest Leon Rivas sighs for the same oblivion:

> 'They have forgotten us,' Aquine said.
>
> 'If only we could believe that,' Father Rivas said. 'To stay here . . . forgotten . . . forever. . . . It would not be so bad, would it?'[65]

The thriller-hero, like the bull-fighter, courts death in order to defy it; Greene's heroes sigh for the relaxation of their mortal burden.

Greene, then, is incurring a two-fold risk: he must maneuver his reader into accepting both the coincidences of the thriller and the illogic of events shaped by Providence. Thus his characters can be weakened by being actors simultaneously in a Morality and in a thriller. They can be too bare, and above all, too predictable. Their characterization can suffer as much because they serve Greene's moral theme as because they rely upon the action of the plot for definition.

A further danger of this thematic shaping of character is that Greene will merely substitute some of the stereotypes of the Catholic novel (for example, that of the "sanctified sinner" with its attendant romanticizing of sin) for those of the crime novel. Whatever the theological dangers that accrue to this notion, the literary danger is an unnecessary reliance upon paradox. Greene, of course, has precedent for the religious tradition of paradox in Tertullian theory: "It is certain because it is impossible." At times Greene handles this paradox very successfully: e.g., in a pivotal scene in *The Power and the Glory* the priest experiences epiphany in the stinking cell in which he is imprisoned. At other times, however, this reliance on paradox dwindles to a weary mannerism.

Greene also borrows from the Catholic novel and allegory in general the conception of character defined by function and revealed by names. He uses several techniques: the repetition of names, which robs many female characters of individuality (Anne or Anna, Mary or Marie, Rose); the specifically allegorical name ("everyman" Brown, Smith, or Jones; "everyman" Mr. Surrogate, the Boy, D.); and the repetition of roles (the lonely isolated man, the child-woman, the grotesque). A more subtle example is the name Wilditch ("Under the Garden") which may be a combination of "wild" plus "ditch," or possibly "wild" plus "eldritch." This subordination of character development to function recalls the construction of other allegorical forms. "While the *dramatis personae* of the fairy tale vary, their allegorical function does not." We can apply what Archibald Coolidge said of Dickens: "Suppose we try substituting Wemmick for Noggs, Smallweed for Bounderby. Can the story go on as before? Certainly." Suppose *we* try substituting Brown for Fowler, Else for Rose. Can the story go on as before? Certainly. What saves these people from becoming abstractions, and the fiction itself from remaining abstract, besides certain stylistic merits to which we have already alluded, are the author's personal obsessive notions which individualize his narratives. Like the hero *manqué,* the other characters who stud his novels and entertainments with strange persistence, personalize them.

One such character is the child-woman, pathetic, gawky, and vulnerable, a modern variant of Dickens' child-brides. The bony knee, the worn slipper, are what wrench the heart. "The greying hair, the lines of nerves upon the face, the thickening body held him as her beauty never had. She hadn't put on her mosquito-boots, and her slippers were badly in need of mending. It isn't beauty we love, he thought, it's failure. . . ."[66] The women in Greene's fiction who elicit our sympathies are never alluring. Indeed, the physical aspects of love emanate most often from the desire to comfort (Conrad Drover, Scobie, Querry, Plarr), not from any fantasies of the erotic. (Scobie imagines his wife under the coverlet as a side of beef.) At best, sex stirs feelings of pity (like those of Scobie for Helen Rolt); at worst, revulsion (Pinkie for Rose). Furthermore, the pathetic and vulnerable are aspects of failure which have always attracted Greene, since he links them to

Christian contrition. Behind this attitude is the hidden equation:

$$\frac{\text{pity}}{\text{mercy}} \quad \frac{\text{(human)}}{\text{(divine)}} = \frac{\text{sex}}{\text{love}} \quad \frac{\text{(human love)}}{\text{(divine love}}$$

The idea of God as an implacable lover in pursuit of His desire, a metaphor familiar in Donne and Herbert for example, operates differently for Greene. The reader is left with an impression of the author's distaste for the physical, as if human love were a travesty of the sacred form, not a preparation for it.

The child-women (Rose in *The Living Room,* Mme. Rycker in *A Burnt-Out Case,* Helen Rolt in *The Heart of the Matter,* Else in *The Confidential Agent,* Clara in *The Honorary Consul*), are continuations of the lost childhood—seeking security, courageous, under no illusions (it is their realistic appraisal of their chance for happiness in life that undercuts the nominally happy ending), and yet retaining hope of man's goodness. The nostalgia which surrounds the child obtains partly because the child is still a believer, hoping for goodness. (As I commented before, the child has forgivable innocence.) Anthony and Kate in *England Made Me,* Mr. and Mrs. Fellowes in *The Power and the Glory,* are Babes-in-the-Wood.

Though the figure of the lost child and the child-woman recur with such frequency, the counterpoise figure of the benevolent guardian, father, grandfather, so familiar in fairy tale and so featured in Dickens, is missing. The lack of such a figure partially explains what in the lost childhood has been lost. The child-hero, such as Coral or Rose, may recall a Platonic state of harmony, a fairy-tale world. For Greene, childhood, like the allegorical narrative, provides a temporary reconciliation between the individual and society. But these figures are also psychologically explicable as the incarnation of Greene's own obsessions: "Like Dickens, he . . . found images of childhood fears that are never outgrown."[67]

In his imaginative reconstruction of the child-victim as lost-child, Greene resembles Dickens (Scobie's dead daughter, the child in Querry's parable). "He could hear the heavy, uneven breathing of the child. It was as if she were carrying a weight with great effort up a long hill: it was an inhuman situation not to be able to carry it up for her."[68] This description of the shipwrecked child in *The Heart of the Matter* echoes uncannily Dickens' description of the boy Jo's death in *Bleak House:* "For the cart so hard to draw is near its journey's end, and drags over stony ground. All round the clock, it labors up the broken steps, shattered and worn."[69]

Not only the child-women are rendered appealing because of their vulnerability. Male characters in the novels frequently bear marks of their childhood: Raven and his harelip, Philip and his painful precocity. "The adult world prematurely forced upon Philip a sense of responsibility and an awareness of the horrors of violent action."[70] Minty and Wilson touch us with their frailties; Krogh's baffled attempt to establish rapport with his workers animates him for a single moment; Mr. Surrogate's posturing at the mirror reveals a man behind the platitudes.

Greene's motif of the lost childhood merges with his concern for the alienated, isolated individual, which, as J.H. Plumb tells us, holds that centrifugal place in literature today which the concern with beneficence held in the eighteenth century. Like Conrad's Razumov, Kurtz, Lord Jim, and Heyst, Greene's Rowe, Raven, D., and Czinner are all solitaries. Nor is isolation preempted by the criminal. Although many characters in Greene's fiction are isolated because they are outlaws (e.g., Czinner, Raven, and Hale), Conrad Drover is isolated by his intelligence; Louise, Minty, Anthony, Kate, and Wilson are isolated because they are displaced persons.

Just as these isolated individuals share a common guilt and a common loneliness, they are often shaped into a common physical clump, labelled Bystanders: Bystanders are in the background of Jim Drover's calamitous defense of his wife; Bystanders comprise the holiday throngs in *Brighton Rock* and *The Ministry of Fear;* Bystanders are the Roman soldiers standing-by at the Crucifixion, Scobie thinks. The literary associations are those of the nameless, faceless mass hurrying over London Bridge in *The Waste Land.*

Greene continually relies on the map metaphor to illustrate the struggle his characters experience in establishing an identity separate from "the nameless, faceless mass." Though Ida's face is

195

"a map of experience," she has no map for understanding Rose and Pinkie, no map for Hell. In *The Heart of the Matter,* Scobie's map has been borrowed by one of the younger officers; Scobie mistakenly believes that he knows the district "by heart." In *The Confidential Agent,* D. perceives his world in terms of the map: Where can I belong? Where am I safe? The fugitive Czinner carries a map whose meaning he cannot read. The superimposition of the metaphoric upon the literal level is seen most clearly in the metaphor comparing the human heart to a geographical territory: Greene speaks of Africa as being "roughly the shape of a human heart"; he maintains that just as there are blank spaces on the maps of Mexico and Africa, so there are blank spaces on the map of the human heart. The epigraph of *The Heart of the Matter* reads, "Man has places in his heart which do not yet exist, and into them enters suffering in order that they have esistence." Greene also quotes from Kurt Heuser's African novel *The Inner Journey* to amplify his meaning. " 'The interior': that might signify the heart of a continent, but also the heart of things, the mystery: and finally, the comprehension of himself in nature and in time."[71] From this one might infer that Greene would endow his characters with an historical sense necessary for a synthesis of identity. But in fact Greene's characters remain captives of their own time, with no conscious historical perspective. While the author's own interest in the primitive may be partially an attempt to recapture a sense of racial history, his characters do not seem to benefit from it in their searches for identity.

In the context of Greeneland, men have lost touch with each other. The fear of betrayal, the acknowledgment of duplicity, make man a loner. As we noted before, ". . . suspicion, distrust, treachery and fear are signs of the great aboriginal calamity."[72] But primarily loneliness betokens man's spiritual exile. While isolation may result from outlawry (secular law) or displacement (Fate), it stems most importantly from a condition outside Grace: isolation from God. The recognition man seeks which is most precious is a token of a compact with God, not the approbation of a community.

Gracelessness is mimicked in the arrested, grotesque natures of many of the characters: Drewitt, Acky, Minty, Rennitt, the

196

diabolical child in *The Power and the Glory*. "These stunted, perverse natures come from the same place as Dickens' Quilp or Krook, but Greene is more aware of their origin and the serious use to be made of them."[73] These are not the easily deflatable caricatures of Dickens, though a list of their occupations sounds remarkably Dickensian. Greene himself observed, "the truth is seldom tragic, for human beings are not made that grand way. . . . [Truth] is nearly always grotesque [i.e., part of comedy] as well."[74] Just as the grotesque measures the discrepancy between the norm and an inferior version of it, the whiskey priest and the mestizo who betrays him form a grotesque parallel to Christ and Judas.[75] It is this model behind it which adds such resonance to the novel.

Like Conrad, Greene seldom obfuscates or completely conceals identity (there are exceptions, such as the Nazi in *The Ministry of Fear*, the identity of the villain, Mr. Visconti, in *Travels with My Aunt*), despite the fact that concealment is *de rigueur* in the thriller. This is because the elusive quarry, sometimes at the center, sometimes hovering about the edges of the novel, is not the elusive Pimpernel of romance, but an elusive Deity. The incessant conscience-probing of such protagonists as Conrad Drover, Sarah, and Scobie is proof that for Greene the question of identity is overwhelmingly a moral one. "The identity Greene's heroes seek is that of a conscience that shirks none of the deception or confusion of their natures. If the 'destructive element' of social anarchy threatens them, it is the passion for moral energy which redeems them."[76] It is the blight of self-deception which cripples Rowe and Pyle, Minty and Anthony, not only concealing identity, but, as a consequence, impeding salvation. Furthermore, this personal moral identity must be discovered despite the moral anarchy which surrounds it; indeed, because of the moral anarchy which threatens it.

Kunkel believes the conflict between anarchy and conscience to be the essence of Greene's allegory. In Greene's terms, this is really the conflict between the human, which is anarchic, and the divine, which alone conceives order. The conflict between human-anarchic and divine-ordered is a modern restatement of the struggle in Greek tragedy between freedom and fate. Thus the novels of Greene provide the material for potential tragedy.

The moral identity Greene is concerned with, then, has nothing to do with conventional morality. As Morton Zabel writes, the character may be ". . . marked, hunted, or condemned. He may work for evil or for good. . . ."[77] Thus the individual efforts of Scobie, Sarah, or the whiskey-priest to reconcile all the diversities of their natures, may account for an unheroic posture of recalcitrance. As R.W.B. Lewis informs us, such characters represent the "shifting and interwoven attributes of the Greenean man: a being capable of imitating both Christ and Judas, a person who is at once the pursuer and the man pursued; a creature with a splendid potentiality either of damnation or salvation."[78] Greene himself, discussing Frederick Rolfe, declared, "The greatest saints have been men with more than a normal capacity for evil, and the most vicious men have sometimes narrowly evaded sanctity."[79]

The Scapegoat

Martyrdom is, obviously, the extreme expression of victim-as-hero, the voluntary scapegoat. As we prick ourselves with a pin to insure we are not dreaming, so Greene seems to require perpetual pain as the very test of existence. "I suffer, therefore I am," O'Faolain subtitles his essay on Greene, and accuses Greene's heroes of deliberately seeking martyrdom. In *The Heart of the Matter* Scobie charges: "Christ had not been murdered—you couldn't murder God. Christ had killed himself: he had hung himself on the Cross as surely as Pemberton from the picture rail."[80] Because of his empathic participation in the lives of a multitude of characters—Helen Rolt, Louise, Wilson, the Portuguese captain, Ali, his dead child, the victims he encounters performing his police duties—Scobie's death serves as a communal sacrifice. In his desperate desire to insure the well-being of others, he takes the risk of self-defilement.

Scobie's scapegoat role is explicit. "His eye went back to the letter: My darling, this is serius. Serius—his eye this time read it as servus—a slave; a servant of the servants of God. It was like an unwise command which nonetheless he had to obey." And elsewhere in the same novel:

The lights were showing in the temporary hospital, and the weight of that misery lay on his shoulders. It was as if he had shed one responsibility only to take on another. This was the responsibility he shared with all human beings, but that was no comfort for it sometimes seemed to him that he was the only one who recognized his responsibility.[81]

In exactly the same way, the drunken priest in *The Power and the Glory* feels "like the King of a West African tribe, the slave of his people, who may not even lie down in case the wind should fail."[82] In this passage, Greene connects the priest not just with Christian tradition but also with the earlier sacrificial deities described in *From Ritual to Romance* and *The Golden Bough*: this would seem to confirm O'Faolain's charge that Greene's heroes seek martyrdom deliberately. We would compare the whiskey-priest's role and attitude with the dictum of William Empson about the hero:

The tragic hero was a king on sacrificial as well as Aristotelian grounds; his death was somehow on his tribe's account, something like an atonement for his tribe that put it in harmony with God, or nature.[83]

The Doppelgänger

Greene admired Robert Louis Stevenson (a remote relation), and that author's use of the doppelgänger in *The Strange Case of Dr. Jekyll and Mr. Hyde* and *Weir of Hermiston*. The theme of man's divided nature is dominant in Greene's early work (*The Man Within, Rumour at Nightfall, The Name of Action*) and is captured in the quotation from Sir Thomas Browne which Greene selected as the epigraph for *The Man Within:* "There's another man inside me that's angry with me." In *The Man Within* the dualism of Andrews' nature surfaces in his relationships with two other characters, Lucy and Elizabeth. In *England Made Me,* two brothers, Conrad and Jim Drover, serve this purpose; in *It's a Battlefield* the sister and brother, Kate and Anthony Farrant, project an androgynous whole; in *The Ministry of Fear* Arthur Rowe's amnesia makes one man both murderer and detective, the same double identity which Oedipus assumes.

The most extended and serious treatment which this motif receives is in the figures of the priest and the lieutenant in *The Power and the Glory*. The strength of their hatred establishes a magnetic field in which they struggle, an intensity that leads to intimacy. The two protagonists are even described in terms of each other. Thus, the lieutenant has "something of the priest in his intent observant walk." His room is "comfortless as a prison or monastic cell."[84] They exemplify that special attraction between pursued and pursuer.

In *The Power and the Glory* Greene uses the doppelgänger motif to portray a situation of modern moral anarchy. Though the priest and the lieutenant may be two halves, the lieutenant's half lacks ritual and scope, and he loses his disciple, Luis, to the priest. Throughout the novel the lieutenant pursues the priest and, unwittingly, his own identity. The map metaphor forms in the minds of both characters. Priest and lieutenant each desire a kind of justice; both are slaves to their mission. The recognition of responsibility is part of the burden of the dedicated life.

We are vouchsafed a less conventional form of doubling in *Brighton Rock,* in which one character embodies seemingly antithetical potentialities. Pinkie, Greene's most Dostoevskian character, revolts against God and is obsessed with suicide (like characters in *The Possessed*), yet is closer to God than Ida. Pinkie's Hell is the antithesis of Heaven; Ida understands neither. The whiskey-priest is closer to God than the policeman. "Corruptio optimi est pessima. . . . The worst is a corruption of the best," the priest quavers in *Brighton Rock*.[85] The likeness between the sanctified and the bedeviled and their mutual superiority over the trimmer would seem to rest upon verses 14-16, Book of the Revelation: "I know thy works, that they are neither cold nor hot; I would thou wert cold or hot. So then, because thou are lukewarm, and neither cold nor hot, I will spew thee out of my mouth." In much the same way, Dr. Colin muses about Querry (*A Burnt-Out Case*): "The better the man, the worse the aridity."[86] Thus Greene's identity scheme is really based upon the mutual exclusion of those who live on the natural level of right and wrong, and those who live on the supernatural level of good and evil. The flaw in this scheme, as Francis Kunkel discerns, is that God also created the natural world, and Grace supplements, not supplants, nature. The relationship between Ida's world and that of Pinkie and Rose, writes R.W.B. Lewis, is "the relation Greene had formulated for himself in Liberia, between the 'sinless empty graceless chromium world' of modern Western urban civilization and the supernaturally infested jungle with its purer terrors and keener pleasures."[87] If we wish to appreciate the particular bias of Greene's position, we have but to transplant Ida into a Shakespearian context: beery, blowsy, warmhearted, loving, she would descend straight from the nurse in *Romeo and Juliet*.

The same difficulties which confront the character attempting a comprehensive moral identity—i.e., those difficulties constituent upon denial or deception or confusion—face Greene in his construction of a convincing theology. The problem of reconciling injustice and evil with the existence of a covenant repeatedly leads to paradox and coincidence in his prose, and to theological speculation:

> The God I believe in must be responsible for all the evil as well as all the saints. He has to be God made in our image with a night side as well as a day side. When you speak of the horror . . . you're talking of the night side of God. I believe the time will come when the night side will wither away . . . and we shall only see the simple daylight of the good God. . . .[88]

Greene has arrived at the point where he is employing the doppelgänger motif in his intimation of God.

"There, but for the grace of God, go I" perfectly expresses both Greene's affinity for the doppelgänger and the religious framework in which he sets it.

Recognition

Although Greene is one of the few major contemporary writers who has never forsaken conventional plot development, the religious framework lends his plots a special interpretation: plot as conspiracy—a conspiracy with God, a covenant. It is some recognition of this conspiracy which Greene's heroes seek. It is the foundation of identity. Reynolds Price explains:

> Since *Brighton Rock* (1938) Greene's fiction has been the search for the existence of that conspiracy at the center, a conspiracy on the part of a Creator God and his ministers (human and otherwise) to lure a renegade, reprobate character back to Himself, towards rest. . . .[89]

Confirmation of the plot or conspiracy may be inferred from the image of God as the pursuing lover, but more particularly from the comic format of the later novels, from their resolution through the final administration of justice, albeit delayed or painful.

Unlike Conrad, Greene maintains a distinction between mysterious and mystery, the secrets of conspirators and the arcana of The Great Conspirator. They are consciously juxtaposed in his drama *The Potting Shed,* which Bertram Cottrell calls "the apotheosis of Greene's search pattern," comparing it to *Hamlet* and *Oedipus* and *Crime and Punishment.*[90] The mysteries of divine love are felt as "something outside that has to come in," to use Greene's own definition. In *The Heart of the Matter* Scobie forsakes Aristides the Just in his struggle to accommodate that immanent spirit. And that struggle to respond ennobles the humblest characters: "The scapegoat self-defilement of the Curé d'Ars, the challenge made by Péguy, reappear in the selfless, defiant passion of a little waitress [*Brighton Rock*] ready to forego salvation because her lover must be damned."[91] Greene's work is visionary in exactly the same sense that he brings visions of another world into this one.

The reward of creating a moral identity is, finally, the recognition of a covenant for man inseparable from Poetic Justice. This is the Grail which was sought.

Poetic Justice

Oh, there is a sort of comfort in reading a story where one knows what the end will be. The story of a dream world where justice is always done. There were no detective stories in the age of faith—an interesting point when you think of it. God used to be the only detective when people believed in Him. He was law. He was order. He was

good. Like your Sherlock Holmes. It was he who pursued the wicked
man for punishment and discovered all. . . .

Graham Greene, *The Honorary Consul*

For Graham Greene, there are two kinds of justice, man's and
God's; but only the second matters. *It's a Battlefield* destroys any
hope of a comprehensible idea of secular justice. Milly Drover's
scornful dismissal of legal proceedings, "I don't want justice, I've
seen enough of it, I was in court everyday."[92] recalls not just the
hypocrisy and wastage of Jarndyce vs. Jarndyce in *Bleak House,*
but also Winnie Verloc's more devastating intuition, "Things
don't bear looking into," in *The Secret Agent.* The phrase,
"vengeance is mine, saith the Lord," assumes importance for
Greene in direct proportion to the failure of man's justice. In
Brighton Rock, Ida takes it upon herself to become Hale's
avenger, playing detective, judge, and jury. But, "pursuing 'fun'
rather than the justice she overtly seeks, Ida reveals the weakness
of our secular society"[93] and necessarily fails as avenger. Rowe
practices euthanasia upon his wife, appointing himself judge of
her suffering, and then is tormented by doubts about the purity of
his motives. Rowe (like Scobie in *The Heart of the Matter*) cannot
bear to inflict or watch pain; but this too is a kind of hubris, an implicit denial of God's will. In *It's a Battlefield,* the prison (the visible symbol of secular justice done) is caustically described as a
hybrid of zoo and factory; and the Inspector from Scotland Yard,
a former Colonial adminstrator, wished himself back amidst the
simplicities of the jungle. The conflict between sympathy and duty
is one of the skirmishes of the battlefield, leaving the protagonist
irresolute in his attempts to administer justice.

Both the priest in *The Living Room* and the priest in *The Heart
of the Matter* speak against the obvious condemnation of hero or
heroine. "We can't tell," is even the considered consolation of the
institutionalized Church. Pity, too, constitutes a kind of judgment
and is to be abjured. "Who were they to pity him?" the Boy asks
himself in *Brighton Rock.* Pity is the debasement of mercy.

Man has neither the omniscience to arrive at a judgment, nor the
omnipotence to execute justice. In the entertainments, even a
spokesman for justice is frequently lacking. In the novels,
however, one of the characters is usually "on God's side"—for

example, Sarah in *The End of the Affair*. Sometimes Greene presents us with a devil's advocate, a plausible spokesman for secular justice—e.g., Dr. Colin in *A Burnt-Out Case*.

Repeatedly, Greene brings the worlds of imperfect justice and Poetic Justice into collision. (Secular justice, as Chance, is parodied in ferocious games of chance—e.g., the chess game of *Our Man in Havana*, the poker game of *England Made Me*, the dice game in *The Quiet American*.) As the detective story and the tragedy intertwine in *Brighton Rock*, "we find ourselves in a universe wherein seeming opposites—good and evil—become closely allied, and seeming likenesses the good and the right—are totally opposed."[94] Their only possible relation is the paradox of the Catholic novel. What Greene has done in *Brighton Rock* is to take the pivotal murder of a detective novel and demonstrate instead "the workings of providential justice through the logical implications of a crime."[95]

Obviously, the workings of providential justice stand revealed in the conclusions. We have seen that secular justice (the detective novel) is unacceptable to Greene, but even the probability of providential justice (the Catholic novel) fails to provide completely reassuring conclusions; behind the happiness of lovers finally united stands the history of violence which preceded their union. Though Rivas in *The Honorary Consul* derives solace from the perusal of a detective novel, Greene does not allow his readers this specious security.

Greene's private vision focuses on evil. As a result, his conclusions are often equivocal, occasionally tragic, although in Greene, as in Dostoevsky, "the promise of salvation lurks behind each novel."[96] The problem which presents itself to Greene is to reconcile the novelist's creativity and the archetypes of Catholicism, the aesthetically pleasing solution and the theologically correct one (one paradox he may not have reckoned with). Thus, though Greene rejects the mechanical contrivance of the detective novel with its invariable solution, his own inflexible formula also relies upon contrivance. The progress toward an ideal moral solution may be too quirky to be felt as convincing, the solution itself too adventitious (particularly the suggestion of Grace as a *deux ex machina*). His preoccupation with damnation leaves us emotionally unprepared for solutions, and though the fallen world no doubt implies a previous, non-fallen state, Greene runs the risk of stranding his reader in the wasteland. When he fails to convince, the unhappy ending seems as forced as the happy one.

Before commencing a close examination of the structural resemblances between the Greenean novel and the crime novel, a few words need to be said about the classification of Greene's "novels" and "entertainments." Though Greene adds the subtitle, "An Entertainment," to certain of his novels, his design is still more than formulaic. Of *The Confidential Agent* (an "entertainment") he declared his desire was to "create something legendary out of the thriller."[97] The distinction between Greene's "novels" and "entertainments" must be held to be inexact. The first American edition of *Brighton Rock* labeled it an "entertainment," though now it is commonly held to be one of his more serious statements. *The Collected Edition of Graham Greene* (which began publication in England in 1971) designates all of his output as "novels," thereby gratifying those readers who have long held that both *The Ministry of Fear* and *The Confidential Agent* are worthy of serious attention.

Because allegory admits of much compression, the entertainments were able to serve as rehearsals for the novels. R.W.B. Lewis writes:

> Each of these three novels *Brighton Rock, The Power and the Glory, The Heart of the Matter* has its correlative entertainment—a mystery story, in the popular sense, that functions ably as a trial run for a mystery drama in a more ancient and theological sense. . . .[98]

Furthermore, characters in the entertainments are often condensations of those in the novels: Raven/Pinkie; D./Major Scobie; Else/Milly Drover. Nevertheless, certain generalizations about the differences may be ventured:

1. The entertainments seem to be more melodramatic because the violence is more sudden and less well rooted in character.

205

2. There is less character development in the entertainments.
3. The entertainments make some concession to the happy ending. (In fact, this compromise consists of a nominally happy ending that is not emotionally convincing.)
4. There are more background characters in the entertainments.
5. The pace of the entertainments is faster.
6. There is a greater reliance on coincidence and generally slacker structure (though there is dependence on coincidence in the novels also).

All Greene's works are entertaining; all are carefully paced and use, variously, befuddlement, concealment, chase, detection. Among the novels it could be pointed out that *The End of the Affair* clings to many of the cliff-hanging devices of melodrama such as retardation, shift in narrative point of view for the prolongation of suspense, and diversionary asides. *The Power and the Glory* is constructed in the episodic fashion which the thriller inherited from the picaresque encounter system; *Brighton Rock,* claims R.W.B. Lewis, betrays a confusion of kinds between entertainment and tragedy (though Greene exploits this disparity to organize the book); *The Third Man* contains a similar confusion of kinds, but in less fortuitous combination; *A Burnt-Out Case* has been termed "a spiritual melodrama" by Francis Wyndham. Conversely, it must be conceded that even the entertainments embody changes of tempo based upon alternation of emphasis between character and action, motive and suspense. They are ingeniously plotted, authenticated by the scrupulous observation of contemporaneous detail and by the inclusion of autobiographical material. The fears about which Greene reminisces in his autobiographical prose (*The Lost Childhood and Other Essays, A Sort of Life*) are consistently woven into his fiction, thereby giving melodrama psychological reality and making obsessions credible. In fact, this is true to such a degree that in a certain sense all Greene's fiction may be read as a serial, whether entertainment, Catholic or political novel. Despite his interest in fairy tale, parable, and legend, Greene does not so much employ cultural archetypes as attempt to render his own inventions archetypal.

First and foremost, however, Greene's novels and entertainments are linked by the fact that both are modeled into allegory. Morton Zabel writes:

> His superiority to the convention in which he worked was clear; if at times it ran uncomfortably close to the jigsaw manipulations which entertainers like Ambler, Hammett and Raymond Chandler make so readable and finally so trivial, there was always working in it a poetry of desperation and an instinct for the rudiments of moral conflict that lifted it to allegoric validity.[99]

And it is the allegory which is in some measure responsible for the insistent melodrama. What Lord David Cecil said of the plays of John Webster can be applied verbatim to the fiction of Greene: ". . . the battle of heaven and hell cannot be convincingly conveyed in a mode of humdrum everyday realism. . . . The wild and bloody conventions of Elizabethan melodrama provided a most appropriate vehicle for conveying his hell-haunted vision of human existence."[100]

Nevertheless, Greene wrote in the Preface to *The Third Man* that the entertainment was "too light an affair to carry the weight of an unhappy ending," claiming that he used reality, in such fiction, only as a "background to a fairy tale." The true fairy tale usually does end happily; Greene's entertainments in a similar fashion, have a nominally happy ending, but even these contain many hints of Purgatory. For example, Rowe (*The Ministry of Fear*) will be returning to a world which has lost its innocent burnish forever. This kind of tempered ending is also found in *The Confidential Agent, This Gun for Hire,* and *The Third Man.*

The serious view of life which is our expectation of the novel means, functionally, that the element of irony is taken seriously, not viewed as accidental or coincidental, but as a commentary upon life, to be interwoven with the attributes of the characters. It is this that enables Greene's novels to become tragedies, when they do. Conversely, the entertainments may be less affecting because their rapid tempo precludes a causal relationship between character and event. The entertainments may induce sadness in the reader, but not reach tragedy. Though the novels may utilize the same melodramatic incidents and effects, the composition as a whole is altered by an alteration of emphasis. R.W.B. Lewis cites *The Heart of the Matter* as the final transmutation of entertainment into novel bcause such melodramatic components as the suicide of Scobie, the death of a child, a shipwreck, and the murder of Ali, are all subordinated to the ''drama of Scobie's soul.'' This shift of balance from entertainment to novel is reflected, as well, in the more digressive, discursive pace of this book.

Structural Resemblances

Throughout his career, Greene borrowed freely from the devices of the crime novel. The parallelism between entertainment and detective novel is predictable: the device of delay in *This Gun for Hire,* where the real motive is not disclosed until more than halfway through the book; Else's last-minute rescue of D. as he is being interrogated in *The Confidential Agent,* and her adventitious appearance at an unlikely time and place; the closed community of *Orient Express. The Ministry of Fear* immerses us immediately in mystery and melodrama. For whom was the clue in the cake intended? Why does it portend danger for Rowe? What is Rowe's own secret? But further documentation of crime novel technique in the entertainments is superfluous. The surprise lies in how much Greene has retained, how little abandoned, of the structural characteristics of the crime novel in his more serious fiction:

1. the sprinkling of clues, and/or the false solution
2. deliberate retardation
3. alternation of plot lines for the prolongation of suspense
4. concealment of relevant information
5. the use of sensation
6. the interview
7. the confrontation

The chase is Greene's favorite plot line, and the above devices, singly or in combination, implement its suspense. The choice of milieu—an underworld peopled by spies and police and agents —he inherits from the *roman policier* and the romance, renewed by the vogue of cinéma vérité (whose technique parallels closely that of the *roman policier*). Cinéma vérité, as we have said, may well be responsible for Greene's visual heightening of suspense by the use of the odd angle of vision and/or the disquieting juxtaposition.

Although Allott and Farris claim that "in the last period of Greene's work it is easy to detect some contempt for the *mise en scène* of the detective story or the spy story,"[101] Greene was not successful in sloughing them off, if such were his intention. Greene's novels and plays consistently resort to the catalyst of violence. *The Honorary Consul* (1973) focuses on a political kidnapping, and one of the characters, Rivas, is committed to political violence as a considered philosophy. Melodrama even surfaces in the metaphors: "When he bent to kiss her cheek he could smell the hot chocolate in her cup like a sweet breath from the tomb."[102] Violence also produces the adventitious ending of melodrama: *A Burnt-Out Case* is "solved" by the death of Querry; *The Power and the Glory* is "solved" by the death of the whiskey-priest. The death of Conrad Drover in *It's a Battlefield* is a sensational death; the physical details are dwelt upon in such a way as to heighten the shock.

The End of the Affair affords the most interesting example of the "kidnapping"[103] of crime novel technique, for it was Greene's declared intention to forswear melodrama in that work. Yet we find it contains pursuit and a detective, the sprinkling of clues (e.g., Sarah's fingerprints on the doorknob), a false solution (Sarah's love interest). The heroine strikes a self-sacrificing bargain with God, in itself a melodramatic idea. The novel utilizes the service of a grotesque boy-detective, reminiscent of the legion of demon imps in Dickens. Furthermore, as Ursula Spier notices, by concealing from the reader the fact of Sarah's Catholic birth, her motive for renouncing her lover Maurice in order to 'love the sores of the leper' remains mysterious. "Greene holds out the information until the proper time exactly as does the author of a detective story."[104] Spier asserts that Greene adds the cliff-hanging suspense of melodrama to the device of concealment when he delays revelation through the insertion of authorial marginalia:

Henry says, 'Bendrix, I'm worried.' 'Tell me,' answers Bendrix.

But Greene isn't going to let Henry reply so quickly. He discusses first whether it is the rum the men have been drinking that is going to be responsible for Henry's willingness to confide. And then he relates some interesting details about Henry that help characterize him—his sleeping habits, a birthmark, the significance of his near-sightedness and his reluctance to wear glasses in public. Then he lets Bendrix wonder if Henry knows how much Bendrix knows about him. Only after all this is Henry allowed to say something again: 'I'm worried about Sarah, Bendrix.' One would think that suspense had really been heightened sufficiently by now. But Greene chooses to make some comments about the bar, and about Henry's eyes, and then Henry says, 'Bendrix, I can't talk here.'

So we must go with the two men across the Common, after the drinks are paid for, and Greene stops to remark upon how Henry is about money, and how different it is for him to accept someone's hospitality. Then we go into Henry's study, and the decor of the room and the significance of the books and furnishings are discussed. Only when the men have settled in their armchairs and drinks have been poured do we get a little more. 'What's troubling you, Henry?' Bendrix asks. Henry answers, 'Sarah.' But just exactly what is troubling him about Sarah is not disclosed until several pages further on.[105]

Such instances can be readily multiplied. The point is that this novel, ostensibly a love story, tricked out as a pursuit story, but actually a parable about grace, does not successfully discard the formulaic except insofar as it turns its back on both the exotic locale and Greeneland and substitutes the suburban setting that figures again in *The Complaisant Husband* and *Travels with My Aunt*. Greene has set the familiar machinery of melodrama in gear, even though the interest of the novel purportedly lies in the emotions of the characters. But it is not a novel of manners, and it has nothing whatever to do with morality. It is a Morality. " 'Adultery' and 'remorse' like 'private detective' and 'the unknown man' are stock properties Greene takes over to explore a theme connected neither with morality nor detection."[106]

Again, in *The Power and the Glory* Greene employs the techniques of the crime novel to convey his Catholic message. This novel utilizes a flight and pursuit pattern and the mystery novel's deliberate retardation. The continuous motion of the priest's escape is interrupted by a quiescent interlude: "The Mission across the mountain on the further side of the border has something of the effect of Pilgrim's stay in the House Beautiful in *Pilgrim's Progress.*"[107] The Mission functions as a midway station, affording a glimpse of the lost Eden; it also permits that momentary lull which, by effectively postponing the dénouement, increases the narrative's suspense.

In *Brighton Rock,* Greene retards progress by switching narrators continually. The closer we come to the climax, the more frequent the alternation, frustrating the *éclaircissement,* a familiar Dickensian practice.

In *The Potting Shed,* a search for a lost identity replaces a literal chase and evasion with a psychological one, and the action thriller is transmuted into a psychological thriller. Mystery is present in abundance: what event precipitated the protective layering of forgetfulness? Does some crime lie concealed in the past? Clues are distributed and pieced together, tempting the audience to a false conclusion. The crime, in fact, was an abortive suicide attempt, a spiritual crime, not a civil one. Francis Wyndham, observing this combination of form and content, has dubbed the drama a "spiritual detective story."[108]

In the crime novel the confrontation between the forces of good and evil is often enacted by the archetypal figures of the law-giver and the law-breaker. In Greene's case this is subtly altered, for the representative of secular law may, ironically, also be the law-breaker. Thus in *The Comedians* the Ton-Ton Macoute, the official government police, are cruel travesties of the constabulary. The entire book operates as a series of magic lantern slides of interviews and confrontations—the interview of the detective novel whose purpose is to glean information, and the confrontation of the allegory whose purpose is to throw its dialectic into relief. There is an interview between Brown and Jones on the ship; a confrontation between Brown and his mistress; a confrontation between Brown and the Presidential Condidate; a confrontation between the Presidential Candidate and the Ton-Ton Macoute; an interview between Brown and his mistress's husband; an interview between Brown and his mother's lover; a confrontation between Brown and an officer of the Ton-Ton Macoute in a brothel; an interview between Jones and the Presidential Candidate while the former is in jail; an interview between Brown and Dr. Magiot. Nor is *The Comedians* singular in this regard; the confrontations between the whiskey-priest and the lieutenant (*The Power and the Glory*), like engagements in a moral duel, come to mind; the self-revelatory interviews between Scobie and the Portuguese captain (*The Heart of the Matter*); Sarah's supernatural confrontation with God, objectified by her bargain (*The End of the Affair*). It may be objected that the interview, and indeed the confrontation, are indispensable to any novel with individual characters, and do not belong exclusively to the crime novel. If they are, however, they are put to the same purpose in all novels—that is, to slowly release morsels of information so as to increase tension; the story is alternately obscured and illuminated.

In Greene's fiction the revelations of the interview and the confrontation are augmented by the confession (*The Third Man, The End of the Affair*), which has the advantage of simultaneously imparting information and tidying up the conclusion, much in the manner of the detective novel's exegesis.[109] Greene's use of the exegetical confession has its roots not only in the spy story but also in the pathos of the romance. The most obvious of Greene's models for the exegetical confession is the actual religious ritual of confession.

The confession which finds no audience is conveyed to the reader through the dream mechanism. In *The Confidential Agent,* for example, Raven's dreams are fused with the desperate need he feels (like that of the child), to confess. Greene's travel books recount his own dreams; in *The Ministry of Fear* a whole chapter is devoted to that state of semi-somnolence between sleeping and waking. But whereas the dreams in Conrad's novels seem involuntary, seem to contain a truth buried too deep for words or daylight observation, Greene's have an air of arrangement and seem an obvious authorial strategy. In his short story "Under the Garden," Greene shows only a marginal interest in the dream as a revelation of the unconscious. The character Wilditch asserts ironically, "A dream can only contain what one has experienced, or if you have sufficient faith in Jung, what your ancestors have experienced."[110] Greene's faith in Jung is clearly limited; the dreams he creates contain few archetypal images, all of which seem to be planted dangerously close to the surface.

Francis Kunkel makes a distinction between the manner in which dreams function in the entertainment—exaggeration of reality—and in the novel—intensification of reality. Except for *The Power and the Glory* and *The Heart of the Matter,* in which the dream is extended by quotation and reverie, Greene's dream generally remains external, an internalization of the action of the novel. For example, Martins, Harry Lime's friend in *The Third Man,* is looking for Lime under circumstances that create suspicion and great anxiety, and Martins dreams:

> He was tired: he realized that when he stretched himself out on his bed in his boots. Within a minute he had left Vienna far behind him and was walking through a dense wood, ankle-deep in snow. An owl hooted, and he felt suddenly lonely and scared. He had an appointment to meet Harry under a particular tree, but in a wood so dense as this how could he recognize any one tree from the rest? Then he saw a figure and ran toward it; it whistled a familiar tune and his heart lifted with the relief and joy at not after all being alone. Then the figure turned and it was not Harry at all—just a stranger who grinned at him in a little circle of wet slushy melted snow, while the owl hooted again and again. He woke suddenly to hear the telephone ringing by his head.[111]

Greene does not generally succeed in conveying that sense of nightmare which we associate with the thriller, because for him dream remains a minor fictive device.

Curiously, one of the more effective uses of the dream in Greene's fiction is the simulation of a sensation of nightmare in a waking situation. Thus Mather (*This Gun for Hire*), knowing that Anne is in great danger, dreads lest he be too late to avert disaster. The conviction of lateness, of impotence in the face of tangible danger, is one of the classic shapes of nightmare (which the thriller has incorporated into the chase) and one of the few instances in which Greene's description of a trance-like state approaches Conrad's success.

The conventions of the crime novel, to which Greene has adhered in the course of a long career, have not inhibited his artistry. They have proben amenable to combination with conventions we do not associate with this order of fiction. Like Conrad, for example, Greene leans upon a recurrent metaphor to transmit his vision, and his metaphor of the cross gains meaning incrementally as it recurs in his work: the Cross upon which Christ died, the cross of ordinary human love and responsibility and duty, the double-cross or betrayal, the cross-referencing and cross-purposing of human life. Greene also invents a system of leit-motifs more sophisticated than the thriller usually allows. Raven's life and situation are punctuated by a gramophone record, Harry Lime's by a tune; the allusions to childhood reading in *The Ministry of Fear* constitute another leit-motif; the repeated references to Scobie's constabulary duties outside his office make up the leit-motif of his burden. The thriller has supported the weight of Greene's theology and given dramatic shape to his political jeremiads. His novels are as entertaining as his entertainments because of two lessons the entertainment taught him: the power of plot and the power of excitation. "If you excite your audience first, you can put over what you will of horror, suffering, truth."[112]

Greene's success in all his writings—whether entertainment, Catholic or political novel—is inseparable from the use he has made of the crime novel. His content attests to this; as Allott and Farris comment, "certain types of incident are repeated—pursuit, acts of suicide, brutal violence and . . . betrayal."[113] These incidents are the very stuff of mystery and melodrama. His technique also reflects it; as R.W.B. Lewis writes, "His technique is one of befuddlement—a technique that makes for a delightful apprehension in his mystery stories, but which is charged with a double purpose and intensity in his mystery dramas."[114]

This "delightful apprehension," the same upon which the Gothic novelists capitalized, lies behind Edmund Burke's theory of the sublime. Robert Kiely explains:

> Taking pain to be stronger than pleasure, Burke argues that whatever excites a painful idea is a source of astonishment, the sublime

passion. The mind is so filled with its object that it cannot entertain any other; there is a momentary suspension of rational activity and of unrelated emotion. One is delivered, at least temporarily, from self-consciousness and mixed feeling and therefore, as long as the pain remains imaginary and not actual, the response may be considered desirable.[115]

Although Gothic fiction stopped short of aesthetic theorizing, it shared with Edmund Burke the preoccupation with the fearful. Burke argues that death, or its apprehension, is the source of all ideas upon the sublime; by the continuous exacerbation of this fear (as well as by innovations in language and setting), the Gothic novelist wished to dispense with the social grounding and realistic detail of the eighteenth-century novel.

Greene has reunited the realistic novel and the romance, wedding theatricality and verisimilitude, concreteness and imagination. His weakness is not a result of being hobbled by outmoded or unbelievable conventions, but a failure of freshness. We recognize these characters, we can identify this world, we know this solution; not because they are the characters, world, and solution of the crime novel, but of Greeneland.

Note 1
CHAPTER V

The Country and the City - Raymond Williams, Oxford Univ. Press, N.Y. 1973, p. 249

But the true fate of the country-house novel was its evolution into the middle-class detective story. It was in its very quality of abstraction, and yet of superficially impressive survival, that the country-house could be made the place of isolated assembly of a group of people whose immediate and transient relations were decipherable by an abstract mode of detection rather than by the full and connected analysis of any more general understanding. Sometimes the formula is merely instrumental, as inAgatha Christie and others. Sometimes, as in Dorothy Sayers, it is combined with middle-class fantasies about the human nature of the traditional inhabitants. But tradition, elsewhere, is reduced to old architecture, old dress, and the occasional ghost. It seems to me very fitting that a mode of analysis of human relationships which came out of Baker Street, out of the fogs of the transient city, should find a temporary resting-place in this facade way of life, before it returned eventually to its true place in the streets. For the country-house, while it retained its emotional hold, was indeed a proper setting for an opaqueness that can be penetrated in only a single dimension: all real questions of social and personal relationship left aside except in their capacity to instigate an instrumental deciphering. In very recent times it had been leased again as a centre for criminal planning or espionage or the secret police. But the point is that the country-house, in the twentieth century, has just this quality of abstract disposability and indifference of function. The real houses can be anything from schools and colleges and hospitals to business retreats, estate offices, and subsidized museums. In the same way, emotionally, they can be the centres of isolated power, graft, or intrigue, or what are called the 'status symbols'—meaning the abstractions—of success, power and money which are founded elsewhere but left conveniently out of sight. It is not a sad end; it is a fitting end. The essential features were always there, and much of the history that changed them came out of them, in their original and continuing domination and alienation.

The Evening Colonnade, Cyril Connolly, "Deductions from Detectives," (David, Bruce and Watson, London, 1973), pp. 493-4.

And this brings me to the second great virtue of detective stories. They are the last repository of our passion for the countryside. . . . Suddenly I realized that here was the ideal medium for describing scenery. Here were books where the stress was taken off the countryside (which then seemed to spring up like trodden grass), and conveyed to the events which took place in it; where local color was

216

not an overworked sentimental symbol, but a place where loveliness was enhanced because it was accidental, like the metaphors of 'Paradise Lost,' or the landscapes in 'Tales of the Hall.' . . . And the country houses, the great parks dripping in the autumn weather, the brilliant company, the rooms I have slept in, finding my way from the map on the first page.

NOTES
CHAPTER V

[1]Graham Greene, *In Search of a Character* (London: Bodley Head, 1961), p. 48. Greene employs the Conradian linkage of abstract and concrete: "I thought I knew what it was that held me. It was the smell of innocence." Graham Greene, "The Innocent," (*Viking Portable Library Graham Greene,* New York: Viking Press, 1972), p. 51. Or, "Hope creaked in his chest like a piece of rusty machinery." Graham Greene, *The Honorary Consul* (New York: Simon and Schuster, 1973), p. 2.

[2]As quoted in Gwenn Boardman, *Graham Greene: The Aesthetics of Exploration* (Gainesville, Florida: University of Florida Press, 1971), p. 137.

[3]Kenneth Allott and Miriam Farris, *The Art of Graham Greene* (London: Hamish Hamilton, 1951), p. 40.

[4]Graham Greene, *The Lost Childhood and Other Essays* (New York: Viking, 1951), p. 79.

[5]*The Art of Graham Greene,* p. 70.

[6]Sean O'Faolain, "Graham Greene," *The Vanishing Hero* (London: Eyre and Spottiswoode, 1956), p. 95. Greene designated his novel, *The Quiet American,* a "Morality."

[7]*The Honorary Consul,* p. 116: " 'In a wrong society,' Rivas said, 'the criminals are honest men.' "

[8]John Davison as quoted by John Berryman. *The Freedom of the Poet* (New York: Farrar, Strauss, Giroux, 1976), p. 289.

[9]Graham Greene, *Collected Essays* (New York: Viking Press, 1969), p. 23.
[10]*Ibid.*

[11]*Craft and Character in Modern Fiction,* p. 285.

[12]Graham Greene, *The Lost Childhood and Other Essays,* p. 17.

[13]An example of how Greene melodramatized religion: " 'I'm all right,' he said, the old longing pricking at his eyeballs, and looking towards the cross on the altar he thought savagely: take your sponge of gall. You made me what I am. Take your spear thrust." *The Heart of the Matter, Viking Portable Library Graham Greene,* p. 320.

[14]Samuel Hynes, "Introduction," *Graham Greene: A Collection of Critical Essays,* ed. Samuel Hynes (New Jersey: Prentice-Hall, 1973), p. 1.

[15]Graham Greene, "François Mauriac," *Viking Portable Library Graham Greene,* p. 555.

[16]Graham Greene, *The Ministry of Fear* (New York: Viking Press, 1943), p. 190.

[17]*The Art of Graham Greene,* p. 67.

[18]*Craft and Character in Modern Fiction,* p. 278.

[19]As quoted in *The Art of Graham Greene,* p. 63.

20Gwenn Boardman, *Graham Greene,* p. 35.

21"The Cinema," *Spectator,* June 17, 1938.

22"Tram Cars or 'Dodgems,' " *Times Literary Supplement,* Feb. 25, 1955, p. ii.

23*Craft and Character in Modern Fiction,* pp. 267-8. See also Auden's poem "New Year Letter" (1941) for a similar statement.

24Graham Greene, *Journey Without Maps* (London: Heinemann, 1950), p. 10.

25*Craft and Character in Modern Fiction,* pp. 280-181.

26*Anatomy of Criticism,* p. 48.

27One of Graham Greene's favorite quotations taken from Cardinal Newman: "What can be said of this heart-piercing, reason-bewildering fact? I can only answer, that either there is no Creator, or this living society of men is in a true sense discarded from His presence . . . if there is a God, since there is a God, the human race is implicated in some *terrible aboriginal calamity.*" Quoted in anonymous essay, "The Man Within," *Graham Greene,* ed. Samuel Hynes, p. 13.

28Graham Greene as quoted in *The Art of Graham Greene,* p. 174. The subterranean seems to exercise a grip on Greene's imagination: e.g., his short story, "The Basement Room"; the scent of *The Third Man* located in the sewer system of Vienna; the prison cell in *The Power and the Glory.* In view of this it is most interesting to read François Mauriac's insight into the nature of Greene's faith: "We feel it is a hidden presence of God in an atheistic world, that subterranean flowing of Grace which dazzles Graham Greene much more than the majestic façade which the temporal Church still erects above the people." "Graham Greene," *Graham Greene,* ed. Samuel Hynes, p. 77.

29Graham Greene, *Brighton Rock,* (N.Y.: Bantam Books), p. 138.

30"The Heresy of Our Time," *Graham Greene,* ed. Samuel Hynes, p. 93.

31Graham Greene, "The Lesson of the Master," *Viking Portable Library Graham Greene,* p. 541.

32Graham Greene, *The Lost Childhood and Other Essays,* p. 189.

33Anonymous essay, "The Man Within," *Graham Greene,* ed. Samuel Hynes, p. 12.

34Graham Greene, *Journey Without Maps,* pp. 10, 8, 10.

35Graham Greene, "Propos de table avec Graham Greene," *Dieu Vivant* 16, (1950), pp. 127-137.

36"Before the Attack," *Spectator,* April 16, 1954, p. 456.

37"Bombing Raid," *Spectator,* Aug. 18, 1959, p. 249.

38*The Life of the Drama,* p. 204.

39*The Ministry of Fear* (New York: Viking Press, 1943), p. 90.

40Graham Greene, *The Lawless Roads* (London: Heinemann, 1955), p. 216.

41*The Nature of Narrative,* p. 219.

42In this connection it is interesting to read: "Existentialism (which the French critics urge is Greene's philosophy), itself, says Guido de Ruggiero, 'deals with existence in the form of a thriller.' " *The Art of Graham Greene,* p. 164, fn. 1.

[43]*The Art of Graham Greene,* p. 127.

[44]*The Labyrinthine Ways of Graham Greene* (New York: Sheed and Ward, 1959), p. 118.

[45]Derek Traversi, "The Earlier Novels," *Graham Greene,* ed. Samuel Hynes, p. 25.

[46]Greene neatly ties together the quest, the journey and the dream: "Any journey, like a form of dreaming, is an attempt to express the pain (of the past) in harmless images, slipping it past the censor in the shape of a casino, a cathedral, a pension at Rapallo." Quoted by Gwenn Boardman, *Graham Greene,* p. 18.

[47]Karl Pattern, "The Structure of *The Power and the Glory*" (*Modern Fiction Studies,* Autumn, 1957, Vol. III), p. 233.

[48]The detective novel, also a movement toward the ideal, chooses to manipulate the temporal dimension, and therefore is more dependent on rituals of time: time tables, railway schedules, alibies for specific hours.

[49]Graham Greene, *A Burnt-Out Case* (New York: Bantam Books, 1961), p. 73.

[50]Graham Greene, *The Lost Childhood and Other Essays,* p. 189.

[51]"Minty's Day," *Viking Portable Library Graham Greene,* p. 49.

[52]Gwenn Boardman, *Graham Greene,* p. 80.

[53]*The Art of Graham Greene,* p. 203.

[54]Graham Greene, *The Heart of the Matter, Viking Portable Library Graham Greene,* p. 218.

[55]Graham Greene, *The Heart of the Matter, p. 128.*

[56]Graham Greene, *A Burnt-Out Case,* p. 182.

[57]Gwenn Boardman, *Graham Greene,* p. 168.

[58]Gerard Manley Hopkins, "God's Grandeur," *Modern American-Modern British Poetry* (New York: Harcourt, Brace and Co., 1942), p. 43.

[59]Graham Greene, *The Power and the Glory, Viking Portable Library Graham Greene,* p. 77.

[60]Lines taken by Greene from a poem by AE, (George Russell):
In Ancient shadows and twilights
Where childhood had strayed
The world's great sorrows were born
And its heroes were made.
In the lost boyhood of Judas
Christ was betrayed.
As quoted by Martin Shuttleworth, "The Art of Fiction: Graham Greene," *Graham Greene,* ed. Samuel Hynes, p. 155.

[61]Graham Greene, *The Power and the Glory,* p. 77.

[62]As quoted in *The Art of Graham Greene,* p. 31.

[63]*The Vanishing Hero,* p. 91.

[64]R.W.B. Lewis, "The Trilogy," *Graham Greene,* ed. Samuel Hynes, p. 54.

[65]*The Honorary Consul,* p. 253.

[66]Graham Greene, *The Heart of the Matter,* p. 359.

[67]Anonymous essay, "The Man Within," *Graham Greene,* ed. Samuel Hynes, p. 14. See "The Young Dickens," *The Lost Childhood and Other Essays,* pp. 51-57.

[68]Graham Greene, *The Heart of the Matter,* p. 219.

[69]Charles Dickens, *Bleak House,* (London: Collins, 1953), p. 590.

[70]Gwenn Boardman, *Graham Greene,* p. 93.

[71]*Journey Without Maps,* p. 8.

[72]*The Art of Graham Greene,* p. 140.

[73]*Ibid.,* p. 22.

[74]"The Cinema" *Spectator,* Jan. 10, 1936, p. 50.

[75]This is not unlike the grotesquerie implicit for Greene in the earlier equation:

$$\frac{\text{pity}}{\text{mercy}} \quad \frac{\text{(human)}}{\text{(divine)}} = \frac{\text{sex}}{\text{love}} \quad \frac{\text{(human love)}.}{\text{(divine love)}}$$

[76]*Craft and Character in Modern Fiction,* p. 294.

[77]*Ibid.,* p. 281.

[78]R.W.B. Lewis, "The Trilogy," *Graham Greene,* ed. Samuel Hynes, p. 52.

[79]Graham Greene, "Frederick Rolfe," *Viking Portable Library Graham Greene,* p. 566.

[80]*The Heart of the Matter,* pp. 285-6.

[81]*Ibid,* pp. 295, 216.

[82]Graham Greene, *The Power and the Glory,* p. 15.

[83]*Some Versions of Pastoral,* p. 29. "The hero of our modern tragedies is no king whose death brings about the salvation of society. Our modern hero is a man searching for himself." Carolyn Heilbrun, *Towards a Recognition of Androgyny* (New York: Alfred Knopf, 1973), p. 93.

[84]*The Art of Graham Greene,* p. 186.

[85]Graham Greene, *Brighton Rock,* p. 247.

[86]*A Burnt-Out Case,* p. 175.

[87]R.W.B. Lewis, "The Trilogy," *Graham Greene,* ed. Samuel Hynes, pp. 54-55. The same point is made in a short story, "The Return," *Viking Portable Library Graham Greene,* p. 21: "This may explain the deep appeal of the seedy. It is nearer the beginning; like Monrovia its building has begun wrong, but at least it has only begun; it hasn't reached so far away as the smart, the new, the chic, the cerebral."

[88]*Graham Greene* as quoted by Reynolds Price, review of *The Honorary Consul* by Graham Greene, *NY Times Book Review,* Sept. 9, 1973, p. 18.

[89]*Ibid.* Curiously, in a metaphysical detective story, "Death and the Compass," by Jorge Luis Borges, a similar imputation stands that God is the Great Conspirator.

[90]"Second Time Charm: The Theatre of Graham Greene," *Modern Fiction Studies,* Vol. III, p. 254.

[91]*The Art of Graham Greene,* p. 123.

[92]Graham Greene, *It's a Battlefield* (London: Heinemann, 1934), p. 139.

[93]Gwenn Boardman, Graham Greene, p. 41.

[94]Derek Traversi, "The Earlier Novels," *Graham Greene,* ed. Samuel Hynes, p. 25.

[95]R.W.B. Lewis, "The Trilogy," *Graham Greene,* ed. Samuel Hynes, p. 58.

[96]Frederick Hoffman, *The Mortal No,* p. 269.

[97]Anonymous essay, "The Man Within," *Graham Greene,* ed. Samuel Hynes, pp. 11-12.

[98]"The Trilogy," *Graham Greene,* ed. Samuel Hynes, p. 50.

[99]*Craft and Character in Modern Fiction,* p. 287.

[100]*The Art of Graham Greene,* p. 33, fn. 1.

[101]*Ibid.,* p. 162.

[102]*The Honorary Consul,* p. 168.

[103]Cawelti's term for the use of crime novel technique by authors with wider intentions. *Adventure, Mystery, and Romance.*

[104]Ursula Spier, "The End of the Affair," *Modern Fiction Studies,* (Autumn, 1957) III, p. 237.

[105]*Ibid.*

[106]Ian Gregor, "The End of the Affair," *Graham Greene,* ed. Samuel Hynes, p. 113.

[107]*The Art of Graham Greene,* p. 125.

[108]Francis Wyndham, *Graham Greene,* Writers and Their Work Series (London: British Council and the National Book League, Longman, Green and Co., 1962), p. 24.

[109]Roy Fuller believes that the treatment of "the mugs" in *The Third Man* is comparable to that in Ben Jonson's *Volphone* and *The Alchemist;* in other words, the seriousness of the message is not congruent with the superficiality of the form. *Times Literary Supplement,* Feb. 25, 1955.

[110]Gwenn Boardman, *Graham Greene,* p. 163.

[111]"The Third Man," *Viking Portable Library Graham Greene,* p. 286.

[112]Graham Greene, as quoted in Introduction, *Graham Greene,* ed. Samuel Hynes, p. 1.

[113]*The Art of Graham Greene,* p. 11.

[114]R.W.B. Lewis, "The Fiction of Graham Greene," *Kenyon Review,* 1957, p. 68.

[115]Robert Kiely, *The Romantic Tradition in the English Novel,* (Cambridge, Mass.: Harvard University Press, 1972), p. 17.

CHAPTER VI
CONCLUSION

I have attempted to show that the eidetic imagery, archetypal characterization, and the allegorical mode of the crime novel not only permit its two major forms, detective story and thriller, to become the instruments of other, larger, intentions and sensibilities than crime fiction is normally considered to express, but also prove actively, symbiotically, useful. After the close examination of the works of Dickens, Conrad, and Greene, it seems to me unmistakable that the influence and durability of crime fiction derive both from the largely unrecognized universality of its magic protagonists and the centrality of its symbolic action: the allegorical confrontation of good and evil.

With analyses of generic structure and style and particular adaptations behind us, what generalizations may we propose? Two attractions immediately recommend the crime novel. First, its dependence upon corroborative detail provides us with valuable social history. Cyril Connolly writes:

> . . . in a hundred years our thrillers will have become text-books . . .
> the most authentic chronicles of how we lived. For the detective story
> is the only kind of book now written in which every detail must be

right; nobody cares in fiction, even in biography, what make of car the hero uses, or where he gets his clothes, but in the compression of the detective story where every touch must add something to our knowledge of the characters, their walk in life, their propensities for crime, such incidents become of extreme importance, they must render an accurate delineation of the business of living.[1]

This statement was written nearly five decades ago; the situation, if anything, has intensified. We can indeed say the crime novel provides not only the minutiae of social history, but the *zeitgeist*. Prose experimentation has moved in the direction of divesting the novel of its material bonds and affiliations, its bourgeois predilection. John Weightman explains:

> Any realism of the social context is out of the question, because reality is infinite and multifarious and can only be rendered linguistically by partial, and often mutually exclusive grids.[2]

The conventional detective novel still attempts to represent a social whole.

One of the attractions that the Sherlock Holmes stories affords is immersion in a social record. With Holmes, the armchair detective can also be peripatetic. Undoubtedly nostalgia for a by-gone world plays its part in certain of these fictions, but so, too, does the enjoyment of geographical particularization. Both Gertrude Stein and Cyril Connolly have attested to this. "During the Occupation, when she [Gertrude Stein] could go through only the books already read, she enjoyed re-reading detective novels by paying particular attention to the geographical locations which had previously been unregarded."[3] The detective novel, Cyril Connolly claims, has remained "the last repository of our passion for the countryside."[4] (See Note 1, Chapter V.)

Second, the reader of a crime novel may assume a measure of readability. All aesthetic creations, as Wolfgang Iser points out, alternate between induction and deduction. One of the paramount pleasures of the crime novel is that it totally engages the reader's deductive powers. It also gratifies that delight in mystification which mankind displays ontogenetically in the nursery—for example, in the fairy tale and riddle—and never abandons.

Conclusion

This type of fiction retains the belief in cause and effect, and therefore in chronology. 'Once upon a time' inevitably leads us to a satisfying conclusion: 'and then they lived happily ever after.' "Perhaps literature as a whole," writes Northrop Frye, "ends in much the same place that it begins": the gratification of a static condition. Until this resolution, the suspense of the detective novel (or fairy tale) prevents the reader's interest flagging, and we "may be very close to the experience of a child listening to a story, too spell-bound to question the narrative."[5] Chronology enables us to participate in the progression of the fictional scheme; "*peripeteia* depends on our confidence of the end."[6]

Furthermore, the necessity for relevance requires an economy of style which also secures the reader's interest. Cyril Connolly comments:

> . . . it can be said for the detective novels that they are the most advanced, the nearest approach to pure form of any work being produced today. While the novel grows more and more sprawling, dragging from incident in incident, volume to volume, weltering in emotions, the typical unplanned exuberant Romantic achievement, so its sister the detective story grows ever more classical, as the characters, the scene, the actions are more strictly compelled by the writer's rigid subordination to plot.[7]

Paradoxically, this economy of style is part of the sense of magical significance in the detective novel, in which "every detail is an omen and a cause."[8] This lack of ambivalence and extravagance we feel to be magical precisely because it contradicts our experience of the real. There are no loose ends; we solve the puzzle; confusion is conquered, for we are in the realm of magical causation which explains all things. Beyond the dual achievement of social documentation and readability, then, the detective novel is rooted in our common magical associations, as numerous modern writers perceive:

> Like his beloved Chesterton, who made the Father Brown stories a vehicle for Catholic theology, Borges uses mystery and the surprise effect in literature to achieve that sacred astonishment at the universe which is the origin of all true religion and metaphysics.
> **James Irly**, "Introduction," *Labyrinths, Jorge Luis Borges*

225

A Common Spring

For [Gertrude] Stein, mystery and detective fiction . . . metaphorically stated the mystery behind creation and life itself.

Lawrence Stewart, "Gertrude Stein,"
Mystery and Detection Annual, 1972

In the preceding chapter we confronted a parallel belief in Graham Greene's opinion that "murder is a religious subject." Yet the very branch of literature whose special domain it is—crime fiction—is most often pronounced "frivolous" (because escapist) and "self-consuming" (because its solution destroys its reason for existence). How can these paradoxes be explained?

Those who charge the crime novel with frivolity often cite its adventitious solutions, frequently the by-product of melodrama. The evasions of melodrama are the natural outcome of its own dependence upon accident. "Melodrama in the novel is a way of covering up, of getting around an emotional block or conflict which the novelist and perhaps his society are unable to face or resolve."[9] Or as Gertrude Stein saw it, melodrama "covers up one's bottom nature."[10]

The crime novel has also been labeled "frivolous" because it depicts a series of adventures, predominantly physical, which are never connected to any moral issues or ultimate problems, or to any final reckoning. Comparing Stevenson and Conrad, Robert Kiely sums up the case:

> . . . in the former [the mere boyish adventure tale] the act of dissociation or disobedience permits the escapade without permanent consequences. . . . It is the wonderful, pathetic, and perennial dream of being born into a world without death [of which I take punishment to be the adumbration]. At all levels of sophistication, adventure [homologous here to the thriller] turns on disobedience—on breaking of a law. . . . The realization that the authority, whether it assumes the name of God, father, superego or romantic ideal is inescapable . . . brings the adventure into the realm of universal human experience regardless of bizarre locale and unlikely quality of incident.[11]

Conclusion

As Kiely perceives, escape lies not in the exoticism or the derring-do, which merely adorn the dream, but in the absence of futurity. The dream can continue; the waking never comes.

But these limitations are not the enemy of serious fiction. They have been accepted by authors like Dickens, Conrad, and Greene, all of whom extended the range of melodrama and the thriller in the socio-political novel, using it for prognostication and social analysis; the crime novel objectifies the experience of our time. Paradoxically, the crime novel, though formulaic, provides distinctive opportunities for interpreting society and the individual.[12] This is true because the individual's relationship to society, the nature of evil, the quest for identity, the problem of justice, the response to transgression all cling to this genre; it offers the advantage of a set of *a priori* questions. In the conventional crime novel, be it thriller or detective story, they may be evaded or settled by formula. But this need not be so. "The detective story presents a framework into which almost any depth of literary expression can be fitted."[13]

Society and the Formula

Both the detective story and the socio-political novel share a quest for a wholesome, unified society. They both treat of an everyday world gone wrong in a circumscribed way. For the former, a specific and individual crime provides the narrative impetus; for the latter, a specific social wrong in a specific place at a specific time. Both introduce sins of transgression (Kiely's "dissociation" or "disobedience"). The criminal of the detective story and the segment of society which is excoriated in the socio-political novel share the role of transgressor against the common weal. Both forms are concerned with setting things aright, and therefore share a temporal urgency, the anxiety of forestalling a dire situation. Rex Warner, W.H. Auden, and Liam O'Flaherty, among others, have written serious works of political or social commentary set in the framework of the thriller or detective story.

Warner's *Men of Stones* (1949), a political allegory whose subtitle "A Melodrama" links it with Wilkie Collins and Victorian melodrama, uses a Gothic setting and an exotic aura of Orientalism to depict the demise of Christian liberalism and prophesy the rule of supermen. Numerous familiar themes and devices are employed: for example, there is a hunt similar to the Grail quest, for a picture. The unspecified crime and unspecified setting of this novel lend it allegorical flavor. Warner uses the closed setting of the university (*The Professor*—1939) or the rural village (*The Aerodrome*—1941) for the same reason the detective novel does: to commence from an organic unity, in which life may resume only after the disruptive element has been removed. This goal is accomplished, for example, by the death of sterile force (the Air Vice Marshal in *The Aerodrome*).

Warner's characters—the Chancellor, the Air Vice Marshal, the Professor, the Commodore—are identified by function, like those of the detective novel. In *The Aerodrome* we meet a detective-surrogate, Dr. Faulkner, who, paralleling the conventional disinterested detective, questions suspects, challenges the criminal, and is free to act for the restoration of peace. The Flight Lieutenant, though he is not a conventional criminal but Warner's symbol of authoritarianism, repeatedly commits transgressions against the society. He is the disruptive element, and the communal attitude toward him is compounded partly of fear and partly of attraction, just as it is toward the criminal in the thriller. Furthermore, Warner accepts the crime novel's criterion of relevance; none of the characters is introduced gratuitously. Even the "locals," sitting outside the pub in *The Aerodrome,* are not extraneous, but are representative of the community which is being threatened. We find, too, a parallel between the vindication of villagers in the same novel (symbolized by the return of the hero, Roy, to his village sweetheart, Bess) and the vindication of innocent suspects in detective fiction.

In yet another Warner novel, *The Wild Goose Chase* (1938), the author presents us with a fairy tale, complete with three brothers and a quest. We have easy and direct symbolism—for instance, physical giants = supermen—and a highly stylized language like that of legend. But with its sophistication of viewpoint, its Swiftian detachment, irony, and interpolation of imaginary places for the purposes of satire, it tells an anti-fascist didactic tale about the perils of authoritarianism and the loss of individual liberty.

Written during the 1930s, the period of Auden's strongest belief in the social voice of the poet, the play *The Dog Beneath the Skin* (1935) by Auden and Isherwood also dresses political as well as moral problems in the flashier raiment of the detective story. (As Auden begain his famous 1941 "New Year Letter": "The situation of our time/surrounds us like a baffling crime.") With unmistakeable elements of the fairy tale (the hero has mysterious adventures, rescues the maiden, overthrows the giant), *The Dog Beneath the Skin* reveals, via the creaky mechanism of a missing heir, the corruption of bourgeois London. It draws, too, upon archetypal figures and images which add richness and suggestiveness. Joseph Warren Beach writes:

> The main image of the mysterious two perpetually watching, from left and right and over the garden wall, is the begetter of a number of related images (the woods, the scissor-man [Peer Gynt, Atropos?], the woman in dark glasses, the hump-back) that build up the shivery atmosphere of mysterious threatening powers. . . .[14]

In *On the Frontier* (1938) by the same authors the vocabulary of conspiracy, the presence of spies and guards (a delight in the game of conspiracy was Auden's from boyhood), is employed to reinforce Marxian grammar. In just such a way the limited view of morality native to the detective story can be used by the socio-political writer to focus his own work upon any single bias—thus a simple equation of capitalism and villainy or democracy and truth can be construed.

Employing the thriller form, Liam O'Flaherty dramatized the political scene in Ireland (1928) in *The Assassin* and *The Informer*. A social melodrama, *The Assassin* is fast-paced and suspenseful, increasingly so as it is told by the assassin from a narrowing margin of safety. The acceleration of narrative tempo is the obverse of the device of retardation; paradoxically, both produce suspense. An atmosphere of sordidness and doom is created beyond the necessity of the plot; danger and death (even a raincoat is described as "looking like a shroud") convey the message: the impossibility of life in Dublin.

Religion and the Formula

Father Ronald Knox, G.K. Chesterton, Dorothy L. Sayers, and
Charles W.S. Williams all attempted to infuse their versions of the
crime novel with an ardent Christianity, combining the transgression against God and the transgression against society with a tone
of lighthearted sophistication, yet never straying far from the
bounds of the detective tale. Chesterton in particular was bend on
achieving this union and went so far as to enlist a priest, Father
Brown, as his detective hero.

Chesterton, like Greene, bases his detective stories on the
religious dichotomy between good and evil or God and the devil.
Yet Chesterton has been the butt of criticism from Greene and
others for his naive resolutions of these tensions. Greene dismissed
Chesterton as a sentimental writer of fairy tales (though Greene
sees parallels between all detective fiction and fairy tale), viewing
the ratiocinative solutions of Chesterton's Father Brown as a per-
former's trick and that detective's Christianity as a mere novelty
for the reader. Greene's novels, though less steadfast to the articles
of Catholic faith, achieve a deeper Christian spirit by permitting
each character to struggle for faith rather than to enjoy Chesterton's facile moral victories. We feel that Chesterton must have only sublimated the devils that haunted him, or, as Gavin Lambert
comments, "unlike Chesterton, who joined the Church to escape
from Hell, Greene will continue to live in it."[15]

Part of Chesterton's "sentimentality" lies in his portrayal of the
criminal as an artist *manqué*, an individual of unusual sensibility
with whom it is a privilege, albeit an illegal one, to joust (e.g.,
Flambeau). Chesterton's romantic notion of the criminal confers a
glamour upon him totally absent from the shabbiness of
Greeneland types. And instead of Greeneland we find ourselves in
an innocent London. Though Dickens had discovered many years
before the corrupt and squalid core of city life, Chesterton continues to fantasize, as Cawelti notes:

> No one can have failed to notice that in these stories the hero or in-
> vestigator crosses London with something of the lonelines and

liberty of the prince in a tale of Elfland, that in the course of that in-
calculable journey, the omnibus assumes the primal colors of a fairy
ship. The lights of the city begin to gleam like innumerable goblin
eyes, since they are the guardians of some secret, however crude,
which the writer knows and the reader does not.[16]

This version of the city as something mysterious and beckoning,
a place as exotic as Conrad's islands and tropics, contrasts further
still with the scene in which the secular tough-guy thrillers of
Chandler and Hammett take place. In these, the city impinges
upon the mind, causing a ravaging of the soul. By the time Raymond Chandler had invented Philip Marlowe, that trip across the
city had changed to a car chase through the ugly slums and "mean
streets" of a sprawling boom-town, Los Angeles. Perhaps an
answer to Greene's criticism of Chesterton's naiveté had already
appeared in the writings of T.S. Eliot, who managed eventually to
reconcile his vision of the city as a wasteland of desperation with a
personal piety.

In the dramas of T.S. Eliot, there are a surprising number of af-
finities to detective fiction. There are particulars such as the crime-
novel title, *Murder in the Cathedral,* and the inclusion in the same
play of the quotation from Conan Doyle's "The Musgrave
Ritual":

> Whose was it?
> His who is gone.
> Who shall have it?
> He who shall come.[17]

Even the discussion among the four knights toward the conclusion
of this play, when the fourth knight pointedly inquires, "Who killed the Archbishop?", closely resembles the revelation at the conclusion of the detective novel. These, it may be objected, are
superficial likenesses, but the choice of murder as the central
event, the stichomythic query and answer, the conspiratorial
whispers, the mounting of suspense, testify that the author is
aware of the contributions of detective fiction and melodrama. In
similar fashion *The Family Reunion,* also organized around the

event of a death which turns out to be murder, uses the classic detective setting of the country house, with its limited cast of characters. In this play we encounter Agatha, a character whose role plainly corresponds to that of detective-as-seer, as does that of Sir Harcourt-Reilly, the psychiatrist in Eliot's *The Cocktail Party* (1949).[18] Cawelti comments more broadly on *The Cocktail Party*, "These analogies between psychoanalysis and the detective story suggest to me a common concern with hidden secrets and guilts that may reflect a cultural pattern of the period."[19] In any case, Eliot may have chosen the figure of the detective because his profession demands a detachment Eliot favors for the artist.

In these, as in his other dramas, Eliot insists upon the same distinction Greene makes between secular and sacred laws. "What we have written is not a story of detection/Of crime and punishment, but of sin and expiation."[20] This is the final formulation of Eliot's theatre, but the passion of sin and expiation is worked out in the secular terms of crime and punishment: the melodramatic use of coincidence, of concealment, of disguised identity, of the sleuth, of the group gathered for the final disclosure.

Epistemology and the Formula

I have already discussed the limited view of the world presented by the so-called "realist" writers of crime fiction, Hammett and Chandler. Their vision of a sprawling metropolis infested with criminality in both underworld and police bureaucracy was another allegorical station, the "Great Wrong Place," one reality. In his three detective stories, "Death and the Compass," "Theme of The Traitor and the Hero," and "Emma Zunz," Jorge Luis Borges explores his notions of a complex and ambiguous "reality" by selecting the literal mode of investigation.

Borges, himself a Catholic, also finds fault with Chesterton, but not on religious grounds. Chesterton's Catholicism, Borges maintains in his essay "On Chesterton," is a disguise for the Poe or Kafka in him, the suppression of nightmare in a paean to reason. David Gallagher explains:

232

Conclusion

In the Father Brown stories . . . an apparently supernatural crime is
always solved by the sober common sense of the eponymous hero.
. . . In the Father Brown stories, moreover, the world is presented as an
apparent fantasy which, however, becomes easily explainable when
subjected to the scrutiny of reason. In "Death and the Compass" it
is the reasoning mind [of the detective Lönnrot] that turns a perfectly
commonplace event into a recondite fantasy. By presenting the
Father Brown pattern in inverted form, Borges [like Greene before
him] is therefore implying a criticism of Chesterton's faith in
reason.[21]

For Borges, the correct interpretation of appearance and reality
is subjective; there is no omniscience. "One of his favorite expe-
dients to symbolize or re-enact the problems of the limitation of
knowledge is to present us with a detective with a limited command over the limited evidence at his disposal."[22] In all detective
fiction, the evidence is incomplete. Gertrude Stein, a reader,
writer, and analyst of detective fiction, considers the detective
story an appropriate metaphor for the difficulty of arriving at a
single conclusion: "the corpse can never be revived. It cannot
answer questions, it cannot confirm deductions or substantiate
hypotheses. . . . Death concludes the evidence."[23] Yet most of
these fictions produce a single comprehensive interpretation of the
evidence. Borges posits a complex world in which the human, falli-
ble detective can never account for all the variables. "Death and
the Compass," for instance, is a parable about the vanity of the intellect. It is a detective story, a parody of a detective story, and a
"meditation upon its [the detective story's] implications."[24]
Borges retains all the clichés and conventions and inverts them or
uses them as points of departure for his own metaphysical specula-
tions: the mysterious telephone call; the deserted house; the final
revelatory dénouement; a super-logician sleuth, Lönnrot, who
compares himself to Dupin. But—the detective here does not solve
the puzzle, he invents it. Faced with a straightforward case of
murder for gain, the investigator rejects such a banal explanation.
For Lönnrot, as for his creator, "the more complicated the game,
the happier he is."[25] Thus personal preference upsets the science of
logic; logical deduction in this story proceeds only after a fantastic
hypothesis is made. Lönnrot makes his own case, his own reality,

233

enabling Borges to demonstrate the unwritten law behind every literary detective story: it must be an "interesting" case. Borges' phrase, "the innocence of reality," applies to the reality of the detective genre, "innocent" because it yields without exception to reason. Borges uses the prototypical circumstantial situation, the crime of formulaic detective fiction, to dramatize the impossibility of explanation. Lönnrot is killed as the result of his own baroque reasoning. It is as shocking as to say—Holmes failed, or Dupin failed!

In Borges' fiction the confusion of appearance and reality finds its central metaphor in the labyrinth. Gallagher writes:

> Borges has said that he uses the labyrinth rather than any other image to express the bewilderment of man because labyrinths are places that have been constructed artificially and deliberately to confuse. The confusion of those that enter it is the labyrinth's sole purpose. Now a good criminal is like a labyrinth-maker. If he plants false clues for the detective it is so as to lead him down false trails—for the planting of false clues is a skill that all Borges' criminals possess.[26]

For Borges, the metaphor of the labyrinth is often amplified with the metaphor of the mirror. He combines the two in "Death and the Compass":

> Lönnrot explored the house. He traveled through antechambers and galleries to emerge upon duplicate patios; several times he emerged upon the same patio. He ascended dust-covered stairways and came out into circular antechambers; he was infinitely reflected in opposing mirrors. . . . *The house is not this large, he thought. It is only made larger by the penumbra, the symmetry, the mirrors, the years, my ignorance, the solitude.*[27]

Borges finds in the mirror a second visualization of the complexity of reality. The view aslant, unawares, or partial; the sameness of mirror image and original, all express his conviction of reality's diffusion, whereas the detective story is, *sui generis,* incapable of allowing complexity of viewpoint. And the mirror, of course, is also a means of suggesting the doppelgänger theme on which "Death and the Compass" is based. (Borges, an admirer of Poe, uses the same motifs of the doppelgänger and the mirror that can be found in Poe's "William Wilson" and "The Imp of the

Conclusion

Perverse.'') And Jung sees still another significance in the mirror:

> In dreams a mirror can symbolize the power of the unconscious to 'mirror' the individual objectively—giving him a view of himself he may never have had before. Only through the unconscious can such a view (which often shocks and upsets the conscious mind) be obtained—just as in Greek myth the Gorgon Medusa, whose look turned men to stone, could be looked upon only in a mirror.[28]

The sense of reality Borges strives to summon with the aid of the mirror metaphor is unpredictable and often shocking.

In "Emma Zunz" and *"Theme of the Traitor* and the Hero,'' the evidence is faked: yet is it reality that is altered or just appearance?

> Actually, the story was incredible [the recital of her crime which Emma told the police and neighbors] but it impressed everyone because it was substantially true. True was Emma Zunz's tone, true was her shame, true was her hate. True also was the outrage she had suffered; only the circumstances were false, the time, and one or two proper names.[29]

Emma Zunz's "case" is never resolved. When the crucial facts of evidence which ordinarily comprise "reality" are shown to be alterable, even disposable, Borges again demonstrates the impossibility of reaching reality through external evidence.

Another aspect of the appearance/reality dilemma is inherent in its relationship to identity. Like Poe, whom he in some ways resembles, Borges frequently engages this problem by means of the doppelgänger. In his book *Poe Poe Poe Poe Poe Poe Poe* Daniel Hoffman says:

> Yet a further inference from Poe's duplicity in the treatment of so many of his themes is this: Chief among his themes is duplicity itself. The doubleness of experience. How can we tell the reality from the mirror, the world from its picture in a work of art, the image from its image? . . . Identity itself, the very vessel of perception, may be fatally flawed, fatally broken in twain. One of Poe's themes is the fate of the man haunted by his own double, his anima, his weird. Which is the real consciousness, the 'I' who speaks or the doppelgänger who pursues him?[30]

In Borges' "Theme of the Traitor and the Hero" doubling occurs again, but all his traitors are heroes. In this story the Irish hero Kilpatrick initiates an investigation that uncovers his own calumny and condemns him to death, the Oedipal doubling of scapegoat and detective.

In "Death and the Compass" the detective and the criminal, who are doubles, finally come together in a shoot-out. "The killer and the slain," writes Borges in a commentary on this story "whose minds work in the same way, may be the same man."[31]

Alain Robbe-Grillet, practitioner of the *nouveau roman,* also used the formulae of the detective novel as a point of departure from which to write anti-novels. What does his fiction, which Roland Barthes has compared to the surrealist attack upon rationality, retain or discard of the older form? In his novel *Jealousy,* Robbe-Grillet uses an atmosphere of suspense and an investigative narrator; the sense of impending violence requires explanation that such a narrator would customarily reveal. But we are never given adequate means to decipher the mystery; even with the detective novel's famous *aide-de-memoire,* the plans of the house, included, we are unable to locate the event. *The Erasers* retains still more of the detective novel's apparatus: an assassin, a victim, clues, concealed identity. Robbe-Grillet admits he modeled this novel after Simenon's Inspector Maigret series. But more significantly, Robbe-Grillet has kidnapped the plot of the world's oldest murder mystery—the Oedipus drama. The investigator in *The Erasers* unwittingly becomes the assassin he is seeking. Yet, unlike Sophocles, Robbe-Grillet provides no scene of cathartic recognition. Simultaneous, equally plausible, interpretations preclude recognition. The author leaves the reader, along with the protagonist, puzzling over the mystery.

Robbe-Grillet's most significant rejection, then, is of the resolution that allegorical forms require, and which the reader's own epistemological preconceptions demand. Robbe-Grillet claims that *The Erasers* and *Jealousy* will not enact an "ideal order," and certainly he has abandoned the allegorical progress toward the ideal. In both novels his method has been to establish expectations for resolution and to confound them almost from the start. This is accomplished mainly through his manipulation of the passage of time. The classical temporal sequence—beginning, middle, and end—has no place here, and hence we perceive no certain causality. The world of his novels is spatial (grids that never intersect) rather than temporal; and although Robbe-Grillet invents many new temporal systems it is the absence of sequential time that disconcerts the reader.

This does not mean that the Robbe-Grillet novel is either irrational or oneiric. Roland Barthes argues that these novels "exist outside time"; but in a way, all fictions do, creating the time of their own world, counter-realities. It is not because they exist "outside time" that his works produce an extra sense of bafflement in the reader. (The fairy tale, which exists 'once upon a time,' does not disconcert the reader because it holds to a familiar linear progression.) It is because Robbe-Grillet chose a formulaic fiction, the crime novel, which, to an even greater degree than the non-formulaic novel, promises reconciliations, satisfying exegeses, and an overriding sense of determinism through sequential time. Kermode maintains that "great [novelists] retreat from reality [chronicity] less perfunctorily than the authors of novelettes and detective stories."[32] Paradoxically, having chosen the method of the detective novel, Robbe-Grillet moves his narrative even further away from paradigmatic form than the ordinary novel does.

Confounding of such expectations constitutes a tremendous change in contemporary literature. In Samuel Beckett's *End-Game,* both the title and the content inform the reader that a game is being enacted on stage. However, we are never told the rules and the form is not congruent with the substance. Hence the end of *End-Game* seems arbitrary; we have experienced many possible endings preceding the actual one. Our powers of deduction are deliberately defeated; we have traveled a long distance from the gamesmanship of the Golden Age. In Beckett's *Waiting for Godot,* mystery is spun out into mystification. Confused audiences insist upon investing the work with an allegorical meaning (e.g., Godot = God), dissatisfied with the fact that waiting has to be perceived as an end in itself, rather than as an epistemological means. We share in what Wolfgang Iser terms "the impetus toward meaning."[33]

The Formula as Cathexis

> Because mythic narrative is the expression in story form of deep-seated human concerns, fears and aspirations, the plots of mythic tales are a store house of narrative correlatives—keys to the human psyche in story form—guaranteed to reach an audience and move them deeply.
>
> **Scholes and Kellogg,** *The Nature of Narrative*

Man is separated from myth more now than ever before, and depends more upon those fictions which can reconnect him to it. Myth imbues man with a sense of permanence that his individual life lacks by attaching him to interpretations outside himself. Since we exist in time, we sense that we are *in media res,* but from the middle we cannot formulate satisfactory perceptions of the whole. Myth does just this: the Book of the Revelation enjoins us, "Write the things which thou hast seen, and the things which are, and the things which shall be hereafter." Since myths offer explanations maintained through ritual, which are both retroactive and projected, they provide the concord which man seeks to make of this life. They are what Kermode calls "agents of stability."[34]

The first mythic tales we meet are the fairy tales of the nursery, in which violence and terror are so prevalent (for example, the tales of Grimm and Andersen) as to lead Jonathan Gathorne-Hardy to surmise that such a diet must provide some necessary sustenance for children.[35] He reasons that though ". . . the violence and terror must be insulated and removed, whether by improbability, by exaggeration, by symbolism, by humor, by time, by fantasy . . . [fairy tales] introduce the children to the mystery of death, to the polarities of good and evil."[36] Thus fairy tales are moral, cautionary tales. (The same "insulation and removal" is, of course, accomplished by the "gamesmanship" of detective fiction.)

Not only children have strong attachments to pattern making. We are forced to continually reshape the connections between beginning, middle, and end, to accord with our changing experiences of reality. If all "fiction is for finding out" as Kermode believes, this cathetic process is most explicit in the crime novel.

238

Conclusion

Similarly, if fictions counteract the ambivalence, ambiguity, and inconclusiveness of life, the need for that fiction which supplies concord most definitively, will persist.

In the detective story, as in the fairy story, good and evil are polarized; good is rewarded and evil is punished. In the detective story, as in the fairy story, there is a struggle for success, and a quest and/or test. The teaching by precept in the fairy tale exists under the integument of the adventure/thriller, and occasionally in combination with the riddle; the teaching by precept in the detective story exists under the integument of the puzzle. (Both derive from the "enigma.") If we look at the examples Jacques Barzun summons to illustrate his definition of the "tale"—*The Arabian Nights,*[37] *The Decameron, Don Quixote, Robinson Crusoe,* the fiction of Thomas Love Peacock,[38] and the inventions of Poe, Kleist, Kafka, and Borges—we can make a generalization about it: the tale (to which classification the detective story still belongs) is not mimetic drama. W.H. Auden classifies the detective story as "Dream Literature" (which classification will comfortably accommodate most of the works Barzun denominates "tales").[39] "For the writing of Dream Literature, though it includes many works like detective stories and opera libretti which are, formally, 'feigned histories,' the primary requirement is the gift of a mythopoetic imagination."[40]

Both Barzun and Auden, from their separate beginnings, arrive at the same conclusion about characterization in this type of literature. Thus Barzun: "The characters it [the tale] presents are not persons but types, as in the Gospels: the servant, the rich man, the camel driver. . . ."[41] And Auden:

> In comparison with his colleague, the novelist of our social waking life, the novelist of dream life is freer in his choice of events but more restricted in his choice of characters, for the latter must all be variations on a few 'archetypes,' the Wise Old Man, the Wise Old Woman, the Harlot-Witch, the Child-Bride [Dickens, Greene], the Shadow-Self [Conrad, Poe, Borges].[42]

The recurrence of these archetypes, with their pleasurably easy identification and accretive meanings, is one of the fundamental

239

appeals of both the fairy tale and the detective tale. The core figures of the detective tale are the scapegoat-victim, the law-breaker-villain, and the law-giver-rescuer. Except for the detective, who has little but a transient connection with the other characters, a fact often signified by his importation from outside their circle, the characters are submerged sufficiently in a group existence so that the final accusatory finger often seems arbitrary. As I noted earlier, Northrop Frye claims that one major difference between a detective novel and a novel such as *Crime and Punishment* is that in the latter the crime is a signature of the character. It is worth recalling two earlier points about characterization: first, we react primarily to events and not to character in detective fiction; and, second, the detective story, even when expanded to novel length, deals with an episode and not a life, thereby effectively forestalling character development. The characters do not interest us except as suspects; once dismissed, they fade from memory.

In the thriller, which, like the fairy tale, is more expansive, the outcome is determined partly by fate, but fate can also be derived, at least in part, from character. If the hero of a fairy tale defeats the wicked adversary, or succeeds in enlisting the help of some magical agency in so doing, it is because he is more patient, or more compassionate, or more unswerving in his purpose—in short, more deserving. In a perfect coincidence of fate and character in the novel *Crime and Punishment,* "a man reveals what he is in what he does, or what happens to him is a revelation of what he is";[43] the reader's interest in the event and the development of character are inseparable.

We have already viewed the crime story, a moral allegory, progressing toward the ideal. For overwhelming reasons it cannot be "realistic." The "feigned history" to which Auden alludes in his account of Dream Literature is the attempt to provide the illusion of realism. For instance, in the detective story and the thriller the fantastic gains verisimilitude by the inclusion of minute details of scenery and costume, and by accurate diagrams and measurements (Poe and Stevenson). For the same reason, Borges includes Swiftian appendages of pseudo-erudition. Though the action of the

Conclusion

thriller is not illusory, the impression of the hero as a man of action frequently is; the active protagonist, upon closer inspection, does not generate events. They simply befall him. In the detective story the sense of historical time imparted to the reader is also spurious. We know that time is supposed to be important by the attention the author pays it, by the elaborate timetables that are given us of the movements of the characters. But this is a special time in which the present is distinctly secondary, existing mainly as a time in which to unravel the past and to await the resumption of an unequivocal future. The past usurps the present, since the focal point of the book, the murder, took place then, or at least the history which led up to it was being enacted then.

The past is also the primary tense of the fairy tale. The introductory "once upon a time" not only signals that something happened in an imaginary and indefinite past, but also that the action of the story has been completed in the safety of the pluperfect tense. The emphasis upon the past in both the fairy story and the detective story has the effect of disengaging the reader, thus "insulating and removing" him from the violence and terror. The thriller, on the contrary, which exists primarily for the present, as do most adventure stories, not only immerses the reader in violence and terror, but simultaneously provides an escape through its very absence of futurity and punitive consequences. Thus no realistic sense of the passage of time can be approximated in either the detective tale or the thriller; the former treats of what has happened and is waiting to happen—i.e., the timeless—and the latter treats only what is happening now—i.e., the timely. The gratification and escapism in the crime novel is manifold. It lies in the exercise of ratiocinative powers, in the ineluctable motion towards Poetic Justice, in the creation of a doppelgänger onto whom we may project our less worthy desires or a superman hero who enables us to transcend our own powers. But I believe the crucial fact is that the book *ends* in the present. No formulation of futurity need be constructed; its potential or possible is not projected and not to be coped with. In this absence of futurity, we escape into an ideal world.

241

In sum, the crime novel, like the fairy tale and the folk legend, stems from the mythopoetic imagination, a common spring, and contains a mythos of its own. The dream spawns its own reality. This is in no way dependent upon the aesthetic excellence of any particular example. What are the events and images of the crime story? The event is murder. And—"Murder is unique among human events. It plays a ritual part, exorcising the one desire we keep most deeply hidden."[44] This ritual basis joins the crime novel to the fairy tale and myth.

"One of the major non-literary social functions of myth," writes Northrop Frye:

> is to explain or rationalize or provide the source of authority for rituals. We do this now, myth says, because once upon a time, etc. The ritual is, so to speak, the epiphany of the myth, the manifestation or showing forth of it in action. In literature itself the mythos or narrative of fiction, more especially of romance [Frye's categorization which subsumes the crime novel] is essentially a verbal imitation of ritual or symbolic human action.[45]

The crime novel's sources are in the archetypal situations of flight and pursuit, escape and struggle, guilt and expiation. Archetypal images have become increasingly important to the writer as the number of common acquired cultural references dwindles in modern times. (In the past decade, the Latin-American fabulists, led by Garcia-Marquez, have been freeing writers from the confines of private imagery.)

And so the crime novel must accomplish for the adult what the fairy tale does for the child; it is a method of expressing and perhaps thereby banishing universal, libidinal, and perennial fears and guilts. "We all have our guilty secrets, our secret shames; the two are always watching us over the garden wall."[46] Gavin Lambert quotes Eric Ambler: "In most human beings the idea of spying and being spied upon touches fantasy systems at deep and sensitive levels of the mind."[47]

Northrop Frye asks why the detective story, an epiphany of law set in a comic context, does not contain, as do the fairy tale and myth, the reassuring cyclical view of existence which relates man to his observations of the natural world. The recognition of the murderer at the end should cancel out the corpse discovered at the beginning. Frye charges that there is not the sense of well-being that cyclical explanation usually confers: "Devotees of detective stories tell me that there is usually a sense of anti-climax when the murderer is identified, an anti-climax only resolved by reaching for another story." He deduces that the reason for this insatiable need for reassurance is that the law is not justice. "In literature as in life the only real justice is poetic justice [a timeless idealization] and the triumph of the law [in the crime novel] does not quite achieve this."[48]

Frye's rather dismissive judgment does not account for the sense of recovery such fiction provides. To hold reality and justice in the mind simultaneously it is necessary to impose a plot. It is not frustration but satisfaction that is the impulse behind a reader's repeated choice of such infallible fictional consonances. We require images of our ending. Of all that we know least about, the ending is surely primary. But in fiction, and particularly allegorical fiction, the end is made to seem knowable. The progression does not have to be cyclical, as Frye maintains, it may be a linear progress toward the ideal. Gertrude Stein found "a continuing present" in the detective novel—a satisfactory substitute for the cyclical pattern.

The human fears which were discussed at the beginning of this study, and their reappearance in individual literary permutations, suggest that fear is an inescapable fact of human life. As Darwin and William James have testified, it is one of man's principal emotions.[49] Chesterton makes no separation between adult and childhood fears: "The healthy lust for darkness and terror which may come on any of us walking down a dark lane."[50] We can recall from Chapter III Dickens' championing of fairy tales, and pillaging them for his own adult fiction. And Graham Greene asserts, in his *Journey Without Maps*, "the child possesses an ancestral fear of the devil, who dances while he [the child] sleeps."[51] This devil, a "fact of life" for every child, became an archetype for Greene. Thus the crime novel is less an escape from reality than a rehearsal of it in which we can confront our fears. It is an anagogical pattern which we must have continually re-enacted for us, in order that we may achieve moments of fearlessness. Dorothy L. Sayers writes,

> It may be that [in crime novels, man] finds a catharsis or purging of his fears and self-questioning. The mysteries made only to be solved, these horrors which he knows to be mere figments of the creative brain, comfort him by subtly persuading that life is a mystery which death will solve, and whose horrors will pass away a tale that is told.[52]

Thus the intellectual puzzle serves to convince us that a pattern of life and death is being composed for us; the insatiable appetite for this kind of literary material stems not only from a delight in its ratiocination or its violence, but from man's need to ritualize his fears and provide for them a context in which Poetic Justice operates.

Notes
CHAPTER VI

[1]Cyril Connolly, *The Evening Colonnade* (London: David, Bruce and Watson, 1973), p. 490.

[2]John Weightman, *The Concept of the Avant-Garde: Explorations in Modernism* (London: Alcove Press, 1973), pp. 312-3.

[3]Lawrence D. Stewart, "Gertrude Stein and the Vital Dead," *Mystery and Detection Annual, 1972*, ed. Donald K. Adams (Pasadena, California: The Castle Press, 1972), pp. 111-112.

[4]Cyril Connolly, *The Evening Colonnade*, p. 493.

[5]*The Secular Scripture*, p. 51.

[6]Frank Kermode, *The Sense of an Ending*, p. 18.

[7]Cyril Connolly, *The Evening Colonnade*, p. 494.

[8]Borges, "Narrative Art and Magic," *Tri-Quarterly Review* No. 25, Fall 1972, p. 215.

[9]V.S. Pritchett, *Balzac* (London: Chatto and Windus, 1973), p. 163.

[10]Lawrence Stewart, *Mystery and Detection Annual, 1972*, p. 121.

[11]Robert Kiely, *Robert Louis Stevenson and the Fiction of Adventure* (Cambridge, Mass.: Harvard University Press, 1965), p. 264.

[12]For example, Joseph Warren Beach comments, "As in Auden the physical, tangible illness is often a sympton of psychic malaise, so the outward trappings of melodrama may be used for spiritual or psychological depiction." Joseph Beach, *The Making of the Auden Canon* (Minneapolis, Minn.: University of Minnesota Press, 1957), p. 16.

[13]David Daiches, *A Study of Literature*, (Ithaca, New York: Cornell University Press, 1948), p. 122.

[14]Joseph Warren Beach, *The Making of the Auden Canon*, p. 160.

[15]*The Dangerous Edge*, p. 134.

[16]Cawelti, *Adventure, Mystery, and Romance*, p. 169. Taken from G.K. Chesterton, "A Defiance of Detective Stories," from *The Defendant* (London 1901), quoted also in Haycraft ed., *The Art of the Mystery Story*, p. 4.

[17]T.S. Eliot, *Murder in the Cathedral* (London: Faber and Faber, 1935), p. 28.

[18]Simenon has invented the same type of agent. He says in his notebook, "For almost as long as I can remember, I have felt an anguish over spoiled lives, which made me invent, and describe, when I was fourteen, maybe in 1917, the profession 'restorer of destinies,' a sort of Maigret doctor, psychiatrist, etc., a kind of consulting God-the-Father. . . ." (Lambert, *The Dangerous Edge*, p. 176).

[19]Cawelti, *Adventure, Mystery, and Romance*, p. 95.

[20]T.S. Eliot, *Collected Plays* (London: Faber and Fabor, 1935), p. 28.

[21]David P. Gallagher, *Modern Latin American Literature* (London: Oxford University Press Paperback, 1973), p. 109.

[22]*Ibid.*, p. 96.

[23]Lawrence Stewart, *Mystery and Detection Annual, 1972* pp. 109, 112.

[24]David P. Gallagher, *Modern Latin American Literature*, p. 109.

[25]André Maurois, "Preface," Jorge Luis Borges, *Labyrinths*, ed. Donald A. Yates and James Irby, (N.Y.: New Directions, 1964), p. xi.

[26]David P. Gallagher, *Modern Latin American Literature*, p. 193.

[27]Jorge Luis Borges, *Ficciones* (New York: Grove Press, Inc., 1962), p. 138.

[28]Jung, *Man and His Symbols*, p. 218.

[29]Jorge Luis Borges, *Labyrinths*, ed. Donald A. Yates and James Irby, p. 137.

[30](Garden City, N.Y.: Doubleday and Co., 1972), p. 211.

[31]David Gallagher, *Modern Latin American Literature*, p. 105.

[32]*The Sense of an Ending*, p. 51.

[33]*The Implied Reader*, p. 269.

[34]*The Sense of an Ending*, p. 39.

[35]For a thorough examination of this theory see Bruno Bettelheim's *The Uses of Enchantment* (New York: Random House, 1977).

[36]*The Rise and Fall of the British Nanny* (London: Hodder and Stoughton, 1973), p. 285.

[37]Although Mr. Barzun does not specifically cite R.L. Stevenson in his list, it is interesting to note that Stevenson was the author of *New Arabian Nights*.

[38]Thomas Love Peacock labeled his tales "entertainments," the same word chosen by Graham Greene.

[39]That the tale, or what Auden calls Dream Literature, would seem to have at least a subtle connection with fantasy, is suggested by the frequency with which Borges' four devices of fantasy (the work within the work, the contamination of reality by the dream, the voyage in time, and the double) appear in the works listed above. Incidentally, Dream Literature should not be understood as synonymous with oneiromancy.

[40]W.H. Auden, *Forewords and Afterwords*, selected by Edward Mendelson (New York: Random House, 1973), p. 268.

[41]Jacques Barzun and Wendell Hertig Taylor, *A Catalogue of Crime* (New York: Harper and Rowe, 1956), pp. 7-8.

[42]W.H. Auden, *Forewords and Afterwords*, pp. 269-270.

[43]*Ibid.*, p. 207.

[44]Jonathan Gathorne-Hardy, *The Rise and Fall of the British Nanny*, p. 293.

[45]*The Secular Scripture*, p. 55.

[46]Joseph Warren Beach, *The Making of the Auden Canon*, p. 185.

[47]*The Dangerous Edge*, p. 104.

[48]*The Secular Scripture*, p. 137.

[49]Eric Bentley, *The Life of the Drama*, p. 205.

[50]Lambert, *The Dangerous Edge*, p. 69.

[51]Lambert, *The Dangerous Edge*, p. 69.

[52]*Adventure, Mystery, and Romance*, p. 123. Cawelti quotes Dorothy L. Sayers from her book, *The Omnibus of Crime*.

SELECTED BIBLIOGRAPHY

Primary Sources

Auden, W.H. *The Collected Poetry of W.H. Auden.* New York: Random House, 1945.

Auden, W.H. and Isherwood, Christopher, *The Ascent of F-6.* London: Faber and Faber, 1936.

_____. *The Dog Beneath the Skin.* London: Faber and Faber, 1935.

_____. *On the Frontier.* New York: Random House, 1938.

Borges, Jorge Luis, and Casares, Bioy. *Six Problems for Don Isidro Parodi.* Buenos Aires: Sur, 1942.

Borges, Jorge Luis. *Labyrinths: Selected Stories and Other Writings.* New York: New Directions, 1962.

Camus, Albert, *The Rebel.* New York: Vintage Books, 1956.

Chandler, Raymond. *The Big Sleep.* New York: Alfred A. Knopf, 1939.

_____. *Farewell My Lovely.* New York: Alfred A. Knopf, 1940.

_____. *The Lady in the Lake.* New York: Alfred A. Knopf, 1943.

_____. *The Long Goodbye.* New York: Alfred A. Knopf, 1954.

Collins, Wilkie. *The Moonstone,* Intro. by T.S. Elliot. London: Oxford University Press, 1928.

_____. *The Moonstone.* Intro. by Dorothy Sayers. New York: Dutton and Dent, 1944.

_____. *The Woman in White.* New York: Random House, Modern Library, 1937.

Conrad, Joseph. *Almayer's Folly.* New York: Doubleday, Doran, 1928.

_____. *Chance.* New York: Doubleday, Page, 1914.

_____. *An Outcast of the Islands.* London: T. Fisher Unwin, 1919.

_____. *Great Short Works:* "An Outpost of Progress," "The Nigger of the *Narcissus,*" "Youth," "Heart of Darkness," "Typhoon," "The Lagoon," "The Secret Sharer." New York: Harper and Row, 1967.

_____. *Lord Jim.* New York: Random House, Modern Library, 1931.

_____. *Nostromo.* Intro. by Dorothy Van Ghent. New York: Holt, Rinehart and Winston, 1961.

Conrad, Joseph and Hueffer, Ford Madox, *Romance.* (London: Smith, Elder, 1903)

Conrad, Joseph. *The Secret Agent.* New York: Doubleday, 1953.

_____. *Under Western Eyes.* New York: Doubleday, 1963.

_____. *Victory.* New York: Doubleday, Doran, 1928.

Dickens, Charles. "The Detective Police," "On Duty with Inspector Field," "Three Detective Anecdotes," *Lamplighter's Story and Other Nouvelettes.* Philadelphia, Pennsylvania: T.B. Petersen, 1861.

_____. *Barnaby Rudge.* New York: Coward McCann, 1950.

_____. *Bleak House.* London: Collins, 1953.

_____. *Great Expectations.* New York: James Gregory, 1861.

_____. *Little Dorrit.* Boston, Massachusetts: Ticknor and Fields, 1867.

_____. *Martin Chuzzlewit.* London: Oxford University Press, 1951.

_____. *The Mystery of Edwin Drood.* New York: Doubleday, 1961.

_____. *The Old Curiosity Shop.* London: MacMillan, 1908.

_____. *Oliver Twist.* London: MacMillan, 1897.

Dostoevsky, Feodor, *Crime and Punishment.* Trans. Constance Garnett. New York: MacMillan, 1928.

_____. *The Possessed* "Afterword" by Marc Slonim. New York: Signet Classics, New American Library, 1962.

Eliot, T.S. *The Cocktail Party.* New York: Harcourt, Brace, 1950.

_____. *Collected Poems.* New York: Harcourt, Brace, 1936.

_____. *The Confidential Clerk.* London: Faber and Faber, 1953.

_____. *The Family Reunion. Collected Plays.* London: Faber and Faber, 1962.

_____. *Murder in the Cathedral.* New York: Harcourt, Brace and World, 1938.

Ford, Ford Madox. *Vive le Roi.* Philadelphia, Pennsylvania: Lippincott, 1936.

_____. *Bodley Head Ford Madox Ford.* Intro. by Graham Greene. London: Bodley Head, 1962.

Green, F.L. *Music in the Park.* London: M. Joseph, 1942.

Greene, Graham. *A Sort of Life.* New York: Pocket Books, 1973.

_____. *Brighton Rock.* New York: Viking Press, 1968.

_____. *The Comedians.* New York: Viking Press, 1971.

_____. *The Confidential Agent.* New York: Viking Press, 1958.

_____. *The End of the Affair.* New York: Viking Press, 1955.

_____. *England Made Me.* London: Heinemann, 1935.

_____. *The Honorary Consul.* New York: Simon and Schuster, 1973.

_____. *It's a Battlefield.* London: Heinemann, 1934.

_____. *The Living Room.* London: Heinemann, 1953.

_____. *The Man Within.* New York: Viking Press, 1971.

_____. *The Ministry of Fear.* New York: Penguin Books, 1943.

_____. *Our Man in Havana.* New York: Viking Press, 1970.

_____. *Orient Express.* New York: Viking Press, 1955.

_____. *The Portable Graham Greene.* Edited by Philip Stratford. New York: Viking Press, 1973.

_____. *The Potting Shed.* New York: Viking Press, 1957.

_____. *The Power and the Glory.* New York: Viking Press, 1954.

_____. *The Quiet American.* London: Heinemann, 1955.

_____. *This Gun for Hire.* Harrisburg, Pennsylvania: Superior Reprint, 1945.

_____. *A Burnt-Out Case.* New York: Viking Press, 1960.

Selected Bioliography

Hammett, Dashiell. *The Big Knockover.* Edited by Lillian Hellman. New York: Random House, 1962.

_____. *The Maltese Falcon.* New York: Alfred A. Knopf, 1930.

Ionesco, Eugene. *Three Plays: Amédée, The New Tenant, Victims of Duty.* Trans. by Donald Watson. New York: Grove Press, 1958.

O'Flaherty, Liam. *The Assassin.* London: Jonathan Cape, 1928.

_____. *The Informer.* London: Jonathan Cape, 1925.

Peake, Mervyn. *Titus Groane.* New York: Reynal and Hitchcock, 1946.

Poe, Edgar Allan. *Collected Works of Edgar Allen Poe.* New York: Stoddard, 1894.

_____. *Little Masterpieces of Edgar Allan Poe.* Edited by Bliss Perry. New York: Doubleday and McClure, 1901. [This volume comprises: "The Fall of the House of Usher," "Ligeia," "The Cask of Amontillado," "The Assignation," "Ms. Found in a Bottle," "The Black Car," "The Gold-Bug."]

Sayers, Dorothy L. *Lord Peter.* Edited by James Sandoe. Coda by Carolyn Heilbrun. New York: Avon/Flare Books, 1972.

Simenon, Georges. *The Bells of Bicêtre.* New York: Harcourt, Bruce and World 1964.

Stevenson, Robert Louis, *Dr. Jekyll and Mr. Hyde.* Leipsis: Tauchnitz, 1886.

_____. *Weir of Hermiston.* New York: Chas. Scribner, 1896.

_____. *The Wrecker.* New York: Chas. Scribner, 1908.

Warner, Rex. *The Aerodrome.* Philadelphia, Pennsylvania: J.B. Lippincott, 1946.

_____. *Men of Stones.* New York: J.B. Lippincott, 1950.

_____. *The Professor.* London: Boriswood, 1938.

_____. *The Wild Goose Chase.* New York: Alfred A. Knopf, 1938.

Williams, Charles. *The War in Heaven.* London: Victor Gollancz, 1930.

_____. *The Place of the Lion.* New York: Pellegrini and Cudahy, 1951.

Secondary Sources

Adams, Donald., ed. *Mystery and Detection Annual.* Pasadena, California: Castle Press, 1972.

Allott, Kenneth and Farris, Miriam. *The Art of Graham Greene.* London: Hamish Hamilton, 1951.

Alloway, Lawrence. "Frankenthaler as Pastoral." *Art News,* November 1971, pp. 69-70.

Alvarez, A. *The Savage God: A Study of Suicide.* New York: Random House, 1972

Arendt, Hannah. *The Origins of Totalitarianism.* New York: Harcourt, Brace and World, 1966.

249

A Common Spring

Atkins, John. *Graham Greene*. London: John Calder, 1957.

Aubry, Georges-Jean. *The Sea-Dreamer: A Definitive Biography of Joseph Conrad*. New York: Doubleday, 1957.

Auden, W.H. *Forewords and Afterwords*. Edited by Edward Mendelson. New York: Random House, 1973.

————. *The Dyer's Hand and Other Essays*. New York: Random House, 1962.

Aylmer, Felix. *The Drood Case*. London: Rupert Hart-Davis, 1964.

Baker, Richard. *The Drood Murder Case*. Berkeley, California: University of California Press, 1951.

Barzun, Jacques and Taylor, Wendell Hertig. *A Catalogue of Crime*. New York: Harper and Row, 1971.

Barzun, Jacques. *The Energies of Art*. New York: Harper and Row, 1956.

Beach, Joseph Warren. *The Making of the Auden Canon*. Minneapolis, Minnesota: University of Minnesota Press, 1957.

Bentley, Eric. *The Life of the Drama*. New York: Atheneum, 1946.

Bergler, Edmund. *The Writer and Psychoanalysis*. New York: Doubleday, 1950.

Boardman, Gwenn. *Graham Greene: The Aesthetics of Exploration*. Gainesville, Florida: University of Florida Press, 1971.

Boileau, Pierre and Narcejac, Thomas. *Le Roman Policier*. Paris: Payot, 1964.

Buchan, John. "The Novel and the Fairy Tale." *English Institute Essays* 76 (July 1931): 1-16.

Callois, Roger. *Le Roman Policier*. Buenos Aires: Sur, 1941.

Cawelti, John G. *Adventure, Mystery, and Romance*. Chicago, Illinois: Univ. of Chicago Press, 1976.

Chandler, Raymond. *Raymond Chandler Speaking*. Edited by Dorothy Gardiner and Katherine Sorley Walker. London: Hamish Hamilton, 1962.

————. "The Simple Art of Murder." *The Art of the Mystery Story*. Edited by Howard Haycraft. New York: Simon and Schuster, 1946.

Chesterton, G.K. *Appreciations and Criticisms of the Works of Charles Dickens*. Port Washington, New York: Kennikat Press, 1966.

Collins, Philip. *Dickens and Crime*. Cambridge Studies in Criminology. London: MacMillan, 1962.

Connolly, Cyril. *The Evening Colonnade*. London: David, Bruce and Watson, 1973.

Coolidge, Archibald C., Jr. *Charles Dickens as Serial Novelist*. Ames, Iowa: University of Iowa Press. 1967.

Cottrell, Bertram. "Second Time Charm: The Theatre of Graham Greene." *Modern Fiction Studies* Vol. III (Autumn 1957): 249-255.

DeQuincey, Thomas. "Murder Considered as One of the Fine Arts," *Little Classics*. Edited by Rossiter Johnson, V. 2 Boston: James P. Osgood, 1847.

Selected Bibliography

DeVitis, A.A. "Allegory in *Brighton Rock.*" *Modern Fiction Studies.* Vol. III

Durham, Philip. *Down these Mean Streets a Man Must Go.* Chapel Hill, North Carolina: University of North Carolina Press, 1963.

Eliot, T.S. *Selected Essays.* London: Faber and Faber, 1932.

Empson, William. *Some Versions of Pastoral.* London: Chatto and Windus, 1935.

Fanger, Donald. *Dostoevsky and Romantic Realism.* Cambridge, Massachusetts: Harvard University Press, 1965.

Fleishman, Avrom. *Conrad's Politics.* Baltimore, Maryland: Johns Hopkins University Press, 1967.

Fletcher, Angus. *Allegory: The Theory of a Symbolic Mode.* Ithaca, New York: Cornell University Press, 1970.

Flores, Angel, ed. *The Kafka Problem.* New York: New Directions, 1946.

Ford, Ford Madox. *Portraits from Life.* Boston, Massachusetts: Houghton Mifflin, 1937.

Forster, John. *The Life of Charles Dickens.* London: Everyman's Library, 1927.

Friedman, Norman. "The Shadow and the Sun: Notes Toward a Reading of *Bleak House.*" *Boston University Studies in English* Vol. III (Spring 1957): 147-166.

Frohock, Wilbur M. *The Novel of Violence in America.* Dallas, Texas: Southern Methodist University Press, 1950.

Frye, Northrop. *Anatomy of Criticism.* Princeton, New Jersey: Princeton University Press, 1971.

_____. "The Archetypes of Literature." *Kenyon Review* (Fall 1951): 92-110.

_____. *The Secular Scripture.* Cambridge, Mass.: Harvard Univ. Press, 1976.

Gallagher, David P., ed. *Modern Latin American Literature.* London: Oxford University Press, 1973.

Gathorne-Hardy, Jonathan. *The Rise and Fall of the British Nanny.* London: Hodder and Stoughton, 1973.

Graves, Robert, *Good-bye to All That.* New York: Doubleday, 1957.

_____. *The Long Week-end.* London: Faber and Faber, 1940.

Greene, Graham and Glover, Dorothy. *A Catalogue of Victorian Detective Fiction.* London: Bodley Head, 1966.

Greene, Graham. *Collected Essays.* New York: Viking Press, 1969.

_____. *The Lost Childhood and Other Essays.* New York Viking Press, 1962.

Guérard, Albert J. *Conrad the Novelist.* Cambridge, Massachusetts: Harvard University Press, 1958.

A Common Spring

Hagan, John Jr. "The Design of Conrad's *The Secret Agent.*" *Journal of English Literary History* XXII (June 1955): 148-164.

Haycraft, Howard., ed. *The Art of the Mystery Story: A Collection of Critical Essays.* New York: Simon and Schuster, 1946.

————. *Murder for Pleasure.* New York: Appleton, Century Crofts, 1941.

Hoffman, Daniel. *Poe Poe Poe Poe Poe Poe Poe.* New York: Doubleday, 1972.

Hoffman, Frederick. *The Mortal No.* Princeton, New Jersey: Princeton University Press, 1964.

Holloway, John. "Dickens and the Symbol," *Dickens 1970.* Edited by Michael Slater (New York: Stein and Day,) 1970.

Hyman, Stanley Edgar. *Poetry and Criticism.* New York: Atheneum, 1961.

————. *The Tangled Bank.* New York: Atheneum, 1962.

Hynes, Samuel B., ed. *Graham Greene.* New Jersey: Prentice-Hall, 1973.

Iser, Wolfgang. *The Implied Reader.* Baltimore: Johns Hopkins University Press, 1974.

Kermode, Frank. *The Sense of an Ending.* New York: Oxford University Press, 1968.

Kiely, Robert. *Robert Louis Stevenson and the Fiction of Adventure.* Cambridge, Massachusetts: Harvard University Press, 1962.

————. *The Romantic Novel in England.* Cambridge, Massachusetts: Harvard University Press, 1972.

Kunkel, Francis, *The Labyrinthine Ways of Graham Greene.* New York: Sheed and Ward, 1959.

Lambert, Gavin. *The Dangerous Edge.* New York: Viking Press, 1976.

Lauriat, Lane, Jr. "Dickens and the Archetypal Villain." Ph.D. dissertation, Harvard University, 1953.

Leach, Edmund. *Claude Lévi-Strauss.* New York: Viking Press, 1970.

Leavis, F.R. *The Great Tradition.* New York: Doubleday, 1954.

Levin, Harry. "Motif." Lecture notes presented Harvard University, 1970.

————. "Some Meanings of Myth." *Daedalus.* (Spring 1959): 223-232.

Lewis, C.S. "High and Low Brows." *Selected Literary Essays.* Cambridge, England: Cambridge University Press, 1969: 266-279.

London Times Literary Supplement Feb. 25, 1955 special supplement "Detective Fiction," i-xii; June 23, 1961 special supplement "Crime Detection and Society," i-xii.

Macdonald, Ross. *On Crime Writing.* Santa Barbara, California: Capra Press, 1973.

Macdonald, Ross. Review of *A Catalogue of Crime,* by Jacques Barzun and Wendell Hertig Taylor. *N.Y. Times Book Review,* 16 May 1971, p. 3.

Selected Bioliography

Melchiori, Giorgio. *The Tightrope Walkers*. London: Routledge and Kegan Paul, 1956.

Miller, J. Hillis. "Dickens' Symbolic Imagery." Ph.D. dissertation, Harvard University, 1952.

Morse, Robert. "Our Mutual Friend." *Partisan Review* (March 1949): 227-289.

Moser, Thomas. *Joseph Conrad*. Cambridge, Massachusetts: Harvard University Press, 1957.

Murch, A.E. *The Development of the Detective Novel*. London: Peter Owen, 1958.

Nevins, Francis M., Jr., ed. *The Mystery Writer's Art*. Bowling Green, Ohio: Bowling Green University Press, 1970.

O'Faolain, Sean. "Graham Greene." *The Vanishing Hero*. London: Eyre and Spottiswoode, 1956: 73-97.

Orwell, George. "Charles Dickens." *Collected Essays*. New York: Doubleday, 1954: 31-87.

Ousby, Ian. *The Bloodhounds of Heaven*. Cambridge, Mass.: Harvard University Press, 1976.

Partlow, Robert B., Jr., ed. *Dickens the Craftsman: Strategies of Presentation*. Carbondale, Illinois: Southern Illinois University Press, 1970.

Patten, Karl. "The Structure of *The Power and the Glory*." *Modern Fiction Studies* Vol. III (Autumn 1957): 225-234.

Phillips, Walter. *Dickens, Reade and Collins*. New York: Columbia University Press, 1970.

Plumb, J.H. *The Death of the Past*. Boston, Massachusetts: Houghton-Mifflin, 1971.

Poe, Edgar Allan. *Complete Works* v. IV: "Barnaby Rudge," *Critical Essays*. New York: Thomas Crowell, 1902: 38-64.

Praz, Mario. *Mnemosyne*. Princeton, New Jersey: Bollingen Series, Princeton University press, 1970.

————. *The Hero in Eclipse in Victorian Fiction*. London: Oxford University Press, 1956.

Propp, Vladimir, "Fairy Tale Transformations." *Readings in Russian Poetics: Formalist and Structuralist Views,* pp. 94-114. Edited by Ladislav Matejka and Krystyna Pomorska. Cambridge, Massachusetts: M.I.T. Press, 1971.

————. *The Morphology of the Folktale*. Translated by Laurence Scott. Edited by S. Pirkova-Jakobson. Bloomington, Indiana: American Folklore Society, Indiana University Press, 1958.

Queen, Ellery [pseud.] *Queen's Quorum*. Boston, Massachusetts: Little, Brown, 1951.

A Common Spring

Raglan, Lord. *The Hero: A Study in Tradition, Myth and Drama.* London: Watts and Co., 1949.

Rank, Otto. "The Double." *Psychoanalytic Review* VI (1919): abstract 450-460.

Reid, Stephen C. "The Hidden World of Charles Dickens." *University of Auckland Bulletin* n. 61, (English Series 10, 1962): 5-47.

Rosenfeld, Claire. *Paradise of Snakes.* Chicago, Illinois: University of Chicago Press, 1967.

Rycroft, Charles. "A Detective Story: Psychoanalytic Observations." *Psychoanalytic Quarterly* V. 26 (1957).

Šklovskij, Viktor. "The Mystery Novel: Dickens' *Little Dorrit.*" In *Readings in Russian Poetics: Formalist and Structuralist Views,* pp. 220-226. Ed. Ladislav Matejka and Krystyna Pomorska. Cambridge, Massachusetts: M.I.T. Press, 1970.

Slater, Michael., ed. *Dickens 1970.* New York: Stein and Day, 1970.

Spier, Ursula. "Melodrama in Graham Greene's *The End of the Affair.*" *Modern Fiction Studies* Vol. III. (Autumn 1957): 235-240.

Spilka, Mark. *Dickens and Kafka.* Bloomington, Indiana: University of Indiana Press, 1964.

Stallman, Robert Wooster. "Life, Art and *The Secret Sharer.*" In *Forms of Modern Fiction,* pp. 229-243. Ed. William Van O'Connor. Minneapolis, Minnesota: University of Minnesota Press, 1948.

_____. ed. *The Art of Joseph Conrad: A Critical Symposium.* East Lansing, Michigan: Michigan State University Press, 1960.

Stein, Gertrude. *Narration, Four Lectures.* Chicago, Illinois: University of Chicago Press, 1969.

_____. *What Are Masterpieces.* Los Angeles: Conference Press, 1940.

Symons, Julian. *Charles Dickens.* London: Arthur Barker, 1951

_____. *The Detective Story in Britain.* London: Longmans, Greene, 1962.

_____. *Mortal Consequences.* New York: Harper and Row, 1972.

Teets, Bruce Earle and Gerber, Helmut, compilers and editors. *Joseph Conrad: An Annotated Bibliography.* De Kalb, Illinois: Northern Illinois University Press, 1971.

Thompson, Stith. "Index of Folk Literature." *Indiana University Studies* v.XIX, Studies 96, 97. Bloomington, Indiana: University of Indiana Press, 1932.

Tindall, William York. *The Literary Symbol.* New York: Columbia University Press, 1955.

Trilling, Lionel. *Sincerity and Authenticity.* Cambridge, Massachusetts: Harvard University Press, 1972.

Tymms, Ralph. *Doubles in Literary Psychology.* Cambridge, England: Bowes and Bowes, 1949.

Selected Bioliography

Van Ghent, Dorothy. "The Dickens World: A View From Todgers.' " *Sewanee Review LVIII, 1950, pp. 419-438.*

_____. *The English Novel: Form and Function.* New York: Rinehart, 1953.

Velikovsky, Immanuel. *Oedipus and Akhnaton.* New York: Doubleday, 1960.

de Vries, Paulus Henri. *Poe and After.* Amsterdam: Drukkerij Bakker, 1956.

Warner, Rex. *The Cult of Power.* London: Bodley Head, 1946.

Weightman, John. *The Concept of the Avant-Garde: Explorations in Modernism.* London: Alcove Press, 1973.

Wellek, René., ed. *Dostoevsky: A Collection of Critical Essays.* New Jersey: Prentice-Hall, 1962.

Wells, Carolyn. *The Technique of the Mystery Story.* Revised ed. Springfield, Massachusetts: Home Correspondence School, 1929.

Weston, Jessie. *From Ritual to Romance.* New York: Peter Smith, 1941.

Wiley, Paul. *Conrad's Measure of Man.* Madison, Wisconsin: University of Wisconsin Press, 1954.

_____. *Novelist of Three Worlds.* Syracuse, New York: Syracuse University Press, 1962.

Wilson, Angus. *The World of Charles Dickens.* London: Martin Secker and Warburg, 1970.

Wilson, Edmund. "Dickens: The Two Scrooges." In *Eight Essays,* pp. 11-91. New York: Doubleday, 1954.

_____. "Why Do People Read Detective Stories?" "Who Cares Who Killed Roger Ackroyd?" In *A Literary Chronicle,* pp. 323-328; 338-345. New York: Doubleday, 1950.

Winters, Warrington. "Dickens and the Psychology of Dreams." *P.M.L.A.* LXIII (1948): 984-1006.

Wölchen, Fritz. *Der Literarische Mord.* Nurnberg: Nest, 1953.

Wyndham, Francis. *Graham Greene.* London: Longmans, Greene, 1962.

Zabel, Morton Dauwen. "Conrad: The Terms of Response." "Graham Greene." In *Craft and Character in Modern Fiction,* pp. 147-227; 275-296. New York: Viking Press, 1957.

INDEX

256

Index

exotic, 119; fairy-tale, 94; of foreboding, 97, 99-100, 194, 229;
Greene's use of, 175; of horror, 8;
of suspense, 236; tainted, 80
Auden, W. H.: quoted, 2, 17, 22-3,
26, 35, 37, 39-40, 43, 62n, 65n,
79, 173, 174, 175, 177, 239, 240,
246n; works discussed, 227-229
Austen, Jane, 165n
Aydelotte, William, 19, 34-5

B

Ballad, 20
Balzac, Honoré de, 6, 73
Barnaby Rudge (Dickens), 6, 15n,
70-74, 76, 91, 97, 99, 101, 105-7,
108n
Barthes, Roland, 236, 237
"Bartleby the Scrivener" (Melville),
88
Barzun, Jacques, 25, 41, 63n, 139
"Basement Room" (Greene), 219n
Battlefield, as metaphor in Greene's
fiction, 176-7, 188, 203
Baudelaire, Charles, 109n, 166n
Beach at Falesá, The (Stevenson), 112
Beach, Joseph Warren, 229, 242, 245n
Beckett, Samuel, 237
"Before the Attack" (Greene), 179
Bentley, A. C., 12
Bentley, Eric, 42, 70, 94, 119, 179
Berkeley, Anthony, 8
Berrigan, Daniel, 31
Bettelheim, Bruno, 246n
Black Mask magazine, 65n
Blake, Nicholas (pseud. of C. Day-
Lewis), 7, 8, 12, 23, 37
Bleak House (Dickens), 5, 11, 31, 70,
72, 73, 74, 76-7, 78, 79, 80, 82, 83,
87, 92, 95-6, 96, 97, 100-103, 105-
107, 137, 154n, 195, 203
Bloodhounds of Heaven, The
(Ousby), 15n

Boardman, Gwenn, 173-4, 186-7, 195
"Bobbies," 5. *See also* Bow Street
Runners
"Bombing Raid, The" (Greene), 179
Book of the Revelation, 200, 238
Borges, Jorge Luis, 3, 17-18, 67n,
221n, 232-6, 239, 240, 246n
Bowen, Marjorie, 171, 172
Bow Street Runners, 5, 73
Bradbury, Ray, 9
Bread and Wine (Silone), 181
Brighton Rock (Greene), 176, 177,
181, 183, 191, 195, 200, 202, 203,
204, 205, 106, 211
Browne, Sir Thomas, 199
Buchan, John, 9, 66n, 186
Bulwer-Lytton, Edward George, 4,
72, 95
Bunyan, John, 40
Burke, Edmund, 214-215
Burnt-Out Case, A (Greene), 172,
179, 184, 185, 194, 200, 204, 206,
209
Byron, George, 4, 70
Bystanders, in Greene's fiction, 195

C

Camus, Albert, 46-7, 48, 66n, 185
Canterbury Tales, The (Chaucer), 100
Carlyle, Thomas, 88
Castiglione, 41
Catharsis, 22-3, 27, 92, 140, 161, 236
Cathexis, the formula as, 238-244
Catholic novel, 182, 192, 204, 206,
214
Cautionary tale, 238
Cawelti, John G., 50, 148, 230-231,
232
Cecil, Lord David, 207
Cervantes, Miguel de, 4
Chance (Conrad), 117, 123, 132-3,
152, 156, 157, 163n

Index

Index

"Fly Paper" (Hammett), 48
Folklore. *See* fairy tale
Folk tale. *See* fairy tale
Ford, Ford Madox, 112, 116, 156
Forest, as archetype, 40, 41, 86, 122, 128. *See also* Wood of error
Formosam, 41
Formulae. *See* Formulaic fiction; Narrative formulae
Formulaic Fiction, 2, 9, 20 defined, 91, 113, 156, 227, 234, 237. *See also* Narrative formulae
Forster, E.M., 112, 119
Forster, John, 69, 95
Francis, Dick, 47
Frankenstein (Shelley), 9
Frazer, Sir James, 33, 145
Freeling, Nicholas, 5, 12, 65n
Freeman, R. Austin, 12
Fremlin, Celia, 12
Frence, Paul, 4
Freud, Sigmund, 34
Frisch, Max, 9, 12
Frisson, 112, 138
From Ritual to Romance (Weston), 33, 199
Fuller, Roy, 181, 222n, 240
Frye, Northrop, 2, 16, 18, 25, 45, 77, 90, 92, 95, 110n, 176, 225, 242-3

G

Gaboriau, Emile, 11
Gallagher, David, 232-3, 234
Gamesmanship, 27, 28, 38, 92, 174, 237, 238
Garcia-Marquez, Gabriel, 242
Garden, 78-9, 80-81, 86, 123, 128, 170, 186, 187, 188-9. *See also* Eden; Hortus conclusus; Paradisal vision; pastoral
Gathorne-Hardy, Jonathan, 238, 242
Gilbert, Elliott L., 15n, 31

Gilliatt, Penelope, 45
Gillon, Adam, 144
"Gold-Bug, The" (Poe), 6, 11
Golden Age, of detective fiction, 7, 8, 87, 173, 174, 237
Golden Bough, The (Frazer), 33, 199
Goncourt, Edmond and Jules, 6
Goodwin, William, 4
Gothic novel, Gothic romance, 4, 7, 8, 9, 22, 36, 70, 72, 84, 99, 138, 146, 214-215, 228
Grace, 129, 176, 180, 189, 191, 196-7, 201, 204-205, 210
Graves, Robert, 8, 174
Great Chain of Being, 41
Great Expectations (Dickens), 70, 73, 101
"Great good place," 39-40, 173, 175
Green, Anna K., 11
Greene, Graham, 3, 9, 32, 43, 44, 46, 51, 103, 110n, 123, 152, 159, 164n, *169-223,* 226, 227, 230, 231, 232, 243, 346n
Greeneland, 43, 175, 177, 179, 186, 191, 196, 210, 215, 230
Green, F.L., 115, 123
Gregor, Ian, 210
Grimm, Jakob and Wilhelm, 40, 238
Grotesque, 82, 95, 129, 146-8, 151, 153, 193, 196-7, 209, 221n
Grouping, regrouping of clues, characters, 50, 98
Guérard, Albert, 114, 120, 124, 139
Guilt, 23, 24, 30, 31, 32-3, 37, 79, 80, 88, 100, 129, 136, 137, 141, 142, 175, 176, 195, 242
"Guilty Vicarage, The" (Auden), 26

H

Hagan, John, Jr., 135
Hall, Adam, 12
Hamartia. See Manifestation
Hamilton, Patrick, 8

261

Index

Index

Political Thriller, 115-116, 123, 159, 170, 206, 214, 227

Possessed, The (Dostoevsky), 200

Potting Shed, The (Greene), 188, 202, 211

Power and the Glory, The (Greene), 170, 178, 181, 183, 184-5, 190, 192, 194, 197, 199, 200, 209, 210-211, 212, 213, 219n

Praz, Mario, 150

"Predicament, A" (Poe), 81

Prefaces (Conrad), 168

Price, Reynolds, 202

Primitivism, 124, 128, 164n, 178-180, 196

Pritchett, V.S., 87, 91-2, 226

Private-eye. *See* Detective hero; Tough-guy hero

Proctor, Maurice, 12

Professor, The (Warner), 228

Progression d'effet, 116, 156

Propp, Vladimir, 16, 18, 19, 39, 83

Protagonist. *See* Hero

Providence, Providential end, intervention, justice, order, 70, 95, 96, 103, 129, 133, 137, 145, 146, 152, 184, 192, 204

Psychological thriller, 8, 211

Psychology, fictive use of, 5, 7-8, 25, 28; in Conrad, 112-113, 115, 124, 138, 150, 156; in Dickens, 69, 72, 89, 90-91; in Greene, 169, 181, 206, 111

"Purloined Letter, The" (Poe), 6,11

Pursuit, 21-23 defined, 24, 242; in Conrad, 123, 142, 143; in Dickens, 76-7, 80, 83, 104; in Greene, 180, 181-4, 194, 200, 202, 209, 210, 211, 242

Puzzle, 8, 10, 70, 74, 92, 98, 100-101, 225, 233, 239, 244

Q

Queen, Ellery, 3

Quest, 20-21, 23-4 defined, 33, 52, 227, 228, 239; in Conrad, 121, 123-9, 130, 144, 145, 152, 159; in Dickens, 76, 77-82, 83, 104, 105; in Greene, 178, 180, 184-9, 220n

Quiet American, The (Greene), 170, 172, 184, 185, 187, 204, 218n

Quintilian, 49

R

Radcliffe, Mrs. Ann, 4, 70, 98

Raffles (Hornung), 11, 38

Raglan, Lord, 19, 21, 33-4

Rasselas (Johnson), 25

Ratiocination, 6, 21, 63, 103, 118, 164, 179, 182, 190, 230, 233-4, 241

Reade, Charles, 72, 73, 95

Realism. *See* "Realistic" thriller

"Realistic" thriller, 27, 43-9, 66n, 148, 215, 232. *See also* Toughguy novel

Rebel, The (Camus), 46-7

Recognition, 28, 52, 105, 133, 144, 181, 201-202, 236, 243

Reid, S.C., 93, 145

Rescue, The (Conrad), 111, 165n

Rescuer, 75, 88, 93, 113, 137, 240

Retardation. *See* Deliberate retardation

"Return, The" (Greene), 221n

Reversal, 26, 53, 114, 152. *See also Peripeteia*

Richardson, Maurice, 65n

Riddle, 22, 27, 52, 224, 239

Ritual, 17, 19, 29, 33, 37, 38, 48, 95, 144, 145, 151, 184, 185, 200, 212, 220n, 238, 242, 244

Robbe-Grillet, Alain, 10, 236-7

Robin Hood, 4, 9, 10, 22

Robinson Crusoe (Defoe), 239

Index

269

Index